The 1923
New York Yankees

The 1923
New York Yankees

*A History of Their First
World Championship Season*

RONALD A. MAYER

McFarland & Company, Inc., Publishers
Jefferson, North Carolina, and London

LIBRARY OF CONGRESS CATALOGUING-IN-PUBLICATION DATA

Mayer, Ronald A., 1934–
    The 1923 New York Yankees : a history of their first world
championship season / Ronald A. Mayer.
        p.   cm.
    Includes bibliographical references and index.

    ISBN 978-0-7864-4404-5
    softcover : 50# alkaline paper

    1. New York Yankees (Baseball team)—History—20th century.
I. Title.
GV875.N4M373   2010
796.357'64097471—dc22   2009042905

British Library cataloguing data are available

Cover photograph: The 1923 New York Yankees

Manufactured in the United States of America

McFarland & Company, Inc., Publishers
  Box 611, Jefferson, North Carolina 28640
    www.mcfarlandpub.com

To my six all-stars: Daniel, Stephanie, Justin, Matthew, Ellen and Andrew ... Hall of Famers all

—Love, Poppy

Acknowledgments

I would like to express my sincere gratitude to the following people for their generous assistance: long-time friend Joe DeFerrari, for providing timely research material; Richie Clark, an Army buddy, for his encouraging comments and valuable assistance selecting photographs at the A. Bartlett Giamatti Research Center in Cooperstown; Beansie, my favorite book scout; Rudy Marzano, author and friend, for his insightful advice on all things baseball; Paul diFrancescantonio and Glenn Mayer, two computer wizards who came to my rescue time and time again when my computer and I were not getting along; research associate Freddy Borowski and photo archivist Pat Kelly at the Giamatti Research Center for their help and advice regarding photographs.

I am also indebted to the Society of American Baseball Research and the Grand Rapids Public Library, especially Marcie Beck for providing information about Wally Pipp. Locally, the Morris County Library and the Rutgers University Library have been wonderful sources for old newspapers and periodicals. A big thank you to George King, reference librarian, at the East Hanover Public Library for his tireless efforts to satisfy my many requests.

Last but certainly not least, a special thanks to my wife Arlene, for her impeccable proofreading and knowing where to put those pesky commas, colons and semi-colons. One and all, you will get your reward in heaven.

Contents

Preface

Why write about the 1923 New York Yankees? I've been asked that question several times. The answer is twofold. First, according to my research, a book about the 1923 Yankees has never been published. The second reason, which is more compelling, is that the 1923 Yankees won the first of the franchise's 27 world championships, changing the fortunes of what had until then been a mostly luckless team history. As the Orioles (1901–1902) and Highlanders (1903–1912), they finished higher than fourth in the eight-team American League three times. And in the Yankees years, things had only recently improved. After eight years of finishing third or lower, the New York team won two consecutive pennants—only to lose five of eight Series games in 1921 and four of five (there was one tie) in 1922.

Were the 1923 Yankees a powerhouse of a club? Not in the sense, say, of the 1927 Yankees, led by the famed "Murderers' Row" of Babe Ruth, Lou Gehrig, Bob Meusel, Earl Combs and Tony Lazzeri, considered by many experts to be the greatest team in the history of the game. Or the 1939 Yankees who won the American League pennant by 17 games with Joe DiMaggio, Joe Gordon, Red Rolfe and Bill Dickey leading the way. Or the 1961 Yankees with the "M and M Boys," Mickey Mantle and Roger Maris. Or even the 1998 team that won 114 regular season games and another 11 in the playoffs and World Series. That's not to say the '23 club was not exceptional. It was. What it had was that indefinable thing called chemistry. Not an abundance of high profile superstars, just talented, hustling ballplayers giving one hundred percent every day with one goal in mind and that was to win. That's what the 1923 Yankees possessed. They were an unstoppable force, winning 98 games and finishing the season 16 games in front of the Detroit Tigers.

During the season the team ran off four winning streaks—two for nine games and two for six games. On May 8 the Yankees began a road trip in

Cleveland one game ahead of the second-place Detroit Tigers. It ended on May 30 in Washington D.C. with New York in front of Philadelphia by seven games. The Yankees won 17 of 20 games on the road. Proving their dominance from start to finish, the Yankees played 39 different series of three games or more during the season. They won 20, split nine and lost 10, a remarkable consistency.

Success with any baseball team begins at the top of the organization. It did with the 1923 Yankees, whose owner was Jacob Ruppert, a man with a strong desire to win. Equally important, he was willing to spend money wisely to acquire skilled players and build a winning club. He was also a keen judge of talent. Ruppert hired Miller Huggins over the strong objections of his partner, Tillinghast L'Hommedieu Huston, and he supported his manager after losing back-to-back World Series to the New York Giants in 1921 and 1922. This loyalty was the final straw that broke the partnership with Cap Huston. Ruppert was proven correct in his judgment. Huggins would be elected to the Hall of Fame in 1964, having guided Yankee clubs to six pennants and three World Series championships in 12 seasons. Ruppert made another wonderful move when he acquired Ed Barrow from the Red Sox as his general manager. Barrow had many years of experience at all levels of baseball and was an excellent judge of talent. He had Ruppert's confidence and worked well with the owner.

On the field the Yankees had the big guy, the Babe, the greatest ballplayer of all time. In 1923, Ruth had a monster year. He led the club with a .393 batting average, 41 home runs, 131 RBIs, 170 walks and 151 runs scored, not a bad season's work. He also drove Miller Huggins nuts trying to control the free spirit. But the team was not totally dependent on Ruth. It was a talented and well-balanced lineup from top to bottom. Whitey Witt, the speedy leadoff man, had a career year in 1923. He batted .314, drove in 56 runs and scored 113. He also led the league with a .979 fielding average. The number two batter, Joe Dugan, was a model of consistency throughout the season and his career. In 1923, he hit a respectable .283 and scored 111 runs. The Pennsylvania native led all third basemen with a .974 fielding average. The clean-up hitter was the veteran Wally Pipp. The slick-fielding first baseman, who often played hurt, batted .304, drove in 108 runs and struck out only 28 times during the season. For years Pipp was the subject of a myth claiming he was replaced by Gehrig because of a headache. Not true. The real reason? He wasn't hitting. Bob Meusel, the man with the rifle arm in left field, batted .313 and drove in 91 runs. Nicknamed "Long Bob" for his lanky build, Meusel provided the key hit in the final game of the World Series. The catcher was Wally Schang, one of the finest handlers of pitchers in baseball. He missed almost half the season with an injury but still managed to hit .276. He caught all six games of the World Series and batted .318. Aaron Ward, who would have been the MVP of the World Series if there were such an award at the time, was an excellent second baseman who batted .284 and drove in 82 runs out of the seven hole. He was a college educated man and one of Huggins' favorites. Everett Scott, the team captain and tireless shortstop, was not noted for his hitting, but defensively he was in a class by himself. He batted only .246, but in 1923 he was the best fielding shortstop for the eighth consecutive year. He also finished the year having played in 1,138 consecutive games. Outfielder Elmer Smith and catcher Fred Hofmann came off the bench in many crucial situations to help the club nail down victories. Smith batted .306 and Hofmann .290 in limited but important roles.

As good as the everyday players were, the pitching was even better. It was the Yankees' strength, proven during the World Series. They had a five-man rotation that was second to none. All five had 16 or more victories, a record at the time and later matched by the 1998 Atlanta Braves of Greg Maddux (18–9), Tom Glavine (20–6), Denny Nagle (16–11), Kevin Millwood (17–8) and John Smoltz (17–3).

Sam Jones led the staff with 21 wins against only eight losses for a .724 winning percentage. His ERA was 3.63. Sad Sam also threw a no-hitter on September 4. Herb Pennock, who would be elected to the Hall of Fame in 1948 (the year he died), even topped Jones' winning percentage with a .760 mark. The only lefty on the club, Pennock won 19 and lost six games with a 3.13 ERA. He excelled in the Series, winning two of the team's four victories. Joe Bush, blessed with a mighty fastball, was the workhorse of the staff, pitching in over 275 innings. His record was 19–15 with a 3.43 ERA. He, too, pitched a gem in the World Series. Young Waite Hoyt, the kid from Brooklyn, had a marvelous season, winning 17 and losing nine while leading the staff with a 3.02 ERA. He publicly stated Huggins was the greatest manager who ever lived. The veteran Bob Shawkey, the opening day winner, won 16 and lost 11 with a 3.51 ERA. He also pitched well in the World Series. The sixth man in the rotation was Carl Mays, a troubled and controversial player, who would wind up in Huggins' doghouse. The little manager had strong suspicions that Mays threw games in the 1921 World Series. Huggins limited Mays' pitching to a little over 81 innings, but the hurler still managed to post a 5–2 record.

Lou Gehrig made his major league debut in 1923 but did little to help the club, playing in only seven games. He was sent down to Hartford to get more playing time and later recalled at the end of the season after the Yankees clinched the pennant. On his return to the Yankees, Gehrig made such a monumental impression (.427 batting average) with both Ruppert and Huggins, the two appealed to Commissioner Kenesaw Mountain Landis to declare

Lou eligible for the World Series. That effort fell flat on its face when Giants manager John McGraw said absolutely not.

As it turned out, Huggins didn't need Gehrig. The Yankees whipped the Giants in six games. Pennock, Bush, Jones and Shawkey led the Yankees pitching staff. The Yankees as a team batted .293 compared to the Giants' .234. Ruth hit .368, scored eight runs and belted three home runs. Meusel batted .269, had two triples and got the key hit in Game Six. Ward batted .417 and played a brilliant second. Joe Dugan batted .280 and played a solid third base. Scott saved his best World Series performance for 1923. He batted .318, drove in three runs and scored two. Pipp, playing hurt, added inspiration to help spark the club. Little Miller Huggins became the man of the hour and the toast of New York City as the Yankees captured their first World Series. The championship delivered a crushing blow to McGraw and the Giants, who were once the dominate club in all of baseball. As author Henry D. Fetter proclaimed in his book *Taking on the Yankees*, "With that World Series victory, the balance of baseball power shifted suddenly across the Harlem River, from Manhattan to the Bronx, never to return."[1]

That "baseball power" that Fetter mentions paved the way for the Yankees to begin a dynasty that would capture the hearts and minds of generations of baseball fans ... and it all started with the 1923 New York Yankees.

1

Ruppert and Huston
Buy the Yankees

Jacob Ruppert and Tillinghast L'Hommedieu Huston bought the New York Yankees in January, 1915, for $460,000. Ruppert was encouraged by American League president Ban Johnson to get involved with the purchase. Johnson was an ambitious leader and wanted an American League winner in the lucrative New York City market. He was unhappy with the ownership of Frank Farrell and William Devery, shady characters at best. Both men were hooked up with Tammany Hall politics and gambling. Once the money from gambling and graft dried up, they could no longer afford to operate the franchise. Their personal relationship also began to deteriorate, so they started looking for a buyer. Ruppert didn't need much encouragement. He loved baseball and, at one point, had considered buying the New York Giants. He was also interested in purchasing the Chicago Cubs, but changed his mind because Chicago was too far from Broadway.

John McGraw, the dynamic manager of the Giants, was Huston's close friend. "And it was through McGraw that Huston met Ruppert at the Polo Grounds to watch the Giants."[1] The Ruppert/Huston partnership was definitely not a marriage made in heaven. They were total opposites. Ruppert was a lifelong bachelor who made millions in his father's brewery and millions more in real estate. He was also a four-term congressman. He earned the title of Colonel because of his involvement in New York State's National Guard 7th Regiment. He raised St. Bernards and exhibited them at the Westminster Kennel Club shows in Madison Square Garden. He owned his own yacht, the "Albatross." He owned a fabulous estate in Garrison, New York, across the Hudson River from the United States Military Academy at West Point.

Ruppert was born into society and loved the good life. He was a fastidious dresser, employed a valet and often had shoes made to order. At all times he was well-groomed as appearance was important to him. Not to be fooled by his stylishness, Jacob Ruppert was a tough negotiator. His German accent often lent stature to his argument. Ruppert was the type person who wanted to be first in all endeavors. He had little tolerance for second best.

Huston was a Captain (thus the nickname "Cap") of Engineers in Cuba during the Spanish-American war. He stayed in Cuba for 10 years after the war and made a great deal of money improving the harbors in Havana and other port cities. Later he was a member of the Sixteenth Engineers during World War I when he was promoted to colonel. Huston also loved baseball.

Huston owned Dover Hill, a hunting lodge in Georgia's Glynn County. It contained 30,000 acres of hunting grounds. Between baseball seasons, his friends, such notables as Boston Red Sox owner Harry Frazee, Brooklyn Robins manager Wilbert Robinson, and Colonel Billy Pipp, father of Yankee first baseman, Wally, would gather at the lodge. He later built a home on Butler Island, Georgia, where he raised okra and iceberg lettuce. Huston's Midas touch eventually turned crop raising into a lucrative business.

On the personal side, Huston, to be perfectly frank, was a sloppy dresser. He would often wear the same suit several times during the week. He particularly didn't care about his appearance and didn't look like a millionaire. Perhaps his weight had something to do with it. He hovered around 300 pounds. He had been everywhere, seen everything and done everything. He was a world traveler. He was outgoing, well spoken and loved the company of baseball writers. He was an accomplished engineer and a savvy business man but sadly no match for Ruppert. Author Donald Honig succinctly summed up both men, "Outside of their interest in baseball, [wealth might also be included] the new owners had little in common. Huston was big, untidy, and gregarious, enjoying the company of ballplayers and sports writers. Ruppert ... was compact, an impeccable dresser, cordial but aloof."[2]

Ruppert, the stronger and more dominant personality as time would prove, became president of the Yankees, and Huston the veep. They would soon discover that buying the Yankees was the easy part. Building a winning team was the real challenge. Since 1903, when the Yankees were called the Highlanders, the best the team finished in the standings was second. That occurred in 1904, 1906 and 1910. In 1911, under the incorrigible, some even called him crooked, player/manager, Hal Chase, the Yankees finished sixth with a 76–76 record. Connie Mack's Philadelphia A's were the class of the league and beat the Yankees in 15 of 21 games. The team could hit, but the pitching was atrocious. Dropping from second to sixth was blamed on Chase. The fact that Farrell and Devery were running out of money was also a huge factor. Whether Chase was the culprit or not, a sleazy reputation didn't help. He was replaced in 1912 by Harry Wolverton, a veteran of the Pacific Coast

League. Under Wolverton the Yankees dropped all the way to the basement, losing an amazing 102 games. The pitching continued to fall apart. Russ Ford, who two years prior went 26–6, finished the season 13–21. Their defense was horrible. They committed 382 errors, tops in the American League. The situation sank so low that Devery was giving Wolverton advice on the finer points of the game. There was a brighter side, however, as two positives came out of the season. First, the Yankees adopted the famous pinstripes with the "NY" logo on the front of the shirt for all home games. The second was leaving Hilltop Park where attendance had dropped. Since plans for a new park were not realistic, the Yankees moved to the Polo Grounds to become tenants of the Giants, a move that would have interesting ramifications years later.

Frank Chance, who led the Chicago Cubs to three pennants in seven years, took over the managerial job in 1913. The Cubs had fired him for finishing third in 1912. Chance signed a lucrative three-year contract for $25,000 a year and 5 percent of the profits. He quickly found out the Yankees lacked talent, finishing seventh in 1913 with a 57–94 record. It was a slight improvement over the previous year. Entering 1914, the Yankees were still a hopeless mess in all facets of the game — offense, defense and pitching. When Chance tried to instill team discipline, the players ran to Farrell and Devery and complained. As the season wound down, Chance couldn't take it any more. He wanted out and offered to forgo the last year of his contract if the two owners would pay him through the end of the season. Harsh words were exchanged between Chance and Devery with the manager once taking a swing at the owner. When cooler heads prevailed, the owners paid Chance through the season and hired 23-year-old Roger Peckinpaugh for the remaining 17 games. His record was 9–8. The Yankees finished seventh again.

The first order of business for Ruppert and Huston was to hire a new manager. At the time the new owners purchased the Yankees, American League president Ban Johnson made promises he would help them build a competitive club. His first effort to keep his promise was his assistance in hiring Wild Bill Donovan, who had ended his pitching career after the 1912 season. In 1914, Donovan led Providence to the International League pennant. Even with that limited managerial experience, the former pitcher quickly realized the Yankees needed quality players. The good news was Ruppert and Huston knew it, too, had the money and were willing to spend it.

With Johnson's help the Yankees began to rebuild by acquiring talent like first baseman Wally Pipp and pitcher Bob Shawkey. It would be nice to say the two acquisitions helped turn the Yankees' fortunes around. They didn't even come close. Donovan led the club to a 69–83 record and a fifth-place finish, a whopping 32½ games in back of the first-place Boston Red Sox. Less than 250,000 fans came to the Polo Grounds to watch the Yankees play.

With the collapse of the Federal League after the 1915 season, the Yankees picked up Lee Magee and later, with the help of Johnson, purchased Frank "Home Run" Baker from Connie Mack. The 1916 Yankees got off to a fast start with Shawkey's pitching leading the way. In spite of a spate of injuries to key players—pitcher Nick Cullop, infielder Fritz Maisel and outfielders Frank Gilhooly and Hugh High, the Yankees remained on the top of the league. Then they went on a road trip and the roof caved in, as they lost 14 of 16. They limped to the finish line with an 80–74 mark and a fourth-place finish, 11 games behind the pennant-winning Red Sox. But with attendance up, it appeared the Yankees had turned the corner.

With the United States entry into World War I in April of 1917, the rise of the Yankees took a deep plunge. Half-owner Cap Huston enlisted. Pipp and Baker slumped, and Donovan, in Ruppert's opinion, lost control of the club. On top of this mess, attendance fell dramatically. The Yankees finished the season in sixth place with a 71–82 record, 28½ games behind the Chicago White Sox. It spelled the end for Donovan as the Yankees manager.

Once again the search for a new field leader began. The next manager would be the Yankees' ninth in fifteen years. This selection, however, would cause a major rift between Ruppert and Huston that never healed. Eventually, it would lead to the ouster of Huston and leave Ruppert the sole owner of the Yankees. Ruppert favored Miller Huggins as the new manager. Huston wanted Wilbert Robinson, his friend and hunting buddy. Actually, one could argue that Robinson was a better and more logical choice. He had been a coach for the New York Giants during their pennant winning seasons of 1911, 1912, and 1913. "Uncle Robbie," as he was affectionately called, also had some managerial experience with Brooklyn in the National League from 1914–1917. The results were erratic except for the pennant in 1916. But Brooklyn lost the World Series to Boston in five games.

Ruppert wanted no part of Robinson. He looked upon Robinson as a Huston crony. Once again, Ruppert was influenced by Ban Johnson, who knew Huggins well. He was also intrigued with the idea of stealing away Huggins from a National League team. Huggins had managed the St. Louis Cardinals the last five years, turning in a mediocre performance. In Huggins' defense, he lacked significant talent. Moreover, Huggins and the Cardinals' president, Branch Rickey, couldn't agree on a contract for the 1918 season. With Huston in France building railroads, Ruppert quickly seized the opportunity. On October 25 he signed Huggins to a Yankees contract. There was little Huston could do but rave and rant to Ruppert and the press from a distant Europe.

Huggins, nicknamed the "Mighty Mite," was a diminutive man, standing 5' 6" (it varies depending on the source) and weighing a mere 140 pounds. He played 13 years in the National League, six with Cincinnati and seven with St. Louis. His lifetime batting average was a modest .265. But what he lacked in power and physical stature he made up in heart and determination. Huggins led the National League in walks four times, on-base percentage and fielding average once each. He was a slick-fielding second baseman who would bunt and steal bases, anything to help his team win. He was not blessed with a great deal of natural ability but made the most of his God-given talent. His future success was not on the field but in the dugout. His experience playing under tough, aggressive and smart managers would serve him well with the Yankees. An abundance of talent wouldn't hurt either. As author Honig states, "He exuded a sense of strength, dignity, and integrity that rendered his slightness of frame irrelevant. Everyone who played for him, including that great unmanageable himself, Babe Ruth, came to admire and respect him."[3]

In 1918 with Miller Huggins at the helm, the Yankees finished a distant fourth, 13½ games behind the pennant-winning Boston Red Sox in an abbreviated season. It was an unusual season to say the least. The nation had finally entered World War I. Unlike the theater and film industries, the government declared baseball to be a nonessential activity. Thus, all able-bodied men had to serve in the military or in an industry essential to the war effort. This resulted in dozens of ballplayers leaving teams and entering military service. The Yankees lost one of their best pitchers, Bob Shawkey and outfielder Sammy Vick. Outstanding players like Hank Gowdy, Christy Mathewson and Casey Stengel also served. Other ballplayers followed from both major leagues. Some teams were affected more than others. The New York Giants lost outfielder Benny Kauff and two pitchers, Rube Benton and Jeff Tesreau. The Chicago Cubs were hardly affected and thus, won the pennant by 10½ games.

In the American League, Boston lost star left fielder Duffy Lewis, pitcher Herb Pennock and even their manager, Jack Barry, to Uncle Sam. With Barry gone, owner Harry Frazee quickly named Ed Barrow as the new field manager. It was a brilliant move by Frazee. Barrow, who had recently failed to raise the capital to buy into the Red Sox, had a long, varied and highly successful career in baseball.

Edward Grant Barrow was born on May 10, 1868, in Springfield, Illinois, to John and Effie Barrow. John gave his son the middle name of Grant because his hero was General Ulysses S. Grant. The Barrows left Springfield and headed to Nebraska to begin a life of farming. The rugged farming life didn't last long due to John's poor health. Eventually, the Barrows (now three sons) pulled up stakes and moved to the city of Des Moines where John worked delivering goods in the feed and grain business.

Young Barrow discovered his love of baseball in high school as a pitcher, but not for long. He had to quit school in his sophomore year because his father's health continued to decline, and he had to earn money to help the family. At age 16, Barrow took a job with the *Des Moines Daily News*. He left the *News* after a few years and joined the *Des Moines Leader*. He performed various tasks at the *Leader*, one of which was reporting on baseball. This assignment strengthened his love for the game and after quitting sand-lot ball due to a sore arm, his involvement with baseball took on more serious off-field challenges.

Joining other baseball enthusiasts, Barrow began organizing amateur baseball leagues. He was quite successful and during the experience met up with outfielder Fred Clarke, who would become a Hall of Famer. Barrow was now beginning to make important contacts in the baseball world. He was a born risk taker and didn't hesitate to jump into a new venture that sounded promising. After several of these endeavors (non-baseball related), some successful and others not so, he finally met up with Harry Stevens, who ran the scorecard concession at various ballparks. Through Stevens, Barrow met Connie Mack, and his association with the game continued to grow. Soon Barrow and friend Stevens became part owners of the minor league Wheeling, West Virginia, franchise in the Inter-State League. Shortly thereafter, Barrow had full control of the club, including being their manager. One of the players he

Ed Barrow joined the Yankees in 1920 as their general manager and would remain with the club for more than 25 years, assembling teams that won 10 world championships. He was also instrumental in converting Ruth from the mound to an everyday player when he managed the Boston Red Sox. (Courtesy National Baseball Hall of Fame Library, Cooperstown, New York.)

signed was the famous author of westerns, Zane Grey. Barrow's next adventure was the purchase of the Patterson, New Jersey, team in the Atlantic League. One of the players Barrow signed was the immortal Honus Wagner. He considered Wagner the best baseball player ever. This is quite a pronouncement considering he was the Yankees' general manager during Ruth's prime.

Barrow's organizational and administrative skills stood him well. In the Atlantic League he rose to become president, a position he held for three years. He was also president of two other minor leagues—the Eastern League and the International League. The talented Barrow was also field manager for the Indianapolis Indians, the Montreal Royals and the Toronto Maple Leafs, all minor league clubs. In the major leagues, prior to Frazee's appointment of him to the Red Sox job, he managed the Detroit Tigers. Not quite 35 years old in 1903, Barrow led the Tigers to a fifth-place finish with a 65–71 record. It was a slight improvement over the previous year when the Tigers finished next-to-last under the guidance of Frank Dwyer. In 1904, halfway through the season, Barrow resigned. He and owner Frank Navin disagreed on a trade Barrow made with White Sox owner Charles Comiskey. Once Navin took the side of Comiskey and cancelled the trade, Barrow's days were numbered.

Back in Boston and eager to succeed in his new job as manager of the Red Sox, Barrow wasted little time. He made several important trades and shifts to the 1918 club, but the greatest and most important was to take Babe Ruth off the mound and put him in the outfield.

In 1917, under manager Jack Barry, Ruth had pitched in 41 games (over 326 innings) with an outstanding record of 24–13 and an ERA of 2.01. In 1918, Barrow reduced Ruth's pitching to 20 games and 166-plus innings. The Babe won 13, lost 7 and had an earned run average of 2.22. When not pitching, he played left field, and in 317 at-bats hit .300 with 11 home runs (most in the league) and drove in 66 runs. The following year the transfer of Ruth to an everyday player was completed. Ruth pitched in only 133-plus innings, posting a 9–5 record with a still low 2.97 ERA, but he had 432 at-bats and hit 29 home runs while driving in 114 runs and scoring 103, all league-leading numbers. He also batted .322. Unbeknown to the Yankees front office or anyone else for that matter, Ed Barrow had set the stage for Ruth to become the greatest baseball player in the history of the game, but regrettably not for the Boston Red Sox.

In 1919, the Yankees didn't have an abundance of talent. Except for Shawkey, who won 20, the rest of the staff was mediocre. The offense was average, too. Baker led the team with 10 home runs. Duffy Lewis batted .272

but drove in 89 runs, the most on the club. The shortstop, Roger Peckinpaugh, was the only .300 hitter, and he barely made it at .305. All things considered, the Yankees were lucky to finish third, 7½ games in back of the Chicago White Sox. During the late summer the Yankees completed an important but highly controversial acquisition by obtaining submarine pitcher Carl Mays from Boston. In return, the Yankees gave the Red Sox two pitchers, Allan Russell and Bob McGraw, and a player to be named later, plus $50,000. Mays was an effective pitcher but as unpredictable as the weather. He was mean and disliked by many players. For his first four years with Boston he turned in an outstanding record of 67–40 with an average ERA of 2.23. But in 21 games in 1919, the right-hander surprisingly slumped to 5–11. The slow start was not Mays' chief problem. It was his short fuse. Prior to the trade, Mays had thrown a ball at a fan who had been heckling him. American League president Ban Johnson immediately fined him $100. Mays refused to pay. The end came on July 13. Mays, pitching against the White Sox, completed the fifth inning and stormed off the mound to the dressing room, angrily saying, "I'll never pitch for this club again."[4] Apparently Boston had enough of Mays' antics and unloaded him to the Yankees.

In 1919, baseball had one of its best years ever in terms of attendance and revenue. No doubt, one of the big reasons was a young man playing for the Boston Red Sox by the name of Babe Ruth. As previously mentioned, Ruth had a fabulous season. This made Boston owner Harry Frazee's announcement on Monday, January 5, 1920, that he sold Ruth to the New York Yankees for $100,000, so shocking. It was the most lucrative cash deal to date. The baseball world was stunned. Frazee tried to justify the sale by blaming Ruth for Boston's sixth-place finish. He also berated the Babe for his shenanigans during the season and said that the Yankees were taking a huge gamble thinking they could straighten out the uncontrollable outfielder. The Boston fans were in shock. How could Frazee sell the greatest baseball player ever? The answer was obvious. He needed money to keep his theatrical interests afloat. Others claimed it was simply another bad baseball deal; if so, this one was a real whopper. Regardless, one unequivocal fact remained—Ruppert, Huston, Huggins and the Yankees' fans were ecstatic and looked forward to the 1920 season. Also, in early 1920 with significantly less fanfare, the Yankees purchased the contract of Bob Meusel from the Vernon Tigers of the Pacific Coast League. It was a shrewd purchase and one that would benefit the Yankees for years to come.

Once again, even with Ruth, the Yankees failed to win a pennant, finishing third in 1920 with a much improved 95–59 record, a mere three games behind the Cleveland Indians. Ruth had a fabulous year. He batted .376 with 54 home runs, 137 runs batted in, 158 runs scored, a .530 on-base percentage and an .847 slugging average. He led the American League in all these categories except batting average. Although Huggins hadn't won a pennant since he became manager of the Yankees, each year the club was inching closer and closer to a first-place finish.

The Yankees of 1921 made some significant changes in the front office and on the field. Ed Barrow, the Boston field manager, left the dugout to join the Yankees as their business manager, (equivalent to today's general manager) filling the vacancy left open by the death of Harry Sparrow. The hiring of Barrow on October 28, 1920, was a stroke of genius. Barrow, who had known Ruppert and Huston through his dealings with them as president of the International League, was a rare individual. He was a large man with bushy eyebrows. He lacked a sense of humor and had little sympathy for slumping ballplayers. Barrow was also a tough negotiator. He came to the Yankees with a world of experience and a skill for organizing and recognizing talent. He and Ruppert would work as a close-knit team regarding trades, player purchases and salary negotiations. Ed Barrow would remain with the Yankees for more than 25 years and contribute significantly to the creation of their dynasty.

Less than two months after Barrow joined the Yankees, he was instrumental in obtaining Waite Hoyt, Wally Schang, Harry Harper and Mike McNally from Boston for Muddy Ruel, Del Pratt, Sammy Vick and Hank Thormalen. The New York press severely criticized the trade. In their opinion it was one-sided in favor of Boston. Some, cynically, believed Barrow was still working for Frazee. Of course, that was not true, and the press was dead wrong. The trade turned out to be a good one for the Yankees. Schang was a solid catcher for the next five years. Hoyt proved to be the gem, winning 19 along with Carl Mays (27–9) and Shawkey (18–12) as the Yankees won 98 games, edging Cleveland in a season-long struggle to win their first pennant in 1921. Mays' 27 victories were the most of any pitcher in the league. Ruth turned in another fabulous season. He hit .378 and still didn't win the batting title, which went to the Tigers' Harry Heilmann at .394. In fact, Ruth finished third behind Ty Cobb, who hit .389. But the Babe led the American League in just about every other category: home runs (59), runs batted in (171), runs scored (177), walks (144), on-base percentage (.512) and slugging average (.846). Bob Meusel chipped in with 24 home runs and 135 RBIs. Ruth was at his peak physically at 6' 2" and a muscular 220 pounds. Teamed with Meusel, the duo formed a formidable one-two punch. The Yankees' attendance reached almost 1.3 million as fans couldn't get enough of the Babe.

The Yankees faced the New York Giants in the World Series, the first of three consecutive confrontations between the two clubs. McGraw was fresh off of winning a spectacular pennant race by coming back from a seven-and-a-half game deficit on August 24 to pass the Pittsburgh Pirates and win by four games. Since the Yankees were still the Giants' tenants, all games were played at the Polo Grounds. The clubs alternated daily as to the home team. It was the last of the five-out-of-nine Series.

The Yankees jumped off to a fast start. Carl Mays pitched the first game and blanked the Giants, 3–0, in spite of Frankie Frisch's 4-for-4 day. Game Two saw the young kid from Brooklyn, Waite Hoyt, hurl a brilliant two-hit shutout for the second 3–0 victory for the Yankees. No doubt some Yankee fans had visions of a sweep. In Game Three, the Yankees scored four runs in the top of the third, but the Giants came right back with four of their own, tying the score and chasing starter Bob Shawkey. The game remained tied until the Giants unloaded on reliever Jack Quinn in the seventh, scoring eight runs and winning the game, 13–5. After a day of rain, the Giants came back and beat the Yankees, 4–2, before a boisterous crowd of over 36,000. Phil Douglas pitched a marvelous clutch game for the Giants. Mays pitched a solid game, too, until the eighth when he gave up three controversial runs that would haunt him for the rest of his Yankees' career. Ruth hit his first World Series home run.

Hoyt and Art Nehf faced each other again in Game Five with almost the same results—the Yankees won, 3–1, and regained the lead in the Series. That victory turned out to be the Yankees' swan song. They lost the next three games, handing the Giants their first World Series championship since 1905. Not to diminish the Giants' victory, but Ruth had developed an abscess on his left elbow, the result of stealing third in Game Two, and was only available as a pinch-hitter the last three games.

Some in the baseball world were happy to see the Yankees lose. There were Yankee haters even as far back as 1921. Fans felt the Yankees were arrogant and had bought a pennant. Sound familiar? Joe Vila, writing for *The Sporting News*, was particularly harsh when he professed to know why Ruth and the other Yankees were knocking the cover off the ball during the season. He opined, "Punk pitching was the real reason, pitching by many half-baked youngsters who knew little or nothing at all about strategy.... But when the Bambino and his ball-smashing companions went up against the Giants' pitchers, Douglas, Barnes and Nehf ... the light was turned on and thousands of deluded fans suddenly realized how badly they had been fooled by the so-called supermen wearing the Yankee uniforms."[5]

Although the Yankees' defeat was a disappointment, the team had little time to brood. Before the 1922 season even began, Ruth signed a lucrative contract to barnstorm around the country. Meusel, Bill Piercy, Mays and Schang agreed to join him. Commissioner Kenesaw Mountain Landis had other thoughts. He convinced Mays and Schang not to go. The other three held firm. Landis took action, finally deciding to enforce the rule that had been in effect since 1911 banning such tours by World Series participants. On December 5, Landis said he would hold back the barnstormers' World Series money, but more importantly, he suspended the three culprits until May 20 of the 1922 season. Eventually the barnstormers received their World Series money, but suspended players, under baseball rules at the time, did not get paid.

Barrow, to help offset the suspensions, traded shortstop Roger Peckinpaugh and pitchers Jack Quinn, Bill Piercy and Rip Collins to Boston for Everett Scott, Joe Bush and Sad Sam Jones. Contrary to Barrow's last trade with Boston, the New York press praised this one. Scott was a slick-fielding shortstop, Bush and Jones were front-end pitchers who could give a team 250 innings or more. Boston owner Frazee had the audacity to claim the trade was beneficial to the Red Sox. "I feel I have considerably strengthened the team and see no reason for discontent," he said.[6]

In February, the Yankees announced they had purchased land in the Bronx from the estate of William Waldorf Astor across the Harlem River from the Polo Grounds for $600,000. The sale price has also been reported as high as $675,000. Whatever the true amount, it was a bargain for a 10-acre site that was previously used as a lumber yard. Why did the Yankees buy the old lumber yard? It's an interesting story that started back in 1903 when the struggling Yankees, known then as the Highlanders, were playing in Hilltop Park, built on a piece of land in Washington Heights. It was a simple, wooden structure that held 15,000 people. It was constructed in a hurry and looked it. It lacked class and fitted in well with the surrounding tenement slums. Hilltop Park could not compete with its neighbor, the Polo Grounds, a mile or so away. In 1913 the Yankees abandoned Hilltop Park and became the tenants of the Polo Grounds, which was owned by the New York Giants. The Yankees paid the Giants $65,000 a year in rent to play their home games at the Polo Grounds. In 1913 the Yankees were a floundering club. Manager John McGraw and the New York Giants were on top of the baseball world. Under McGraw's disciplined leadership, the Giants won the World Series in 1905 and consecutive National League pennants in 1911, 1912, and 1913. They won the pennant again in 1917. It was obvious the Yankees were the second most popular team in New York, and McGraw was not threatened in the least and content to have his friends, Ruppert and Huston, as tenants since the Giants consistently outdrew the Yankees. Once the Yankees obtained Ruth in 1920, the situation changed drastically. Ruth and the Yankees' popularity soared, as did the team's attendance at the Polo Grounds. In fact, the 1919 season was the last the Giants would outdraw their tenants. Here are the attendance figures at the Polo Grounds, pre- and post–Ruth:

	1919	*1920*	*1921*	*1922*
New York Giants	708,857	929,609	973,477	945,809
New York Yankees	619,164	1,289,422	1,230,696	1,026,134

McGraw was becoming increasingly irritated by the Yankees' success. He wanted them out of the Polo Grounds. Eventually, he would get his way. But in the meantime, cooler heads prevailed when Giants owner Horace Stoneham told Ruppert the Yankees could stay at the Polo Grounds in 1921 and beyond but their rent would be increased to $100,000. With little choice, Ruppert agreed to the outrageous new rental fee, but it wouldn't be for long.

On May 5 the White Construction Company began building Yankee Stadium. It was completed in 284 days at a cost of $2.5 million, and the project was finished on time.

Yankee Stadium was designed by the Osborn Engineering Company of Cleveland. This was the same firm that would redesign historic Fenway Park 10 years later. Although it was the largest and most magnificent stadium at the time, the engineers at Osborn made a huge mistake. "The wooden right field fence jutted out 12 feet into fair territory, perpendicular to the right field foul line ... then the 12-foot-high fence ran straight back to the wall."[7] It was aptly called "The Bloody Angle" and created crazy caroms that kept visiting right fielders anxious and frustrated. Mercifully, it was corrected prior to the 1924 season.

Ruppert's dream of a cathedral-like ballpark to match the popularity of the bigger-than-life Babe Ruth, the greatest drawing card in the game, was finally realized. No details were spared. Huston insisted on 10 restrooms for men and six for women. Male chauvinism? Not really. In those days men far outnumbered women at games. A brick-lined vault was buried 15 feet under second base. It housed telephone, telegraph and electrical equipment specifically for the press to function ringside during boxing events. The ultimate touch was the scalloped frieze that capped the grandstand roof.

Sportswriter Fred Lieb cleverly named the Stadium "The House That Ruth Built." However, some thought the colossus should have been more appropriately called "The House Built For Ruth." The distance from home plate to the right-field foul pole measured a mere 295 feet, a checked-swing homer for the Babe. Also, right-center field, the power alley, was 429 feet (still a good poke) compared to 449 feet at the Polo Grounds, another advantage for Ruth. The Stadium was purposely situated so the sun would set in left field, making it difficult to catch fly balls late in the game. Historically, left field at Yankee Stadium has always been known as the "sun field" and is a special challenge to players on visiting teams. This Yankees advantage all but disappeared with the transition from all day games to almost all night games.

Yankee Stadium, the shiny, new palace of the Bronx, was now ready to serve the massive crowds that would soon pass through its turnstiles. Even the word "Stadium" was unique and had a certain panache to it. Baseball fans were accustomed to names like "grounds," "fields" and "parks," mundane at best. But a stadium connotes something on a grander scale, something spacious and breathtaking. Ruppert's dream was now a reality. He simply built the Taj Mahal of ballparks.

In January, 1922, as baseball fans began thinking about spring training and a new season, they were reminded of Ruth's pending suspension. Thousands of New York fans petitioned Commissioner Landis to cancel the suspension. He refused. Ruth made some feeble attempts to contact Landis but to no avail. Even Ed Barrow, the Yankees' general manager, paid a call on Landis. The stern commissioner still didn't budge. On opening day, the crusade continued. Landis was adamant, and the suspension of Ruth, Meusel and Piercy remained.

The Yankees' 1922 spring training camp moved to New Orleans. Big mistake. Apparently the Yankees spent more time at the French Quarter than on the diamond. Huggins couldn't stop them and temporarily lost control of the team. This was not a good situation since Huston was never happy with the signing of Huggins in 1918, and he was still looking for a reason to fire him.

But the Yankees were now a powerful team and could absorb distractions and still be the team to beat in the American League. Barrow, not bashful about spending Ruppert's money, acquired more key players. In April, he purchased Whitey Witt from the Philadelphia A's for a reported $16,000. In late July, the Yankees sent Chick Fewster, Elmer Miller, Johnny Mitchell, Lefty O'Doul and $50,000 to (guess who?) Boston for Joe Dugan (arguably the best third baseman in the league) and Elmer Smith.

It came as no surprise then that the Yankees repeated their winning ways in 1922, edging out the St. Louis Browns by one game for their second consecutive pennant. Ruth had an "off year," batting .315 and hitting 35 home runs while driving in 99, a huge reduction from the previous year. Meusel slowed his pace also. He batted .319 with 16 home runs and 84 RBIs. No doubt the suspension had an effect, but pitching saved the day. Shawkey was 20–12, Hoyt 19–12, Jones 13–13, Bush 26–7, and Mays 13–14. Joe Bush was the difference, more than making up for Mays' off year.

Once again, the Yankees faced the New York Giants in the World Series. With an excellent pitching staff, the Yankees were strong favorites which turned out to mean nothing. The Yankees just didn't lose the Series. They were humiliated. They were swept! The best they could do was tie the Giants in

Game Two, called on account of darkness. Ruth's performance was miserable. He was a complete flop. He batted .118 with no home runs and one RBI, and he went hitless in his last three games. McGraw took credit for Ruth's poor showing. In his autobiography, *My Thirty Years in Baseball*, he explained his pitching strategy to Ruth, "...we pitched but nine curves and three fast balls to Ruth throughout the series. All the rest were slow balls.... Our respect for the way he tears into a fast ball is indicated by our giving him but three to hit at during the entire series."[8] Schang, Scott and Ward all hit under .200 for the Series. McGraw's pitching staff of Art Nehf, Hugh McQuillan, Rosy Ryan, Jack Scott and Jesse Barnes held the hard-hitting Yankees to a .203 team batting average, while the Giants were hitting at a .309 clip. The Giants staff turned in an unheard-of 1.76 earned run average. There is no excuse for the Yankees' poor performance, but an important fact to consider is, as author Noel Hynd stated, "The 1922 edition of the Giants was probably the greatest squad in the history of the franchise.... No fewer than five players—Kelly, Frisch, Bancroft, Youngs and Stengel—were future Hall of Famers, as was coach Jennings and manager McGraw. They'd won more than 60 percent of their games in a difficult league, had hit .305 as a team...."[9]

The Giants' second consecutive World Series victory gave the National League a huge boost in popularity. It was the first time the Senior Circuit had accomplished this feat in 13 years. Since the players shared in only four games rather than the five in 1921, their earnings dropped. The Giants' shares were $4,470 and the Yankees $3,225.

Even though the Yankees' attendance was higher than the Giants' for the last three years, John McGraw and his team still owned New York by virtue of their last two World Series Championships. But not for long. The 1923 team would finally start the New York Giants down the path of eventual mediocrity and, at the same time, launch the greatest dynasty in sports history.

2

Opening Day

In late January, 1923, the Yankees traded Norm McMillan, George Murray and Camp Skinner, along with $50,000, to Boston for veteran left-hander Herb Pennock. After six-plus years with the Red Sox, all Pennock had to show for his efforts was a 60–59 record. The Boston press and fans had mixed reactions to the trade. Some felt it was simply another bad deal, one more example of the Yankees stocking their staff with a veteran Boston pitcher. Others believed that Pennock, who showed flashes of brilliance, didn't have the stamina to be effective for a full season.

The *Boston Post* was particularly critical, reminding all its readers that Harry Frazee promised to rebuild the club when he hired Frank Chance as the new manager. Obtaining three average ballplayers was not considered helping the club and was a sorry beginning to a new season. The *Post* went on to predict Boston fans would be quite upset. The *Boston Herald* looked upon the trade differently. It felt McMillan, Murray and Skinner were promising ballplayers and vigorous prospects and even went so far as to call them "brilliant." Further checking the careers of each revealed the *Herald* might have exaggerated a tad. The *Boston Globe* agreed with the *Post* that the fans would be agitated but somewhat resigned to the fact that what the Yankees want, they usually get, based on past transactions. The Pennock deal was not Frazee's and Boston's finest moment.

For the Yankees the trade turned out to be one more brilliant move. Under Miller Huggins, Pennock would become an outstanding pitcher and go on to a Hall of Fame career. With the addition of Pennock, the 1923 Yankees were now complete. The only players remaining from 1918 when Huggins became manager were Aaron Ward (who played sparingly) and Wally Pipp. The rest had either been sold, traded away or released. If anyone was counting, 11 of the 24 players on the Yankees had been obtained from Frazee. The 1923 Yankees were now poised to make baseball history.

Prior to spring training, the bad feelings harbored in the front office by the Giants' drubbing of the Yankees in the World Series were still lingering. Rumors were circulating in the press that the salaries of several of the stars had been drastically reduced. Names weren't mentioned, however, as to the players who were in jeopardy of a pay cut. One has to remember these were the days of the reserve clause where ballplayers had very little to say about their salary or contract. It was a case of "sign or don't play." Free agency and agents representing the career and financial interests of a player were more than 50 years away.

In a formal statement to the press, Jacob Ruppert categorically denied that certain Yankee players would have their salaries cut. Ruppert went even further to say that not one player was asked to accept an actual reduction. Ruppert went on to state that two or three players would have to "take their work more seriously" if they were to receive the same salary in 1923. What it amounted to was a cute way of saying "We didn't like the way you played in the World Series, and if it continues, it will hurt your wallet."

Cutting through Ruppert's convoluted jargon, the explanation was simple: those two or three players who had to buckle down were offered bonuses if they performed at a certain level. If pitchers win a certain number of games and everyday players hit for a certain average, they will receive the bonus. Here's the cute part. That bonus would only bring the player's salary to the level it was the previous year. It wasn't a cut in salary or a bonus. It was neither fish nor fowl. When it came to money, Jacob Ruppert could bob and weave with the best of them.

At 4:50 P.M. on February 15, a train pulled out of Penn Station headed for Hot Springs, Arkansas. It carried the most famous baseball player in the world—Babe Ruth. Greeting the press in his luxurious Pullman berth, the Babe probably reflected on his previous season in which he hit .315 with 35 home runs and 99 RBIs, a disappointing performance for Ruth, a great year for anyone else. It's possible his thoughts drifted to 1920 and 1921, two seasons in which he captured the hearts and minds of baseball fans around the country. In 1920, he led the American League with 54 home runs, 137 runs batted in, 148 walks, 158 runs, a .530 on-base percentage and a slugging average of .847. His .376 batting average was fourth-best behind the leader, George Sisler of the St. Louis Browns, who posted a sensational .407. The following year he again led the league with 59 home runs, 171 RBIs, 144 walks, 177 runs, a .512 on-base percentage and a slugging average of .846. Ruth finished third in the batting race with a .378 average behind Detroit Tiger, Harry Heilmann, at .394 and teammate Ty Cobb at .389.

Ruth, hardly recognized by anyone other than the press, was in a contrite mood. "I want to tell you fellows that I'm looking forward seriously to my training work in the South. There's nothing funny about it for me. I realize that I made many foolish mistakes last year and did not play up to my form," he confessed. "Whatever else I am going to say to the fans I will say with homers," added Ruth.[1]

Babe Ruth arrived in Hot Springs supposedly to lose weight by hiking, bathing and playing golf. His goal was to get down to 200 pounds. Some people were skeptical about the activities at Hot Springs, especially the golf. He, Carl Mays and Bob Shawkey loved the game. Ruth was planning on a round or two, but his luggage had failed to arrive at Hot Springs, so he settled for a bath and a session with the trainer. He was asked to step on a scale but refused. He said he wanted seven days of golfing, hiking and bathing before he weighed himself. He was concentrating on reducing his waist line and chest measurement.

Ruth was the only Yankee to show up at Hot Springs. There were, however, several players from other major league clubs, namely, Burleigh Grimes and Dazzy Vance of the Brooklyn Robins (the name "Dodgers" first appeared on the team's uniform in 1933) and pitchers Stan Coveleski, George Uhle and Sherwood Smith from the Cleveland Indians. Tris Speaker, the Indians' manager, made it known he had high expectations for his three starters. He was depending on them to win 20 to 25 games each during the upcoming season. Coveleski and Smith disappointed Speaker, but Uhle would lead the league with 26 wins while the Cleveland Indians finished in third place, 16½ games back of the Yankees.

Eventually, most all the Yankees would join Ruth, including owner Cap Huston, who wanted to keep a close eye on his players. Huston was impressed with the splendid condition in which he found the Yankees players. He was particularly satisfied with the condition of Carl Mays, who had lost a considerable amount of weight and was in the best condition since becoming a Yankee. Mays welcomed the compliment and then challenged the owner to play a round of golf for 50 cents a hole the next day, which Huston quickly accepted. Then Mays, Ruth, Bob Shawkey, and Joe Bush played eighteen holes on a somewhat wet course, while Mike McNally and Wally Schang hiked through the mountains. Everett Scott didn't leave the hotel all day. By all accounts, however, it appeared that golf was the preferred form of exercise if you want to call it that.

Prior to leaving for the official spring training camp in New Orleans, Ruth became ill with a slight fever and was ordered to bed by doctor W.T. Wotten. Confined to bed, Ruth amused himself by reading the many telegrams he received from numerous fans. Some even wanted to know if he was still alive. "I think I'll want to die if I don't get out of the bed pretty soon," he said jokingly, "but I just can't make it. An omelette for breakfast, the first solid food I have had since Thursday, helped some, but my efforts must have sent my temperature up because I've had a slight fever ever since."[2] Finally, after four bed-ridden days, Ruth felt well enough to travel to New Orleans and join his teammates. He was greeted by manager Miller Huggins at the Hotel Grunewald. This time Ruth was enthusiastic when he spoke to the press. "I feel great," said Ruth. "But for the next several days I'll take things easy. I don't think I will do any practicing before Saturday. I weigh about 202 pounds now and am ready for the training camp grind and the coming season. I haven't felt so fine in several years."[3] It's safe to assume Huggins was smiling from ear to ear.

Huggins announced that the training day would be from 11 A.M. to 2 P.M. He also told the press he anticipated few changes to the previous year's lineup except for a possible switch of Joe Dugan and Aaron Ward, but it never materialized. He expressed confidence that his club would win a third consecutive American League pennant.

On March 31, the Brooklyn Robins and Yankees began their annual inter-borough spring series. Brooklyn was managed by none other than Wilbert Robinson, the same Uncle Robbie Huston wanted to manage the Yankees back in 1918 when Ruppert outfoxed him and named Huggins instead. The two teams played each other 15 times on the way north, traveling through Louisiana, Mississippi, Texas, Oklahoma and Missouri, an exhausting schedule compared to today's relatively relaxed spring training. The last game was played on April 16 at Ebbets Field in Brooklyn, and the Robins won, 7–3. In all, the Yankees won 9 and Brooklyn 6.

In spite of the Yankees' winning the series from Brooklyn, there was one cause for concern. Shortstop Everett Scott had injured his left ankle. He was running from first to second trying to avoid a forceout when he made a foolish mistake of not sliding. Running hard into the bag, his spikes caught and twisted his ankle. He was carried off the field and treated with ice packs to help reduce the swelling. Torn tendons was the initial diagnosis, and some were even thinking it might be a career-ending injury.

Aside from the concern to Scott's health and career, his streak of playing in 986 consecutive games was in jeopardy since the season opener was only days away. Today, Scott's streak appears paltry compared to those of Lou Gehrig and Cal Ripken, but in 1923 it was a gigantic feat. In fact, it was the longest streak, at the time, in the game's history. Like all fairy tales, this one had a happy ending, too. X-rays on Scott's ankle proved negative, just a sprain. Scott would play short on opening day.

On the same day Scott sprained his ankle, Fred Merkle, former first baseman for the New York Giants, hit four home runs in a game for Rochester in the International League. At age 35, Merkle was back in the minor leagues after 14 seasons in the majors. His name would always be linked to one of the most controversial plays in baseball history. It happened in 1908 and is still discussed and written about 100 years later. Merkle was in his second year playing for McGraw's Giants. On September 23, the Chicago Cubs trailed the Giants by mere percentage points in the standings. Giants great Christy Mathewson was locked in a pitchers' duel with Chicago's Jack Pfiester. The score was 1–1 in the bottom of the ninth. Harry "Moose" McCormick was on first with two out. Merkle singled, sending McCormick to third. The next batter, Al Bridwell, also singled, scoring McCormick with the winning run. Twenty thousand Giant fans went berserk. Not so fast. What happened next was one of the most controversial mixups in baseball history. Thousands of spectators poured onto the field while umpires Hank O'Day and

Fred Merkle, blamed by some for losing the 1908 pennant for the New York Giants, but not by his manager, John McGraw. Regardless, Merkle would forever enter baseball lore with the unflattering nickname "Bonehead." (Courtesy National Baseball Hall of Fame Library, Cooperstown, New York.)

Bob Emslie were running off. Chicago second baseman Johnny Evers seeing that Merkle never touched second base but headed for the clubhouse, called for the ball from center fielder Solly Hofman. Hofman obliged but overshot Evers with the errant toss with the ball landing near shortstop Joe Tinker. Joe McGinnity, coaching third base for the Giants, realized what the Chicago players were up to and wrested the ball from Tinker and threw it into the left field stands. End of story? Not quite.

Mysteriously, a second ball appeared on the playing field! Evers picked it up and touched second base for the forceout of Merkle. Evers demanded a call from umpire Emslie, who claimed he didn't see the play, so he asked his partner, O'Day, who said he did and called Merkle out. The game was still tied, 1–1. When O'Day saw all the spectators on the field, he called the game on account of darkness. It would be replayed if it had a bearing on the pennant race.

This was 1908, and the pennant gods, working overtime, had a real sense of humor. Yes, the season ended in a tie, forcing a replay of the game between the New York Giants and the Chicago Cubs. Much to the chagrin of thousands of Giant fans, New York lost the game and the pennant, and Merkle would forever enter baseball lore with the unflattering nickname "Bonehead."

The day before the unveiling of Yankee Stadium, the Bronx was alive with anticipation. Huge crowds were expected to attend the game against their hated rivals, the Boston Red Sox. Long time Yankee fans had anxiously waited since 1912 for this historic moment. Those were the days when the Highlanders played in Washington Heights in a park with antiquated wooden stands. Now they were eager to enter a monument to baseball put together with concrete and steel—2,300 tons of structural steel, to be specific. The Stadium was the grandest ballpark ever constructed at the time. Dignitaries from all parts of the country were flocking into New York City to attend the grand opening. Yankee fans gobbled up tickets and by the afternoon all the reserved seats were sold. Unreserved seats in the grandstand and uncovered seats were on a "first come, first serve" basis. To accommodate the large crowds, Barrow arranged to have 36 ticket windows and 40 turnstiles ready and waiting for the onslaught. The police were handling the security while additional express trains were provided both on the elevated and subway. It appeared everything was in place and ready for the big event.

Ruppert, Huston and Barrow had done their jobs, now the focus was on the pint-sized manager, Miller Huggins, who announced that Bob Shawkey would be his starting pitcher and that Scott would start at shortstop. Huggins had relented when he found out Scott's ankle had improved significantly. Scott's starting at short would preserve his streak of 986 consecutive games played. The batting order shown below would be used by Huggins every day, except when injuries occurred that were serious enough to keep a starting player out of the lineup. Fortunately, the injuries were kept to a minimum, including those on the pitching staff:

Whitey Witt	CF
Joe Dugan	3B
Babe Ruth	RF
Wall Pipp	1B
Bob Meusel	LF
Wally Schang	C
Aaron Ward	2B
Everett Scott	SS

At game time the sun was shining and the sky was clear, but the temperature was a brisk 49 degrees. People wore sweaters, coats and hats. Viewing

Opening day at Yankee Stadium, April 18, 1923. Even though the *New York Times* reported attendance at 74,200, the actual figure was more like 62,000, which meant 4,000 stood to watch the Yankees beat the Red Sox, 4–1. (Courtesy National Baseball Hall of Fame Library, Cooperstown, New York.)

photographs of the packed Stadium, it is almost impossible to find a man or young boy without a hat or cap. Clearly, a sign of the times. Even back in 1923 the New York Yankees and the Boston Red Sox weren't particularly fond of each other, so a hard-fought game was anticipated and few fans were disappointed.

The *New York Times* ran the headline, "74,200 See Yankees Open New Stadium; Ruth Hits Home Run."[4] Great headline. Not true. Apparently, a zealous head counter overstated the attendance by thousands since the capacity was 58,000. An audit later in the season set the official attendance at 62,000, which means some 4,000 fans stood the entire game. Whatever the final figure, it was a record crowd for a baseball game at the time. It was also reported that 25,000 fans were turned away. The turned-away estimate was probably near accurate.

Cars were parked everywhere imaginable, some on the street, some in empty lots, some wherever there was a space. The well-off had black sedans and limousines lined up on unpaved roads outside the Stadium. Crowds

Opening day 1923: owner Jacob Ruppert flanked by manager Miller Huggins and Boston manager Frank Chance. The Yankees won the historic game 4–1 behind the outstanding pitching of Bob Shawkey and Babe Ruth's three-run homer in the bottom of the third. The Yankees would finish the season 98–54 for their third consecutive American League pennant and then finally beat the New York Giants in the World Series for their first championship. (Courtesy National Baseball Hall of Fame Library, Cooperstown, New York.)

poured out of trains. Even when standing room-only signs were posted at the ticket booths, it didn't stop the hoards of people.

Pre-game ceremonies were elaborate. Red-white-and-blue bunting was draped throughout the Stadium. Manager Huggins hoisted the American flag in center field while the talented and popular John Philip Sousa conducted the Seventh Regiment Band playing the "Star-Spangled Banner." Governor Al Smith threw out the first ball to catcher Wally Schang. Other dignitaries included Commissioner Landis, Ruppert, Huston, Barrow, the great Giants pitcher Christy Mathewson and even Red Sox owner and Yankee trading partner Harry Frazee. Mayor John F. Hylan missed the game due to the flu.

From left to right, Yankees co-owner Jacob Ruppert, Commissioner Landis
and co-owner of the Yankees Cap Huston, some of the many celebrities that
attended opening day, April 18, 1923, at Yankee Stadium. Two months later
Huston sold his half-interest in the Yankees to Ruppert, but still followed the
club throughout the season and into the World Series. (Courtesy National
Baseball Hall of Fame Library, Cooperstown, New York.)

True to his word, Huggins selected veteran pitcher Bob Shawkey to start for the Yankees. In 1922 the right-hander was the workhorse of the staff, pitching in almost 300 innings. He posted a 20–12 record with an ERA of 2.91. The Red Sox went with right-hander Howard Ehmke who was 17–17 in '22 with the Detroit Tigers but would win 20 games this season. In the bottom of the third, the Yankees were leading, 1–0. Whitey Witt was on third and Joe Dugan on first. Ruth came to the plate as the crowd roared. Ehmke was a deliberate, slow-working veteran who could drive a batter and spectator mad waiting for him to deliver the ball. With Ehmke pitching carefully, Ruth worked the count to 2–2, then timed a change-up and lined a home run just inside the right field foul pole to give the Yankees a 4–0 lead. The fans went wild with excitement. Hats were tossed in the air with abandon. At this great moment, who cared where they landed? Men, women and children screamed and howled with joy, dancing in the aisles and jumping on seats. It was a bedlam of happiness as Ruth circled the bases tipping his cap and waving as he touched home plate. The Red Sox scored a run in the seventh, but that's all they could muster as Shawkey dominated, giving up only three hits in the game. The final score was New York Yankees 4, Boston Red Sox 1. Prior to the game Ruth commented, "...he would give a year of his life if he could hit a home run in the first game in the new stadium."[5]

For baseball historians and trivia buffs, there were a number of "firsts" recorded at the new Stadium. The first hit in Yankee Stadium was a single by Red Sox first baseman George Burns in the second inning. This is the same George Burns who would give Waite Hoyt fits when he was on the mound. In a *Saturday Evening Post* article Hoyt explained, "In the language of the dugout, 'he hit me like he owned me.' He was George Burns, Cleveland [he also played for Boston] first baseman, and he was such a pest...."[6] The first Yankees hit was Aaron Ward's single in the third inning, which started the four-run rally capped by Ruth's home run, the first in the new stadium.

It's amusing and informative to reflect on the prices of some items in New York City on April 18, 1923. A first-class postage stamp was 2 cents and for another 2 cents you could read the *New York Daily News* with your morning coffee. The opening day program at Yankee Stadium was 15 cents. With today's baseball memorabilia craze in full swing, one could only imagine what the opening day program is worth now. Bleacher seats were a quarter. You could spend a lovely evening at the Monticello Hotel in New York City for $3.00. During your weekly food shopping at the local market, a loaf of bread cost 9 cents, a quart of milk 14 cents and a dozen eggs 24 cents. Sounds great until you are reminded that the average salary in the United States was $1,393 per year. About all you can say for nostalgia is that it is very entertaining.

Ticket scalpers (called speculators then) were prevalent even back in 1923. Two young men were arrested outside the Stadium before the game started. One man was offering his $1.10 grandstand ticket for $1.25; the other man was more greedy, asking for a $1.50. The maximum penalty was a fine of $500 or one year in jail. In night court both men pleaded guilty, couldn't make the bail and were locked up waiting trial.

The Yankees won the next three games from Boston, sweeping the series. The team was off to a fast start. Joe Bush, Sam Jones and Carl Mays all picked up victories. Bush pitched an exceptionally fine game. The right-hander scattered six hits, walked two and fanned four.

Up and down the lineup everyone was contributing, both in the field and at the plate. Bob Meusel hit in all four games, going 6-for-12. Joe Dugan was batting .333, and even weak-hitting Everett Scott had a fine series. Still recovering from the ankle injury, the shortstop had some key hits in the sweep with a solid .357 average. Wally Pipp, who the Yankees were counting on to help the club to a third straight pennant and first World Series championship, was off to a slow start but would come around as the season progressed.

Ruth had a magnificent series. His big bat won the first and third games, and his triple and walk in game two, were key at-bats in the seven-run sixth inning. It was evident that Ruth was determined not to repeat the disappointing 1922 season. And he wouldn't. In fact, Ruth would have a marvelous year. He would bat .393, highest of his career. He would also lead the American League in home runs (41), runs scored (151), RBIs (131), on-base percentage (.545) and slugging average (.764). He would also lead the league with 170 walks, almost half of them intentional. Ruth even stole 17 bases. He was in his prime at 28 and four years later would set the baseball world on its proverbial ear with an unheard-of record 60 home runs.

Carl Mays completed the Boston sweep for the Yankees, but he needed help in the ninth from Jones. Huggins' selection of Mays to start ahead of Pennock and Hoyt was interesting, considering the manager's dislike for the pitcher. Beside Babe Ruth, Mays was the most unpredictable player on the 1923 club.

Carl Mays was born November 12, 1891, in Liberty, Kentucky. He was one of eight children. His father was a traveling Methodist minister who died when Carl was twelve years old. Left to raise eight children, Mays' mother moved the family to a farm in Kingfisher, Oklahoma, to be closer to her sister-in-law. A cousin, John Long, was instrumental in getting young Carl interested in baseball.

After playing semi-pro ball with various teams, Carl wound up with the Boise, Idaho, club in the Western Tri-State League (Class D). He earned $90 a month. He had a great season, 22–9 with a 2.08 ERA. The following year he played in Portland of the Northwest League where he earned $200 a month. In 1914, Mays was drafted by the Providence Grays, owned by the Detroit Tigers, and later sold to the Boston Red Sox. He and Babe Ruth led the Grays to the 1914 International League pennant.

Mays began his major league career with the Red Sox in 1915 and finished with an unspectacular 6–5 record and an ERA of 2.60, mostly in relief. He did endear himself with manager Bill Carrigan late in the season when he stood up to the cantankerous Ty Cobb. The Red Sox won the pennant and World Series, but Mays saw no action in the Fall Classic. Early on in his career, Mays had the uncanny ability of irritating most people he encountered. He was gruff, hot-tempered and a loner. "He was, as one team-mate described him, a man who always looked as if he had a toothache."[7]

The Red Sox repeated in 1916, edging the White Sox to win the pennant by two games. Carrigan made Mays a full-time starter, and the young right-hander with the unorthodox submarine pitch responded with an 18–13 record and an impressive 2.39 earned run average. His delivery, thrown from an underhanded motion, was so extreme that he would often scrape his knuckles on the ground. It was a difficult pitch to master and few could do it. It was also difficult for a batter to pick up the ball which made it a very effective pitch.

The Red Sox faced the Brooklyn Robins in the World Series. In the opening game, which Boston won, 6–5, Mays relieved Ernie Shore in the ninth and saved the day by getting the final out with the bases loaded. Mays started Game Three, went five innings and lost, 4–3. It was the only game the Red Sox lost as they took the Series handily.

In 1917, Mays had a fabulous year, 22–9 with an unheard of 1.74 ERA. He was nearly unhittable. It was also the year he led the league with 14 hit batsmen. He was quickly building a reputation as a head hunter. "Other players, some on his own team, claimed to have heard Mays boast that he was going to 'dust off' certain batters. They said Mays was unscrupulous in his pitching methods, a beaner with little regard for the consequences of his actions."[8]

Although the criticism from around the league was harsh, it didn't affect Mays' pitching. He turned in another splendid season, 21–13 with a 2.21 ERA. He led the league with 30 complete games and eight shutouts as the Red Sox won another pennant under their new manager, Ed Barrow. Their opponent in the World Series was the Chicago Cubs. The Red Sox won in six games. Mays pitched brilliantly in the Series, winning two games including the clincher. He allowed 10 hits and two earned runs in 18 innings for a phenomenal ERA of 1.00. It brought the Red Sox their fifth world championship in five tries dating back to 1903 when they were called the Pilgrims. Painfully, it would be their last until 2004.

The Red Sox started the 1919 season in a slump, as did Mays. At one point, he lost four of five starts. In those five games, the Red Sox scored a total of nine runs. As the team continued to struggle, Mays became more sullen and then began criticizing his own teammates, claiming they were "laying down" when he was on the mound. By the end of June, Mays' record was a disappointing 5–9. His frustration mounted, finally coming to a head in a game in Philadelphia. The A's had rallied to take the lead. Some exuberant fans began pounding the top of the dugout which annoyed the Boston players. Mays, not pitching that day, jumped from the dugout and fired a ball into the stands which hit a spectator, who later complained to the police, who issued a warrant for his arrest. The matter was temporarily settled when the Red Sox paid the fine.

On July 13, in a game against the White Sox at Comiskey Park, Mays was on the mound, trailing, 4–0, in the second inning. Catcher Wally Schang in an attempt to throw out a base runner at second, accidentally hit Mays in the back of the head. After the inning, a furious Mays left the game, headed for the clubhouse and back to Boston. The Red Sox decided enough was enough. Seven days later Mays was traded to the New York Yankees for pitchers Allan Russell, Bob McGraw and $40,000. The Yankees welcomed Mays to the clubhouse. He responded by pitching effectively, without incident, the rest of the season and finished with a 9–3 record and a 1.65 ERA. His efforts helped the Yankees finish third and participate in the World Series money.

In 1920, with a different club and a new setting, Mays turned in a fantastic year, 26–11 with a 3.06 earned run average. He led the league with six shutouts. The Yankees finished third again, three games back of the pennant-winning Cleveland Indians. Mays' performance during the season was even more remarkable, considering he was booed by fans and taunted by opposing players because of his tendency to throw inside to right-handed batters. He also couldn't play in Philadelphia because of the outstanding warrant from the previous year. The tragic climax came on August 16 at the Polo Grounds when Mays hit Cleveland shortstop Ray Chapman in the head with a pitch. Chapman died the following morning. Later in the morning Mays was informed of Chapman's death and then taken to the Manhattan DA's office. When questioned about the incident, Mays explained, "It was a little too close, and I saw Chapman duck his head in an effort to get out of the path of the ball. He was too late, however, and a second later he fell to the ground.

It was the most regrettable incident of my career, and I would give anything if I could undo what has happened."⁹

In spite of the tragic death of Chapman, Mays continued to pitch. The outrage directed at Mays was enormous. Crowds were hostile towards him wherever he went, and he received nasty and threatening letters from total strangers. Several teams sent petitions to Ban Johnson demanding Mays be thrown out of baseball but to no avail. Through it all, Mays had the respect of Yankees co-owner Huston who admired his toughness and the way he stood up to his critics.

If Chapman's death had any effect on Mays, it did not reveal itself in 1921. The Yankees won their first pennant, and Mays had a remarkable year. He was 27–9 (.750) with a 3.05 ERA. He led the league in wins, winning percentage, games (49), and innings pitched (336⅔).

Mays pitched the opening game of the World Series and blanked the Giants on seven hits, 3–0. It was a brilliant performance. He lost Game Four, 4–2, when the Giants tagged him for three runs in the eighth and one in the ninth. Mays also lost a heartbreaker in Game Seven, 2–1. He allowed only six hits but was outpitched by spitballer Phil Douglas. Mays' earned run average for the Series was 1.73. The Giants won the Series, five games to three.

According to sportswriter, Fred Lieb, in his book, *Baseball As I Have Known It*, he was informed by a Broadway actor that Mays had thrown Game Four. Lieb informed Commissioner Landis, who began a secret investigation. Nothing was mentioned in the press. After the Series, Landis told Lieb that his investigation found nothing to incriminate Mays.

Seven years later, Huston spoke to Lieb, "I wanted to tell you that some of our pitchers threw World Series games on us in both 1921 and 1922," he mumbled.

"You mean that Mays matter of the 1921 World Series?" he asked.

Huston replied, "Yes, but there were others—other times, other pitchers."¹⁰

Years after the Huston conversation, Lieb discovered why Miller Huggins had such a deep hatred for Mays and Bush. Lieb put two and two together and figured Huston was talking about Bush, in addition to Mays, when he made his revelation to him. Since Lieb was the chief scorer for the 1922 World Series, he went back and checked his records. What he found was that Bush lost the first and fifth games after leading in the eighth inning. In both games, he allowed three runs in the eighth and lost. It didn't pass the smell test. The fifth game might have been the tip-off to Huggins. The Yankees were leading, 3–2, when Bush found himself with runners on second and third with two outs. Huggins ordered Bush to walk Ross Youngs, a left-handed hitter, in order to face right-handed hitting George Kelly. The hot headed Bush vehemently objected, cursing at Huggins, who was in the dugout, loud enough to be heard throughout the press box and by many box holders. A brooding Bush walked Youngs but served up a fat pitch to Kelly who singled, driving in two runs. The Giants added another and won the game, 5–3, and the Series. Huggins would never forget the shameful incident.

In 1922, Mays had an off season, dropping to 13–14 with a 3.60 ERA. Regardless, the Yankees beat the St. Louis Browns by one game for their second straight pennant. The Yankees met the Giants again in the World Series with all games played at the Polo Grounds. It was an awful Series for the Yankees as they lost all four games (one tie). Mays lost Game Four, 4–3, with relief help from Sam Jones in the ninth.

The 1923 season was the beginning of the end for Carl Mays as a New York Yankee. Huggins had

Carl Mays won five games for the Yankees in 1923, but was in Miller Huggins' dog house most of the season. The reason? Huggins had strong suspicions Mays threw games in the 1921 World Series, which the Yankees lost to the Giants. (Courtesy National Baseball Hall of Fame Library, Cooperstown, New York.)

strong suspicions that Mays threw games in the 1921 World Series and didn't hide his dislike for the pitcher. He made it very uncomfortable for Mays. He used him sparingly, a little more than 81 innings, even though Mays said he was in fine physical condition. Two or three weeks would pass before he got the call to pitch. Huggins took great delight in humiliating Mays. The classic example came on July 17 when Mays took a beating at the hands of the

Cleveland Indians, 13–0. He allowed 20 hits, and Huggins let him pitch the complete game. It was payback time for the unforgiving Huggins. It was so bad that Wally Pipp and Everett Scott refused to finish the game, protesting Huggins' treatment of Mays. More than likely, Pipp and Scott were unaware of what Huggins suspected. Huggins was not alone on Mays' enemy list. Author Daniel Levitt in his seminal book, *Ed Barrow*, quotes teammate Bob Shawkey on Mays: "He was a stinker. One winter I worked for an insurance company in Philadelphia, and I insured his automobile. He went out and hired a guy to steal it in order to collect on the insurance. He promised the guy a certain amount of money to do it and then never paid him. That's how I happened to find out about it—the fellow called me up and told me what Mays had done. Of course we didn't pay Mays anything. Then he went to Cincinnati and did the same thing with somebody else. That's the way he was. A stinker."[11]

Not coming as a surprise to anyone, in late December the Yankees sold Mays to the Cincinnati Reds. Mays pitched for the Reds for five years. He won 20 games and lost nine his first year and received a $500 bonus from Reds president Gary Herrmann. The following year Mays was injured and pitched in a little over 51 innings with a 3–5 record. Mays came back in 1926, posting a 19–12 record with a 3.14 ERA and helped lead Cincinnati to a second-place finish. He also led the league in complete games. After the 1926 season it was all down hill for Mays. His final two years with the Reds he went 7–8 and wound up pitching for McGraw and the New York Giants in 1929. It was his last hurrah. Mays finished the season 7–2 with a 4.32 earned run average and called it quits.

Several years after Mays retired, he was beset with a series of tragedies. He lost $175,000 in the stock market crash. His mother died, and shockingly his young wife suddenly passed away. He coped with these setbacks well and continued to be involved with baseball. He pitched in the minor leagues for two seasons and scouted for Cleveland, Milwaukee and the Atlanta Braves for 20 years.

After leaving baseball, Carl Mays' greatest desire was to be elected to the Hall of Fame. He believed he deserved it and had the numbers to back it up. He pitched for 15 years with a record of 208–126 (.623) and an ERA of 2.92. He was on four pennant winners and two world champions. It must have been frustrating to see teammates and other contemporaries with less credentials be voted into the Hall—Herb Pennock (1948), Waite Hoyt (1969) and Rube Marquard (1971). Compared to all three, Mays had a significantly higher winning percentage and lower earned run average. The evidence is telling. To his dying day he believed the reason he was kept out of the Hall was because he killed Ray Chapman in 1920.

Not true, according to Fred Lieb, a long-time member of the Hall of Fame's Veterans Committee. "Carl Mays's name has frequently come before the committee, but no one has ever brought up the Chapman tragedy as a reason why Carl should not be in the Cooperstown shrine. Rather, the question mark has often been his performance in the Series of 1921."[12]

Carl Mays died on April 4, 1971, in El Cajon, California. He was 79 years old and is still eligible for induction into the Hall of Fame. As of this writing, Mays is one of 10 finalists being considered by the Veterans Committee.

At this early stage in the season, the Yankees and Indians were all even at 4–0. Pre-season predictions around baseball circles were unanimous that Ty Cobb's Detroit Tigers would give the two-time pennant-winning Yankees the most trouble.

On the same day the Yankees won the last game of the Boston series, a kid by the name of Lou Gehrig was playing baseball for Columbia University against Cornell in Ithaca, New York. The young pitcher/first baseman turned in a performance right out of a Frank Merriwell novel. Pitching for Columbia, Gehrig allowed five hits, three runs and struck out 10 batters. That was only part of his contribution. Batting third in the order, he smacked a long home run and a triple. He also scored two runs. In a few short years, Gehrig would hook-up with Ruth to form the greatest one-two punch in the game's history. For now, the Yankees were content to watch Gehrig play college ball with an eagle eye to the future.

Gehrig first attracted attention as an athlete, not for his baseball skills, but for his football prowess. At 17, Gehrig was attending Commerce High School and was a member of the football team. On Thanksgiving day 1920, Commerce was playing DeWitt Clinton High School at Columbia University's South Field. The stands were packed for a high school football game, more than 10,000 spectators. The game turned out to be a lopsided victory for DeWitt Clinton, but Gehrig played a fine game and seemed to be all over the field. He ran with the ball, tackled hard and even punted. Young Gehrig caught the eye of two football men—Robert W. Watt, Columbia's graduate manager of athletics, and Frank "Buck" O'Neill, the head coach at the University. After the game, Watt and O'Neill talked to Gehrig and his father, Heinrick, who had joined the trio from the stands. They probably talked about Gehrig attending Columbia on a football scholarship. Lou's grades, however, were not good enough for entrance to Columbia. But Watt desperately wanted Gehrig on the football team. So after Lou graduated from Commerce, Watt helped him obtain enough credits to meet Columbia's entrance requirements. "After several months of intensive study, Gehrig completed his extension course satisfactorily and passed the college board examinations. He was then granted a football scholarship."[13]

After Boston left the Bronx licking its wounds, the Washington Senators arrived at the Stadium for a four-game series. Washington was managed by Donie Bush, long-time shortstop of the Detroit Tigers. The team was powerless but possessed some outstanding ballplayers like Sam Rice, Goose Goslin and Muddy Ruel, and they were led by pitching immortal Walter Johnson. The best the fiery Bush could do in 1923 was settle for fourth place (75–78), only a half-game ahead of the St. Louis Browns. Owner Clark Griffith was not satisfied, especially after Bush had an altercation with Griffith's favorite player, Rice. Bush suspended Rice, and Griffith reinstated Rice. That was the kiss of death for Bush as he was replaced in 1924 by second baseman Bucky Harris. At age 27, he was called the "Boy Manager" and for good reason. His Washington Senators won the pennant and the World Series, defeating the New York Giants in seven games.

The Yankees split the series the hard way, losing the first two games, then capturing the last two. The first game was a real thriller. Before a capacity crowd at Yankee Stadium, the Senators edged the Yankees, 4–3, for their first loss of the season. The goat of the game was none other than the Babe himself. The score was tied 1–1 in the top of the seventh with Shawkey pitching a fine game. After fanning Roger Peckinpaugh for the first out, the right-hander lost his stuff. A triple and two singles scored a run and put runners on first and third. Sam Rice, the next batter, hit a high fly ball to Ruth in right. The Babe, in his haste to throw out the runner tagging up, dropped the ball! Now the score was 3–1 and for some unexplainable reason, Shawkey's control left him and he couldn't find the plate. He walked the next two batters forcing in a run, making the score 4–1. Herb Pennock relieved Shawkey and retired the side. The Yankees rallied in the bottom half of the eighth, scoring two runs, but fell short. Ruth went hitless for the second game in a row.

Prior to the game, the huge crowd was entertained by baseball comedian Nick Altrock. Among other antics, he would often perform a one-man wrestling match to the delight of the fans. Lost in his comedic brilliance was the fact that Altrock pitched in the major leagues for 16 years, finishing with an 83–75 record and a solid ERA of 2.67. He turned in some outstanding years. With the Chicago White Sox in 1905, he was 23–12 with a minuscule 1.88 ERA. In 1906 he had another fine season (20–13, 2.06 ERA) and helped the White Sox defeat their cross-town rivals, the Cubs, in the World Series by beating Hall of Famer Mordecai "Three Finger" Brown, 2–1, in the opener. In Game Four, Altrock lost to Brown in another pitcher's duel, 1–0. In spite of the defeat, Altrock set a World Series record for chances handled by a pitcher in one game. He had 11 chances, eight assists and three putouts. Plus, he set another record for most chances (17) in a six-game Series, which was tied by Hippo Vaughn pitching for the Chicago Cubs in the 1918 Series. Hippo, however, needed three games.

Altrock had a reputation as an excellent fielder with an exceptional pick-off move. Legend has it in 1901 lefty Altrock, pitching for Los Angeles in the California League, walked seven men intentionally—then picked off six. The Yankees' Andy Pettitte, with one of the great pick-off moves, would have a difficult time duplicating that feat. Baseball lore often stretches credulity.

After the 1906 World Series, Altrock's career was on a steady decline. He finally wound up in the minor leagues as a third base coach for Kansas City in the American Association. Never one to take baseball seriously, Altrock, while coaching, began to imitate a fighter shadow-boxing, repeatedly hitting himself on the chin, falling down and getting up as the crowd laughed. It was pure entertainment and the fans loved it. The owner, Patsy Tebeau, didn't think it very funny and fined Nick. Hearing about Altrock's antics, Washington Senator's manager Clark Griffith quickly hired Nick as a "comedy coach." A new career was born.

With the press reporting Altrock's performance, word spread and more fans began attending Senators games. Even American League president Ban Johnson got involved. He thought the act was funny and agreed to let Nick continue as long as it didn't interfere with the game. Over the years, Altrock used several partners in his routine before he finally hooked up with Al Schacht. Schacht pitched for the Senators for three years, 1919–21, and posted a 14–10 record with a 4.48 ERA.

The two ex-ballplayers teamed up and performed at games for thousands of baseball fans. They created pantomime acts simulating rowing boats during rain delays, bowling, baiting umpires, golf tricks and other nonsense. It was great family entertainment and the fans loved every minute of it. Altrock and Schacht ended their partnership in 1934 when Al joined the Red Sox. Altrock continued performing on his own for the Washington fans. Often the Senators would let Altrock play in a game at the end of the year. At age 48 in 1924, he tripled in a game with a lot of help from the opposing outfielders. In 1929 at age 53, he singled in a game and in 1933 made his final big league appearance as a pinch-hitter for the Senators at age 57!

Nick Altrock died on January 20, 1965, in Washington D.C. at the age of 88. Schacht, his long-time friend and comedic partner, praised Nick for being an "exceptional entertainer" and a "fine big league pitcher."

The next day the Yankees lost again to the Senators, 2–1. Although Joe Bush took the loss, he didn't pitch badly. It was, however, an embarrassing

Monday afternoon at the Stadium. First, only 5,000 fans attended the game, a far cry from the capacity on opening day. Second, the Yankees appeared listless, sleepwalking through the game. The most the team could manage was three hits and two were of the cheap variety. Ruth went hitless, to the disappointment of the crowd. It was his third consecutive game without a hit, an 0-for-8 skid.

An obscure left-hander by the name of Wallace Warmoth, who pitched in the minors the prior year in Little Rock, blanked the mighty Yankees for eight innings on a mixture of curves and fast balls. Warmoth's nickname was Cy. Not to be confused with the great Cy Young of 511 major league victories. Cy Warmoth had a very short career—129 innings and an 8–4 record. By the end of the season, Warmoth would need another 503 victories to tie Young. But on this day, the 30-year-old lefty did a marvelous impersonation of the real Cy.

In game three, New York hosted the most visible man in the country. President Warren G. Harding was among the small crowd of 8,000 who saw the Yankees bounce back from the previous day's loss to shutout the Senators, 4–0. It was the President's first game ever in New York. Prior to the game, Cap Huston introduced the Babe to the President. They exchanged a few words and then Ruth went into the dugout. New York scored three runs in the third to take an early lead. Then in the top of the fifth, Ruth delighted the fans with a towering home run into the right field bleachers off lefty Jim Brillheart. The most enthusiastic fan was President Harding, who applauded vigorously. In typical Ruthian bravado, after touching home plate and arriving at the edge of the dugout, he removed his cap and bowed to the President. Shortly thereafter, Ruth came back out of the dugout and pinned a poppy on Harding's overcoat. It was a great moment and one both men enjoyed to the great delight of the crowd.

Sam Jones was on the mound for the Yankees, and with a 4–0 lead, the right-hander had more runs than he needed. He pitched a magnificent game with his sharp breaking ball working to perfection. He blanked the Senators on five hits and allowed only two runners to reach third.

Jones was born July 26, 1892, in Woodshield, Ohio. Little is known about his early years. Growing up he played both basketball and baseball, ironically preferring the former. Fortunately for baseball, basketball was not a popular sport at the time. Jones pitched in high school and locally in sandlot games. In 1913, he played for Zanesville of the Inter-State League at $175 a month. He was 2–7 but gaining valuable experience at a young age. The following year he signed with Portsmouth in the Ohio State League. During one of his games, Cleveland Indians scout Bill Reedy was impressed with

Jones' performance on the mound and at bat. He signed Jones for their minor league club in the American Association. In 23 games, he posted a record of 10–4 with a 2.44 ERA. It earned Jones a relief appearance with the Indians, an inauspicious major league debut.

In 1915, Jones appeared in 48 games for Cleveland, mostly in relief, with a record of 4–9 and an earned run average of 3.65. In Lawrence Ritter's classic book, *The Glory of their Times*, Jones praised his teammates. "I'll never forget the fellows on that Cleveland club—Joe Jackson, Ray Chapman, Steve O'Neill, Terry Turner, Larry Lajoie, Willie Mitchel. I'll never, never, never forget how nice those fellows treated me when I first came up. They were just wonderful."[14] Much to his dismay, he was traded to the Red Sox in 1916 along with Fred Thomas and $50,000 for center fielder Tris Speaker. With all due respect to Jones, this trade ranks as one of the worst in baseball history, as Speaker went on to become one of baseball's immortals. Most of the Boston press felt it was not a good deal, either. It left the Red Sox fans totally confused. But not owner Joseph Lannin, who was pleased with the trade and felt that Speaker was on the downside of his career and that his market value would diminish. Nothing could be further from the truth. Speaker's batting average for the 11 years with Cleveland, including a title (.386 in 1916), was a phenomenal .354.

For the first two years with Boston, Jones pitched almost exclusively in relief. He found it difficult to crack the starting rotation of Babe Ruth, Dutch Leonard, Carl Mays and Ernie Shore. In fact, Jones wasn't even sent a contract for the 1918 season. He wrote to new owner Harry Frazee wanting to know what happened. In some strange mix-up, the Red Sox thought he was in the Army. In the end it all worked out. Under new manager Ed Barrow and with Shore and Herb Pennock in the military, Jones was finally made part of Boston's rotation. He helped lead the Red Sox to the American League pennant with a 16–5 record and a 2.25 ERA. His winning percentage of .762 led the league.

Boston faced the Chicago Cubs in the World Series where pitching dominated, beginning with Game One, when Ruth shutout Hippo Vaughn and the Cubs, 1–0. With Boston leading the Series, three games to one, Jones was called on to clinch the championship. He faced the tough left-hander Vaughn but lost, 3–0, as Hippo allowed only five hits. The next day Carl Mays returned the favor and beat Chicago, 2–1, for the title. Ruth was 2–0 in the Series with a 1.06 ERA, and Mays was 2–0 with an earned run average of 1.00. Pitching ruled the entire Series. After six games the Red Sox scored 11 runs and Chicago 10.

Jones struggled the next two years with a weak Red Sox club that played under .500 baseball. His struggles were not in vain. He and manager Barrow developed a mutual respect for each other. Jones admitted years later, "...Ed Barrow and I got along just fine. I'd pitch for him anytime he wanted me to, and he'd do anything for me."[15] Then in 1921, Jones had a breakout year, winning 23 and losing 16 with a 3.22 ERA under new manager Hugh Duffy. Ed Barrow, Jones' former manager, was now in the New York Yankees front office as their general manager. Because of their friendship, it came as no surprise that Barrow would be interested in acquiring Jones for the Yankees if the opportunity arose. On December 20, 1921, Jones received an early Christmas gift compliments of Barrow. He traded Roger Peckinpaugh, Jack Quinn, Rip Collins, Bill Piercy and cash for shortstop Everett Scott, Jones and Joe Bush. At some point during his career, he was given the nickname "Sad Sam" supposedly by a sportswriter because of his glum look. Surely the trade put a smile on his face.

It also reunited Jones with fellow pitchers from the Red Sox days: Babe Ruth, Carl Mays, Waite Hoyt and Joe Bush. The trade landed Jones on another pennant winner. He finished the season 13–13 with a 3.67 ERA, but the Yankees were swept by the Giants in the World Series (Game Two was tied, 3–3.) with Jones pitching sparingly in relief.

Without question, Jones' best season with the Yankees was 1923 when he posted a 21–8 mark and helped lead New York to its first World Series championship. His finest pitched game came early in September when he threw a no-hitter against the A's. The Yankees finally beat John McGraw's Giants in six games. In Game Three, Jones pitched magnificently but lost, 1–0, on Casey Stengel's famous inside-the-park home run. Lack of support was always a problem for Jones in World Series play.

In 1924, nursing a sore elbow for two months, he finished the season with a 9–6 mark in a little over 178 innings, the lowest number in six years. The following year he pitched in over 246 innings, a huge jump for someone who had elbow trouble. Perhaps it was the reason for his miserable 15–21 record and an inflated 4.63 ERA. It was clear the Yankees were losing confidence in Jones. In 1926 New York won another pennant led by Herb Pennock, Urban Shocker and Waite Hoyt while Jones' innings pitched dropped to 161. His earned run average continued to climb to 4.98 with a 9–8 record. His lack of work (one inning) in the World Series, which the Yankees lost to the St. Louis Cardinals, was a clear signal his career in pinstripes was over. In February, 1927, it came as no surprise when Sam Jones was traded to the St. Louis Browns for outfielder Cedric Durst and pitcher Joe Giard. The timing of the trade was personally unfortunate for Jones. He missed out being a member of one of the greatest baseball teams in the history of the game, the 1927 New York Yankees.

Jones pitched a year with St. Louis, then went to the Washington Senators, finally ending his career with the Chicago White Sox. In the nine years with the three teams, he compiled a 94–93 record with his best year being 1928 with the Senators under manager Bucky Harris. That year he went 17–7 with a 2.84 ERA for a team that finished the season 75–79, 26 games behind the New York Yankees. It was a remarkable season at age 36.

In the book *When Boston Still Had The Babe*, author Alex Edelman described Jones' life after baseball in Woodsfield, the small town he loved. "During the time after his career he worked as a delivery man for a grocery store, sold furniture, drove a hearse, labored as a church custodian, was president of his county's World War II draft board and spent part of almost every day sitting in his brother Bob's clothing store, surrounded by friends and baseball pictures."[16]

It is easy to picture Jones in retirement regaling everyone

Right-hander Sam Jones had his best year with the Yankees in 1923 when he posted a 21–8 mark. In early September, he threw a no-hitter against Connie Mack's A's. "I guess I liked playing for the Yankees best of all," he commented after retiring from baseball. (Courtesy National Baseball Hall of Fame Library, Cooperstown, New York.)

with baseball stories. To be sure, one of his tales was his philosophy about holding runners close to first base. His approach was simply to hold the ball. That's it. Just hold the ball. He claimed the runner would eventually lean back to first, then you pitch. Also, the hitter would often step out of the batter's box. He also believed, like the great Philadelphia A's pitcher Eddie Plank, it saves wear and tear on your arm. Perhaps Jones and Plank were onto something. Plank pitched for 17 years in over 4,495 innings. His Hall of Fame record was 326–194 with a low 2.35 ERA. Jones' career spanned 22 years, a remarkable achievement in itself. Pitching in 3,883 innings, he won 229 games and lost 217 with an ERA of 3.84. He participated in three Fall Classics — 1922, 1923 and 1926. His record in World Series play was 0–1 with a 1.38 earned run average in 13 innings. Sam Jones fell short of Hall of Fame recognition, but he did leave an indelible mark on the game. He died July 6, 1966, at age 73.

Shortly before his death, Jones commented on his favorite team. "I guess I liked playing with the Yankees best of all. I was there for five years, 1922 through '26. It was a good club to play for. They always had plenty of money, paid real well, and drew good crowds. And three of the five years I was there we won the pennant."[17]

The final game of the Washington series was a laugher for the Yankees as they won, 7–1, behind the fine pitching of Herb Pennock. He allowed nine hits and four walks but was tough in the clutch as he stranded 10 Washington base runners. All the excitement for Washington came in the fifth inning when Sam Rice drove a ball to right center between Ruth and Witt, bounding to the edge of the bleachers and evading the outfielders long enough for Rice to circle the bases for an inside-the-park home run. It was historic, the first ever in Yankee Stadium and a great question for trivia buffs.

There is, however, a lot more to Sam Rice than an answer to a trivia question. He was elected to the Hall of Fame in 1963 and deservedly so. He played 20 years in the major leagues, 19 with the Washington Senators and on all of their three pennant-winning clubs. Rice was a speedy outfielder with good range and a strong arm. He was a contact hitter with a very respectable lifetime batting average of .322. He hit better than .300 in 14 seasons. He stole 351 bases and led the league in 1920 with 63. Rice rarely struck out. In 1929, he came to bat 616 times and fanned an unbelievable nine times.

After eight games, the Yankees and the Cleveland Indians were tied for first place with identical 6–2 records. The next club for the Yankees was the Boston Red Sox. The Yankees hopped a train for Bean Town and another elaborate opening day.

Not to be outdone by the Yankees' extravaganza a week earlier, the Boston Red Sox put on a grand show on opening day at Fenway Park. Close to 20,000 fans showed up to watch a group of marines from the Charleston Navy Yard give a drill exhibition and then lead a parade across the field for the customary flag raising. Next, an unusual first pitch spectacle. Mayor James H. Curley threw out the first pitch. What's so unusual about that? Curley's toss was to Governor Channing Cox. Hold on. That's not all. Boston manager, Frank Chance, was the batter! He swung and missed. Finally, the game got underway. Waite Hoyt was on the mound for the Yankees and Howard Ehmke for the Sox. In the top of the ninth, the Yankees were losing, 4–2, but scored twice to tie the game.

In Boston's half of the ninth, Bush came on to pitch for Mays who had relieved Hoyt earlier. It didn't take Boston long to redeem themselves. With one out, Joe Harris doubled. Mike Menosky ran for Harris. George Burns, who went 3-for-3 for the afternoon, singled to center scoring Menosky and just like that the game was over, Red Sox 5, Yankees 4. With the defeat the Yankees dropped to second place behind Cleveland as the Indians scalped Chicago, 9–0.

Back in New York at the Polo Grounds, there was another opening day. John McGraw and his world champion New York Giants were hosting the Boston Braves before 25,000 enthusiastic fans. It was an unusual opening day in more ways than one. The Polo Grounds was in the middle of a reconstruction project that wasn't fully complete. It was a typical construction site. Piles of sand and concrete, pneumatic riveters and red-painted girders were all part of the unfinished mess. As 3 P.M. approached, all the workers knocked off and settled in to watch the game from the unfinished upper grandstand as the *New York Times* pointed out, "lending another quaint touch to the celebrations."

And what a celebration! Commissioner Landis and National League president John A. Heydler led a long list of distinguished guests, club owners and politicians. Yankees owner Jacob Ruppert even showed up to show the Giants and New York fans he harbored no animosity towards his crosstown rivals for being booted out of the Polo Grounds. At least on the surface that was the appearance. Inwardly, Ruppert's stomach must have been churning although somewhat appeased by the fact that he turned away as many fans (25,000) as were attending the Giants' opener.

The world champions received a fine reception from their loyal fans. Frankie Frisch, Irish Meusel, Ross Youngs and starting pitcher Art Nehf received the most enthusiastic cheers from the boisterous crowd. As both ball clubs and the dignitaries gathered around home plate, the fans recognized Christy Mathewson, the former Giant great and now Boston Braves president was still in his box seat. They began to holler for him. Mayor John F. Hylan recognized what was happening and walked over to get Matty. As he stepped on to the field, the fans erupted into a spontaneous ovation never seen before for a ballplayer. Young and old stood and clapped, whistled and shouted their love for one of the greatest pitchers of all time. The fans were showing their appreciation for all the wonderful years of thrills and championships "Big Six" helped bring to the Giants and the Polo Grounds. He did it all with grace and class. When Matty reached home plate, he was greeted by a smiling McGraw, his former manager and long-time friend. After the ceremonies concluded, Matty walked back to his box seat amid another outburst of applause. All this admiration and respect for the man who last pitched for the New York Giants in 1916.

Although the Yankees were in second place, there was continued good news coming out of Columbia University. Gehrig and company beat Rutgers, 9–4. The future Hall of Famer hit two home runs, collected four RBIs and scored twice. Although Gehrig was given a football scholarship to Columbia, when spring rolled around, he worked out with the school's baseball team. In an exhibition game against the Hartford Senators, Gehrig cracked two long home runs. The *Hartford Times* compared his second blast to those of Babe Ruth. Eye-opening praise indeed for a young man.

Gehrig's feats with the bat did not go unnoticed. Scouts were now taking an interest in the slugger from Columbia. Word spread to New York Giants manager John McGraw, who after some cajoling consented to take a look at Gehrig. At the time, McGraw, a tough, hard-nosed leader, dominated New York baseball. In fact, baseball was his life. Anything else in McGraw's life had little meaning. He pushed his players hard and often. Short, stumpy and cocky of Irish decent, he was a fan favorite, especially among the immigrants looking to make it in America. It was the author's opinion that if McGraw's life was ever put on film, the actor Charles Durning, a distinguished World War II hero, would have been perfect for the lead role. But at age 85 it is wishful thinking.

Gehrig showed up at the Polo Grounds one morning for the workout with the Giants. Lou hit several good shots into the right field bleachers under the watchful eye of McGraw. After his batting turn, Gehrig jogged to first base. One of the first balls hit to him went right through his legs. According to the story, McGraw told his assistant to get rid of the kid, he had seen enough. Remember, McGraw's style was small ball—hit, bunt, steal, sacrifice—anything to score. He was not impressed with big, bruising sluggers.

That blunder by McGraw has to rank right next to Harry Frazee's sale of Ruth to the Yankees. One can only imagine if the stubborn McGraw would have shown more patience with Gehrig, how the New York baseball scene would have changed over the years. With Gehrig entrenched at first base with the New York Giants, maybe no "murderers' row," maybe no Yankees dynasty. Who knows, but it's fun to speculate.

Lou Gehrig continued to make headlines. He single handily stopped New York University's seven-game winning streak by a score of 7–2. Gehrig gave up six hits, two runs and struck out eight. At the plate, he was 2-for-2 and scored three runs. One of his hits was a home run that landed on 116th Street and was later claimed to be one of the longest ever at South Field.

The Yankees split the next two games with Boston and sunk to third place with a 7–4 record. But Cleveland and Detroit were playing sound fundamental baseball, albeit early in the season. Before heading to the nation's capital to play four games against the Washington Senators, the Yankees had a day off, and like the proverbial mailman who takes a walk on his day off, they played anyway. Ruth and company traveled across the Hudson River to New Jersey to play an exhibition game against the Doherty Silk Sox, a semi-pro team in the Paterson Industrial League. At the time, Patterson was aptly called "Silk City." The name came about because Paterson was the home of hundreds of silk mills. The Silk Sox were sponsored by Henry Doherty, owner of one of the silk mills, an interesting story in itself.

In 1791, Alexander Hamilton and a group of investors created the S.U.M., the Society for Establishing Useful Manufactures. Their objective was to put into productive use the great waterfalls of Paterson. A power system was designed by Pierre Charles L'Enfant, later known for designing the layout of Washington, D.C., which transformed Paterson into an industrialized city. Mills sprung up throughout the city providing jobs for immigrants flooding in from Europe. Soon Paterson became the world's center for the production of cotton, silk and locomotives. At its peak in 1910, there were 25,000 workers in 350 large plants producing 30% of the silk in the United States. Then came the strike of 1913 which ended in capitulation by the workers. Continued squabbles between the silk workers and owners further weakened the industry. By 1925, the mills began to leave, which spelled the end of the great silk industry in Paterson. The mill that was struck in 1913? None other than the Henry Doherty Silk Mill!

The Yankees won the exhibition, 10–6, but never completed the game. The Doherty Oval, where the game was played, held only 6,000, but there were twice that many and they were all there to see the great Babe Ruth hit a home run. Dramatically, in the top of the ninth, Ruth obliged. The crowd went berserk with joy and swarmed the Yankees' bench trying to shake Ruth's hand. Ruth tried to distract the onrush and grabbed some baseballs and threw them into the crowd. It might have slowed down some seniors but the tactic did not stop the youngsters. They wanted to shake the Babe's hand and were determined to do it. Finally, the police came to the rescue before someone was seriously injured. Ruth survived, but it was impossible for the police to clear the field, so the game was called without the Silk Sox batting in the bottom of the ninth.

The Yankees ended the month on a high note, but so did the Indians. The standings in the American League had Cleveland in first place, and the Yankees in third, 1½ games behind. In the National League, the New York Giants had an early 2½ game lead over the Chicago Cubs. The five leading hitters in the American League were:

Player and Club		G	AB	R	H	AVG
Harry Heilmann	Detroit	13	49	11	26	.531
Eddie Collins	Chicago	12	44	7	18	.409
George Burns	Boston	11	44	6	17	.386
Babe Ruth	New York	12	35	14	13	.371
Ty Cobb	Detroit	13	50	9	18	.360

3

Ruppert Buys Out Huston

On May 1, the Yankees made it two in a row over Washington by a score of 8–7 and moved to within a half-game of Cleveland for the American League lead. It was an exciting game that featured Babe Ruth stealing home. In all, the Babe would steal 17 bases in 1923, a fact many fans have a hard time visualizing. The reason can be traced back to most of the old films of Ruth showing him swinging and either hitting a home run or striking out. Plus, these films captured Ruth late in his career when he overindulged in food and drink and would be seen rounding the bases on spindly legs. But Ruth in his younger years was quite the athlete and could steal a base or two as he did in this game to tie the score and allow the Yankees to win in the ninth.

Rube Bressler, a major leaguer for 19 years with a lifetime batting average of .301, had high praise for Ruth's overall athletic ability. Bressler said that Ruth was "one of the greatest pitchers of all time, and then he became a great judge of a fly ball, never threw to the wrong base when he was playing the outfield, terrific arm, good base runner, could hit the ball twice as far as any other human being."[1]

The only game the Yankees lost during the series was to Walter Johnson, nicknamed The Big Train by famed sportswriter Grantland Rice. He shut out the Yankees, 3–0. The great right-hander gave up three measly hits. Ruth, Pipp and Meusel, the heart of the Yankees order, went 0-for-10. Shawkey took the loss.

Walter Johnson, a soft-spoken, modest man, was a pitching marvel. In a career that spanned 21 years, he won 417 baseball games, second in all-time victories to the immortal Cy Young. He accomplished this feat with only one team, the Washington Senators, a second-division club for most of his career. He achieved fame and glory exploiting a marvelous fastball. Author Donald Honig describes the fastball as, "...one so fast that for nearly two decades it was almost as if nobody else threw one, so fast that today tales of its velocity can strain one's credulity."[2]

In Johnson's first five seasons, the Senators finished last or next-to-last, but he still managed to win 25 games in two of the years. From 1910–1919, he won an incredible 265 games with a team that did not win a pennant. During that period he led the league in victories five times! Johnson's durability and patience finally paid off. In 1924 Washington nosed out the Yankees for the pennant and met the New York Giants in the World Series. Johnson lost the first and fifth games but redeemed himself in the crucial Game Seven with a four-inning relief appearance for the victory and the championship. The following season Johnson won 20 and led the Senators to another pennant. This time Washington faced the Pittsburgh Pirates in the World Series. The outcome was different. The Pirates won the Series, beating Johnson in the seventh game. Two more mediocre seasons with Washington and Johnson retired. In 21 seasons, the Big Train's Hall of Fame record (elected in 1936) was 417–279 with an ERA of 2.17 and 3,509 strikeouts, dazzling numbers indeed.

In spite of a marvelous pitching performance by Johnson, the day belonged to Everett Scott. The 31-year-old shortstop played in his 1000th consecutive game dating back to 1916 when he played for the Boston Red Sox. Prior to the game, both teams lined up facing each other forming a lane from the pitchers mound to home plate. Washington Senators president Clark Griffith gave the signal which started the Marine Band marching across the field led by Scott and American League president Ban Johnson. When the parade reached the mound, Scott and Johnson walked down the lane to home plate where they were greeted by Secretary of the Navy Edwin C. Denby. The secretary presented Scott with a gold medal which read in "recognition of his remarkable achievement of playing 1,000 consecutive games at short-stop." It was a most gratifying and memorable day for the young man.

On May 4, the Yankees returned to the Stadium from Washington to meet Connie Mack's Philadelphia A's in a three-game series. The Yankees lost two of the three and remained in first place by a mere half-game. It was a wonderful series that revealed the fickleness of fandom and, as expected, involved Babe Ruth, always at the center of events good or bad.

In the sixth inning of the first game, which the A's won, 8–6, Ruth gave the local fans a real scare. Running after a fly ball, his momentum carried him into the right field stands. He ended up with a pair of legs jutting out into the air. It was a marvelous effort by the Babe with Huggins cringing at the thought of his star player being seriously injured. Ruth missed the catch with the ball bounding away. Emerging from the stands, Ruth ran after the ball, caught it and uncorked a strike to Wally Schang at home to nail the runner and end the inning. As the Babe ran off the field, he held his left arm stiff at his side while his hand was bleeding. Fortunately for the Yankees, Ruth was not seriously hurt, but there were some anxious moments. It reminded one of a similar incident on July 1, 2004, when Yankees shortstop Derek Jeter, playing against the hated Red Sox at the Stadium, fearlessly dove into the third base stands to make a catch. He also emerged bruised and bleeding. Both Ruth and Jeter received huge ovations from their adoring fans.

Freeze frame that Ruthian moment of him basking in the fan's adoration because the next day all hell broke loose and the Babe became a target of disdain. The Yankees beat Philadelphia, 7–2, before 35,000 animated fans to move into first place. That was the good news. The bad news was Ruth's sloppy play, both in the field and at bat. In the first inning the Yankees loaded the bases: Ruth on first, Dugan on second and Witt on third. Pipp singled to left scoring Witt, Dugan stopping at third. When left fielder Bing Miller threw home, Ruth kept on running, forcing Dugan to get trapped in a run down and eventually tagged out. Ruth took third. The fans did not appreciate the Babe's poor base running. In the next inning, Ruth struck out with the bases loaded. More fuel on the fire as the fans' frustration mounted. The *coup de grace* came in the eighth inning. Wid Matthews, leading off the inning, lined a pitch down the right field line. Ruth leisurely trotted after the ball and when it bounced against the wall, he "walked after it" and made a lazy throw to the infield with Matthews running full speed. He landed on third with a triple. "When Ruth walked in at the finish of the inning the fans stood up, groaned, hooted, jeered and gave a creditable imitation of a cat calling to its mate."[3]

This wasn't the first time Ruth was booed by fans and wouldn't be the last. In 1922, after some heated salary negotiations between Ruth and Huston, the two finally settled on an unheard-of $52,000 a year. Actually, Huston offered Ruth $50,000 but he turned it down and asked for $52,000. Huston agreed but wanted to know about the extra $2,000. Ruth explained that he always dreamed of making $1,000 a week. He would shatter that dream years later.

Ruth's record salary was way out of line compared to some of the other Yankees' stars. Wally Schang was making $10,000, Shawkey $8,500, Pipp $6,500 and Witt $4,000. Whether Ruth's salary was justified or not, the enormous amount of $52,000 did not sit well with many of the fans who were earning $75 a week and living comfortably.

This was the year Ruth and others were suspended for the beginning of the season and fined for barnstorming where he earned nearly $50,000 touring the country. When he finally returned to the Yankees on May 20, the fans were anxious to see him but also somewhat dismayed at his greed. Ruth went

0-for-4 on his first day back and he heard the hoots and howls from the fans. The next day, before another huge crowd, he went 1-for-5 and the boos continued. The third day he was booed when he made out and applauded sarcastically when he caught a routine fly ball. Ruth playfully acknowledged the crowd by tipping his cap. The same scene happened later in the game. Finally, he gave the crowd what they were looking for all afternoon. Ruth hit his first home run of the 1922 season and the boos quickly turned to cheers. Circling the bases, the unpredictable Ruth refused to tip his cap in appreciation.

Ruth continued to slump and by the end of the fifth game of his return, he was hitting a paltry .093. On May 25, Ruth's frustration was finally unleashed. Trying to stretch a single into a double, he was thrown out at second. Ruth vigorously protested the call and then threw a handful of dirt in the umpire's face. He was immediately ejected, and when a fan yelled some nasty words at Ruth, the Babe went into the stands after him. It was an unpleasant afternoon and Ruth got away easy as Ban Johnson suspended him for only one game and fined him $200.

The Yankees lost the final game of the A's series, 5–1, before 55,000 frustrated fans. Eddie Rommel, who specialized in the knuckleball, pitched a great game. He developed the knuckler while recuperating from a scalded hand he received working as a steam fitter on a ship in World War I. Rommel's 13-year major league record was 171–119 with an ERA of 3.54, all with the A's. He had two exceptional years where he led the American League in victories. He won 27 games in 1922 and 21 in 1925. He pitched in two World Series, 1929 and 1931. In both he was used sparingly because he was at the end of his career. Rommel retired from baseball in 1932. He resurfaced in 1936 as an umpire in the New York/Penn League. He moved up to the International League in 1937 and was promoted to the American League the following year. For the next 22 years, Ed Rommel was one of the most outstanding and respected umpires to wear the blue suit in the American League. He and fellow umpire Frank Umont are credited with being the first umpires to wear eyeglasses on the field.

After the Philadelphia series, the Yankees embarked on their first western road trip. They traveled by train to Cleveland, Detroit, St. Louis, Chicago and back east to Philadelphia and Washington. It lasted for 24 grueling days but built a cohesive and confident club determined to win its third consecutive pennant. More importantly, it helped ease the bitter and disappointing memories of the previous year's World Series defeat at the hands of the New York Giants. The western road trip was the turning point in the Yankees' season that would establish their dominance in the American League and set the tone for an exciting World Series.

While Miller Huggins and his club were riding the rails to Cleveland, boxing promoter Tex Rickard was at the Stadium, accompanied by Yankees general manager Ed Barrow. It was the beginning of Yankee Stadium hosting some of the great sporting and non-sporting events of the 20th century. Over the years, Yankee Stadium would become so popular and famous that *Sports Illustrated* called it the greatest venue of the twentieth century. Sadly, eighty-five years of unforgettable memories ended on September 21, 2008, when the Yankees played their last game at the Stadium. They beat the Baltimore Orioles, 7–3. Andy Pettitte picked up the victory and Mariano Rivera closed out the game in fitting fashion with a 1-2-3 ninth inning. A new magnificent stadium would be built right next door for a whopping $1.3 billion (or $1.5 billion, take your choice), opening the turnstiles in 2009. But that's a story for another time and book.

Rickard and his cohorts were surveying the big park to determine where to build the boxing ring that wound up over the mound. They also had to determine where to place 10,000 field chairs leading away from the ring in all four directions. The proper amount of security was still another consideration. It would be a gala night of boxing featuring former heavyweight champion Jess Willard, all for the benefit of the Free Milk Fund.

Millicent Hearst, estranged wife of William Randolph Hearst, controversial newspaper publisher, created the Free Milk Fund for the poor in 1921. Tired of her husband's affair with actress Marion Davies, Millicent left Hearst and settled in New York City where she became a leading philanthropist. The Fund provided free milk to the poor for decades and sponsored many fund-raising events.

When the Yankees arrived in Cleveland, the temperature was hovering in the 30's. After taking the first game, 3–2, behind the solid pitching of Bob Shawkey, the next day it began snowing. Cleveland manager Tris Speaker refused to let his players take the field due to the poor weather conditions. He announced the game would be played as part of a doubleheader when the Yankees returned in July. Although the word "immortal" is casually tossed around in baseball circles, in the case of Speaker it is most appropriate. After 22 years in the major leagues, his lifetime numbers were staggering: a batting average of .345 with 3,514 hits, including 792 doubles, most ever among major leaguers. He led the American League in doubles eight times. His first year with Cleveland (1916) after being traded by Boston, he led the league in hitting with a .386 mark, the only time he won a batting crown. It broke Ty Cobb's streak of nine straight batting titles. Cobb went on to win three more titles after finishing second to Speaker with a .371 average.

Baseball fans will argue forever as to who is the greatest defensive center fielder of all time. Without question Tris Speaker's name will be foremost in the discussion. If not the greatest of all time, he certainly was during the deadball era. In an era where the long ball was a rarity, Speaker played a shallow center field to cut down on bloop hits. Other outfielders followed suit. When the deadball era ended, Speaker continued to play an uncommonly short center field with continued success. Author Timothy Gay, in his biography of Speaker, summed up the outfielders' defensive skills in these poetic words, "He was called 'the Grey Eagle,' in part because it described the aviary brilliance with which he presided over center field. He swooped and soared, surmounting the game from an aerie few ballplayers have ever attained."[4]

Speaker should have prayed to the weather gods for another snow storm because the following day, the Yankees routed the Cleveland Indians, 13–4. They pounded out 19 hits off three pitchers. Everyone in the order had at least one hit. Even pitcher Herb Pennock, a notoriously weak hitter, chipped in with two hits. Witt and Ward each were 3-for-5, but the hitting star of the day was Joe Dugan. He doubled in the third, driving in two runs, and in the sixth inning homered into the left field bleachers with Witt on third. It was a good day for the man with the odd nickname of Jumping Joe. Whoever tagged him with that sobriquet knew what he was talking about. On several occasions during the 1921 season with the A's, he was known to disappear without informing the club. Manager Connie Mack would suspend him to no avail. It was Dugan's way of showing his unhappiness with Philadelphia and their losing ways. He wanted to be traded. One could sympathize with Dugan since the A's lost 100 games in 1921 and finished last, a dreadful 45 games behind first place New York.

A Pennsylvania native, Joe Dugan was born in Mahanoy City on May 12, 1897. He went directly from Holy Cross to the Philadelphia Athletics for a $500 bonus. When the A's offered a signing bonus, Dugan remembered his father's reaction. "My father looked at the money," Dugan said, "then glanced at my seven brothers and sisters. He couldn't contain himself. He said, 'For five hundred dollars you can take the whole family.'"[5] He played his first five years under the tutelage of Connie Mack. Dugan played all infield positions except first. He lacked power but was a consistent and steady singles and doubles hitter. In fact, in 1920 Dugan slugged 40 doubles and batted a very respectable .322. In early January, 1922, Boston owner Harry Frazee announced a three-way trade involving Dugan. It went like this: Boston sent Roger Peckinpaugh to the Washington Nationals as their player/manager. Washington sent Frank O'Rourke to Boston and Bing Miller and Jose Acosta to the Philadelphia Athletics who in turn sent Dugan to Boston. Cash was not mentioned in the deal, which is hard to believe since Mack was giving up Dugan and only getting Miller and Acosta in return. Some baseball people generously estimated Dugan's value at around $100,000. Mack was too shrewd a baseball man to let Dugan go without involving a substantial amount of money. Whatever. The Red Sox were elated. Manager Hugh Duffy explained "I am after a hitting club and Dugan rounds out a team of sluggers that is sure to prove successful."[6]

Poor Duffy, Dugan didn't last long in Boston. He played in 84 games and batted .287. Before the season ended he was involved in another multi-player deal. The Yankees acquired Dugan and outfielder Elmer Smith from Boston for Chick Fewster, Elmer Miller, Johnny Mitchell, Lefty O'Doul and $50,000. It turned out to be a good deal for the Yankees. In 1923, Smith played well in a limited role as a back-up outfielder, hitting a nifty .306. Dugan was, however, the key to the trade. He finished out 1922 with a .286 batting average. Both Cleveland manager Tris Speaker and Chicago White Sox manager "Kid" Gleason were furious with the Dugan/Smith trade. Speaker

In 1923, Joe Dugan led all third basemen with a .974 fielding average. He wasn't too shabby at the plate either. He batted a steady .283 with 30 doubles, second only to Ruth. He also scored 111 runs during the season. (Courtesy National Baseball Hall of Fame Library, Cooperstown, New York.)

said, "It's a crime."[7] Chimed in Gleason, "I tried to make a trade with Boston for Dugan, but was told there was nothing doing."[8] Many thought the late acquisition of Dugan the key to the Yankees' winning the pennant in 1922. The trade for Dugan, which occurred so late in the season and stirred up a controversy, resulted in major league baseball setting the trading deadline at June 15.

For the next six seasons with the Yankees, Dugan was a model of consistency, hitting .283, .302, .292, .288, .269, and .276. A solid defensive player, he led all American League third basemen with a .974 fielding average in 1923. Coupled with Scott at short, who also led the league in fielding with a .961 average, the left side of the Yankees infield was rock solid.

After the 1923 World Series, Dugan played in three more for the Yankees—1926, 1927, 1928. The Yankees lost to the Cardinals in '26 but swept both the '27 and '28 World Series from Pittsburgh and St. Louis! Dugan was a big part of the great 1927 club which featured brand names like Ruth, Gehrig, Meusel, Earl Combs and Tony Lazzeri. Dugan would eventually room with the Babe and was reported to be quite the party guy.

In December of 1928, rumors were spreading the Yankees wanted to get rid of Dugan. Apparently, his knee was failing. The plan was to waive him out of both leagues so he would become a free agent and be able to make his own deal. The Chicago Cubs were the leading contenders for his services. So it came as a huge surprise when the Boston Braves failed to pass on Dugan and picked him up for the waiver price.

Some informed baseball people believed there was some chicanery among the owners. They wanted a stronger Boston Braves club. Why? The Braves were trying to get Sunday baseball established in Boston and thought an improved team would help their cause. Supporting this theory was the fact that the Braves also acquired Rabbit Maranville, George Harper and Pat Collins, all probably past their prime but still with a few good years left. The acquisitions didn't improve the team as the Braves finished in the cellar. Dugan played in only 60 games as Les Bell was the regular third baseman. Even in his limited role, Dugan hit .304. In 1930, Dugan was out of baseball due to chronic knee problems. He attempted a comeback the following year with the Detroit Tigers. He played in eight games before finally calling it quits. Out of baseball, Dugan worked for a beer distributorship and owned his own bar and grill. He spent the last years of his life in Norwood, Massachusetts. The man from Mahonoy City died on July 7, 1982, at the age of 85 and took with him some of the greatest moments in baseball history.

It is interesting to note the trade of Roger Peckinpaugh to the Washington Senators made him the fourth player/manager in 1922. The other three were: Tris Speaker (Cleveland), Ty Cobb (Detroit), and Bill Killefer (Chicago Cubs). Today there is not one player/manager, and there hasn't been one in many years. With a full coaching staff, including a bench coach, the game has become so sophisticated it is impossible for one man to play, manage and handle the media at the same time.

The weather in Cleveland failed once more to cooperate, and the last game of the series was rained out as the Yankees headed to Detroit. In New York, where the weather was just fine, Lou Gehrig continued to play excellent baseball as Columbia trounced Cornell, 11–3. Gehrig went the distance, allowing four hits and four walks. He struck out 10. He had a no-hitter through five innings before Cornell touched him up for two runs in the sixth and one in the seventh. He had another superb day at the plate, going 3-for-3, including a massive home run that landed on 116th Street. He was also intentionally walked twice. Nobody said those Cornell boys were dummies.

Opening the four-game series at Navin Field in Detroit the Yankees made it three straight by beating the Tigers, 3–2. Joe Bush won his fourth game with a gritty performance while Babe Ruth hit his third homer of the year—a mammoth shot into the center field bleachers.

In Yankee Stadium, a reported 63,000 came to witness Tex Rickard's extravaganza of heavyweight boxing. Ten of the world's top heavyweights went toe-to-toe for the benefit of the Free Milk Fund. Most of the contenders were vying for a chance to meet the champ, Jack Dempsey, for a shot at the title. Attention was centered on two fighters, Jess Willard and Louis Firpo. The crowd was not disappointed. Willard stopped Floyd Johnson in eleven ferocious rounds. Firpo, the giant Argentinian, knocked out Jack McAuliffe after one minute and two seconds of the third round. Neither Willard or Firpo got a shot at Dempsey. Instead they got each other. Willard and Firpo were matched up to fight sometime in July, the winner to finally get a crack at Dempsey for the heavyweight title. It was the first major event held at Yankee Stadium outside of baseball in 1923. It would lead to many more fight cards and over time to other sporting and non-sporting events.

The Tigers won the second game of the series, 4–1, behind the outstanding pitching of George Dauss, snapping the Yankees' four-game winning streak. Sam Jones was tagged with the loss. Game three was a wild one with New York trouncing Detroit, 16–11, in 12 innings with Bush picking up another win, his sixth of the early season, in relief of Bob Shawkey. The Yankees exploded for eight runs in the 12th capped by Bob Meusel's grand slam. New York won the final game, 9–5, aided by Ruth's two-run homer, his fourth of the season. Carl Mays was credited with the victory. His record was 2–0. New York maintained its 1½ game lead over Cleveland as the team, once again, hit the rails and headed to St. Louis to play the Browns in another four-game series.

In Worcester, Massachusetts, a young grammar school pitcher by the name of Moses Dupruis, pitching for Gates Lane School, struck out 24 batters in a seven-inning game. Despite this feat, Gates Lane lost to the Chandler Street School, 9–2. It wasn't even a close game. Seven of the kids fanned by Dupruis reached first base when his catcher could not hold on to the third strike. Six of them scored! One can only imagine how Chandler Street managed to score the other three runs. Undeterred by the lack of defense, Dupruis hit two home runs to account for all the scoring by Gates Lane. Could young Moses be another Babe Ruth in the making? Alas, an exhaustive check of baseball encyclopedias revealed no Moses Dupruis.

On May 15, it was announced by boxing promoter Tex Rickard that former heavyweight champion Jess Willard would meet Luis Firpo, the Argentinian, in a battle of contenders for a shot at Jack Dempsey's heavyweight crown. No site or date had been finalized. June 30 or July 7 were possibilities either at Yankee Stadium or Boyle's Thirty Acres in Jersey City.

Tex Rickard, famous boxing promoter during the jazz age, lived a most amazing and exciting life. In his early childhood years he lived in poverty in several frontier towns in Texas. At age 11, Rickard left home and worked as a cowhand. He was married and widowed by age 24. Soon after, Rickard, who was growing up fast, left to seek his fortune in gold in the Klondike in Canada. Failing at that endeavor, he worked odd jobs in several Dawson City saloons, eventually opening his own in Rampart near the Arctic Circle.

In 1900, Rickard held a half-interest in Cape Nome's Great Northern Saloon where he became wealthy catering to gold miners. Ever the adventurer, Rickard sold his interest in the Nome Saloon and sailed to South Africa looking for diamonds. That venture failed and he landed in San Francisco, broke.

Rickard married again and in 1906 took his second wife and adopted daughter to Goldfield, Nevada, where his saloon and gambling business thrived. At this point in his life, Rickard entered the fight promotion business in earnest. He made $13,000 staging the lightweight championship of the world between Battling Nelson and Joe Gans.

In 1910, out of the saloon racket, ever the gambler and entrepreneur, Rickard thrust himself on to the world stage by promoting a heavyweight championship bout between the black fighter Jack Johnson and Jim Jeffries. Johnson, an outspoken black man who had a preference for white women, was unpopular with the public at the turn of the century. Jeffries, who came out of retirement for the fight, was called the "great white hope."

The bout was scheduled to be fought in San Francisco, but because of the race issue, the California governor, James Gilbert, conceding to political pressure, stopped the fight. Undeterred, Rickard moved the fight to Reno, Nevada, where Johnson kayoed Jeffries in the 15th round. Johnson's victory resulted in nation-wide race riots. Restless as ever, Rickard next traveled to Paraguay to raise cattle on a 5,000-acre ranch. That venture failed and he returned to the United States, once again busted.

In 1916, back in boxing, he promoted the Jess Willard and Frank Moran heavyweight title bout. After ten rounds, the fight was declared a no-decision. At the time, the gate was deemed the largest in sports history for an indoor event.

Rickard's big break came when he hooked up with young Jack Dempsey, and both of them ushered in the golden age of professional boxing. Dempsey, with Rickard's promotional genius, popularized boxing in the 1920's and made millions for both. Rickard's entrepreneurial spirit led him to become president of Madison Square Garden, which was granted a National Hockey League franchise in 1926. The club was called "Tex's Rangers" and in its second year won a Stanley Cup. Gambler, politician, entrepreneur, hustler, showman, publicist, promoter, call him what you like, and he may have been all of them, Rickard was truly an amazing man who touched and entertained the lives of millions. He died on January 6, 1929, in Miami Beach, Florida, from complications after an appendectomy.

The Yankees marched into St. Louis like storm troopers and demolished the Browns, sweeping the four-game series and extending their winning streak to six. Granted, St. Louis was at a disadvantage. The Browns' brilliant first baseman, George Sisler, was out of the lineup. He was sitting in the stands wearing heavily smoked glasses, no doubt anxious and frustrated watching his team lose to the Yankees. In late January, the two-time batting champ contracted influenza. This led to a severe sinus infection that eventually affected his eyesight. Surgery partially remedied the problem, but Sisler still had to sit out the entire 1923 season. When he finally returned in 1924, he batted .305, a solid year for the average ballplayer but not Sisler, who won the batting title in 1922 with a lofty .420 average. After the eye surgery, he never matched his earlier achievements. Years later, Bob Shawkey explained one of the reasons. "When he [Sisler] was up at the plate, he could watch you for only so long, and then he'd have to look down to get his eyes focused again. So we'd keep him waiting up there until he'd have to look down, and then pitch. He was never the same hitter again after that."[9]

The road trip was developing into a major success with everyone contributing from the top of the lineup to the bottom. The hitting was timely, the pitching outstanding. Hoyt, Bush, Shawkey and Mays all pitched well and recorded victories over the Browns. Wally Pipp was working on a nine-game hitting streak. Ruth was red hot. He homered in three consecutive games and hit five in eight days. Meusel was also on fire. In the four-game series, he went 8-for-15 (.533) including a 4-for-4 day against spitballer Urban Shocker, the ace of the Browns' staff. After the 1919 season, the spitball was banned from professional baseball. Those pitchers using the spitball were "grandfathered" and could continue using the illegal pitch until their retirement. The last pitcher to use the spitball legally was Burleigh Grimes, who retired in 1934. The operative word here is legally. Many pitchers since 1920, however, have been accused of "doctoring" the ball.

Meusel's nickname was "Long Bob" for his lanky build. He also had a brother Emil, who was called "Irish" because of his ruddy complexion and Irish appearance. The brothers opposed each other in three World Series (1921, 1922, 1923), Emil for the New York Giants and Bob for the Yankees. Emil got the better of his brother, winning two of the three Fall Classics and outhitting Bob, .297 to .250.

Regardless, most knowledgeable baseball people believe Bob was the superior player. He was born July 19, 1896, in San Jose, California, the last of six children of Charles and Mary Meusel. He was educated in Los Angeles schools and graduated from Los Angeles High School. He played three seasons with the Vernon club of the Pacific Coast League and also did a hitch in the United States Navy before joining the Yankees in 1920 at the age of 24.

Meusel played 11 years in the major leagues, all but one with the New York Yankees. His lifetime batting average was a respectable .309. His best year was in 1927 when he hit .337. He also drove in 103 runs as a member of the famed "Murderers' Row," which consisted of Babe Ruth, Lou Gehrig, Earle Combs and Tony Lazzeri.

Bob Meusel, the man with a rifle for an arm, batted over .300 in his seven years as a Yankee. Of his great arm, Sam Jones said, "I've seen him throw flatfooted from deep in the outfield all the way to home plate." Meusel delivered the key hit in Game Six of the '23 World Series to help defeat the Giants 6–4. (Courtesy National Baseball Hall of Fame Library, Cooperstown, New York.)

Meusel's best overall year, however, was 1925. Although he batted only .290, he led the league with 33 home runs and 138 RBIs. In seven of his 10 years with the Yankees, he batted over .300, a consistent and dependable performer. He also finished his career with 1,067 RBIs, not a minor accomplishment, in 11 years. Doing the math, that's an average of 97 runs batted in per season.

Bob Meusel was far from the model ballplayer. He probably hung around Ruth too much, who could be a bad influence at times. In 1921, for example, he, Ruth and Bill Piercy ignored Commissioner Landis' edict against barnstorming after the season. For their defiance, each was suspended until May 20 of the new season and had his World Series money held back (which they eventually received). Under baseball rules, however, suspended players did not get paid.

One wonders what Meusel and Ruth did during the early days of the 1922 season. Oddly, Meusel had his tonsils removed on opening day. Ruth, never to be outdone, had his tonsils and adenoids removed at St. Vincent's Hospital on May 4.

Ironically, after the 1922 season, Commissioner Landis changed the barnstorming rules and allowed up to three World Series players to participate. Ruth and Meusel jumped at the opportunity and booked a 19-game tour of western states. Both were paid handsomely: Ruth $1,000 per game and Meusel $800.

It was widely known that Ruth and Miller Huggins were rarely compatible and often fought. Ruth had little respect for his diminutive manager. Apparently, Meusel went along with the big guy's jousting. Carl Mays recalled both Meusel and Ruth sarcastically calling Huggins "Little Boy," particularly during tense moments in a game.

Defense was another very important aspect of Meusel's game. He patrolled left field at Yankee Stadium with a nonchalance that some interpreted as lax or indifferent, a most difficult sun field in the days before night baseball. It was a brutal field to play late in the afternoon with the left fielder staring straight into the sun. Meusel also had a rifle for an arm. In 1921, he and Jack Tobin of the St. Louis Browns tied for the American League lead in outfield assists with 28. The same year, on September 5, Meusel had four assists in a game to tie a another major league record. The following year he led the league with 24 assists. Pitcher Sam Jones, who played with Meusel for several years, remembered his arm very well. "Bob Meusel had a fantastic arm," he said. "Once he got his hands on a ball it was as good as wherever he wanted to fire it. It was as good as there already. I've seen him throw flatfooted from deep in the outfield all the way to home plate. On a line, and very accurate, too."[10]

In 1929, Meusel had his worst year as a Yankee. He batted a mere .261 and drove in only 57 runs, the lowest numbers in his 10-year career. Apparently, the front office didn't like what they saw from the relatively young 33-year-old outfielder. In October, the Yankees waived Bob Meusel out of the league, and Cincinnati picked him up. He played one year with the Reds who finished next to last with a 59–95 record—a far cry from the great Yankees teams of Ruth, Gehrig, Combs, Lazzeri, *et al.* Meusel had a decent season with the Reds. He batted .289, drove in 62 runs and hit 10 homers. Regardless, Cincinnati released him after the season. No major league team was interested in him, so Meusel played in the minors for two more years with the Minneapolis Millers and the Hollywood Stars before he finally retired from professional baseball.

Bob Meusel was widely known as a quiet and reserved man who kept his thoughts and emotions to himself. He was a man of few words. Strangely, at the end of his career he tried to cozy up to the press. Frank Graham, well-known sportswriter for the *New York Sun*, best described Meusel's personality in these words, "Meusel began to say hello when it was time to say goodby."[11] After baseball, Meusel was employed as a security guard at the Navy base on Terminal Island, California. In 1942, he had a cameo appearance in the movie *Pride of the Yankees*, playing himself. Bob Meusel died in Downey, California, at the age of 81.

In the National League, the New York Giants were leading the St. Louis Cardinals by 3½ games. If both New York teams continued their fine play, the result would be another World Series match-up. No love was lost between these two teams, including ownership. Remember, after whipping the Yankees in two World Series, John McGraw booted Ruppert and Huston out of the Polo Grounds. The Yankees were itching for a rematch.

Back in New York, more of the same exciting news was coming out of Columbia. Lou Gehrig hit his seventh homer of the year. This one was the longest ever! It seemed each new home run Gehrig hit exceeded the previous one in length. Here's how the *New York Times* described Lou's home run. "Gehrig's terrific smash rose gently until it was above the border of the infield and outfield, then sailed on a straight line over the centre [sic] field fence into the campus surrounding the School of Journalism building."[12] Oh, by the way, Gehrig also pitched a 3-hitter to beat Wesleyan, 15–2.

The New York Yankees continued their winning ways as they moved into Chicago for a three-game series. The Yankees took the opener, 3–2, behind the outstanding pitching of Sam Jones. The right-hander went the distance, giving up nine hits, but he was especially tough in the clutch. His control was perfect. He didn't walk a batter. It was his fourth win against three losses. Pipp extended his hitting streak to 11 straight games, all on the road. During this period he batted a cool .396.

At third base for Chicago was a rookie named Willie Kamm. Very few baseball fans today recall the name. He enjoyed a 13-year major league career with a lifetime .281 batting average. Why should anyone remember Willie? Well, in 1922, Charles A. Comiskey, owner of the Chicago White Sox, purchased his contract from the San Francisco Seals, a minor league team in the Pacific Coast League, for a whopping $100,000—a record and unheard of amount for a rookie.

Waite Hoyt took the mound the following day and blanked Chicago, 5–0, on seven hits. The Brooklyn born right-hander was now 2–0. Ironically, Hoyt wasn't scheduled to start, but with the cold winds blowing off Lake Michigan, Miller Huggins did not want his prize lefty, Herb Pennock, to be subject to the elements. One wonders what Hoyt thought of the switch.

At any rate, the Yankees had an easy game, extending their winning streak to eight and 11 of the last 12. There was one down side to an otherwise great day. American League president Ban Johnson notified Joe Bush he was suspended indefinitely, pending an investigation, for his altercation with umpire Billy Evans during the May 17 game against the St. Louis Browns. Bush had vigorously objected to a pitch he thought was a strike. Evans took offense and ejected Bush from the game with the bases full and two out. Jones relieved and got the final out to preserve the 9–2 victory for Bush.

The most exciting news of the day, however, was the announcement that Colonel Jacob Ruppert had finally bought out the half-interest of his longtime partner Cap Huston and was now the sole owner of the wealthiest franchise in baseball. Ruppert would not reveal the price he paid for Colonel Huston's half, but it was estimated at $1,250,000. Based on the sale price, it was also estimated the New York Yankees were valued at $4 million. The deal would take effect June 1.

This was the second time the sale of the Yankees to Ruppert was announced. The first was in December of 1922. But the announcement then was withdrawn in early January when the two colonels couldn't agree to the wording of the sale. Lawyers for Ruppert wanted the wording in the agreement to state that Huston would remain out of baseball for 10 years after the sale. Huston objected vehemently. Apparently, Ruppert changed his mind and agreed to let his former partner do as he pleased. Huston was free to do whatever he wanted, even buy another baseball team, even a club that would rival the Yankees. That was highly unlikely based on Huston's comments to the press. "Anyway, I wanted to take a rest. I've done a lot of work in my time, and I was beginning to get tired. In the near future I am going to Hot Springs, Arkansas. After that I will take the family to California for a tour of the State. I am just going to take it easy and have the vacation that I have been promising myself for many years. After that—well, I still have a moral interest in the Yankees and I expect to see more games than the average fellow. And I'll probably enjoy it more if I have to pay my $1.50 at the box office."[13]

It was one of those rare deals where both parties benefit. Each got what he wanted. Ruppert was to be sole owner of the New York Yankees and Huston made a handsome profit and was now able to vacation or seek new challenges.

Although the partnership was not a marriage made in heaven back in 1915, it was without question an overwhelming success. The two colonels took one of the worst baseball teams in either league and made it the best in the American League. The Yankees were now a serious challenger to the Giants for baseball supremacy and fan popularity in the New York market.

When the two colonels acquired the Yankees, they were tenants in the Polo Grounds beholden to McGraw and the Giants' ownership. They now had a magnificent home of their own in the greatest city in the United States. The attendance had gone from 256,035 in 1915 to over a million by the end of the season. It was a marvelous success story. A proud Jacob Ruppert told the press: "The papers have been signed, sealed and delivered. They go into effect on June 1. By law and every other way I am now the sole owner of the Yankees, or at least I will be within another ten days."[14]

The final game of the Chicago series was a classic. In the top of the 15th inning with the game tied at 1–1, George Herman Ruth stepped to the plate with two out and Joe Dugan on first. Left-hander Mike Cvengros, a local boy from Pana, Illinois, started the game and was on the mound for Chicago. With apologies to Mario Puzo, the lefty made an offer to the Babe he couldn't refuse. Ruth parked the ball into the right-field bleachers for a 3–1 lead and eventually the victory. It was the Yankees' ninth straight.

It was a classic pitchers' duel between two left-handers, Herb Pennock and Cvengros, both at the top of their game. Pennock had his curve and change-up working to perfection. He allowed only four hits, walked five and struck out six. Up to this point, Pennock was undefeated with a record of 4–0.

The Yankees were playing outstanding baseball. Miller Huggins had the team going in the right direction—solid defense, clutch hitting and consistent pitching. Their record was 23–8 (.742) and with another Philadelphia (now in second place replacing Cleveland) loss, the Yankees' lead widened to five.

Wally Pipp had another fine day at the plate, going 3-for-8 and stretching his hitting streak to 13 consecutive games. After the game, the Yankees hopped a train and headed back east to Philadelphia for three games against Connie Mack's second-place A's. It was an opportunity for Mack's club to chip away at the Yankees' five-game lead. The previous year the A's finished next-to-last in the American League. Prior to 1922, Mack's A's reeled off seven consecutive last-place finishes. The 1916 club ranks as one of the worst in baseball with a 36–117 record and a 20-game losing streak during the season. Even the 1923 franchise was a far cry from the halcyon years of 1913 and 1914 when Philadelphia dominated the league with their $100,000 infield of Stuffy McInnis, Eddie Collins, Jack Barry and Frank "Home Run" Baker along with Hall of Fame pitchers Eddie Plank and Chief Bender.

The mini-dynasty, however, quickly ended when Mack had a fire sale and decimated his club after the 1914 World Series upset loss to the "Miracle Braves" of Boston in a four-game sweep. These were the Braves managed by George Stallings, led by pitchers Dick Rudolph (26–10), Bill James (26–7) and George Tyler (16–13) and supported by superstars Walter "Rabbit" Maranville at short and Johnny Evers at second.

On July 19, the Braves were in last place! By September, they had moved into first place, then back to third and back to first for good by September 8. They won 60 of their last 76 games, finishing 10½ games ahead of the second place New York Giants.

The break-up of the A's was caused by a combination of factors: rising salaries due to competition from the upstart Federal League and Mack's belief that his club quit on him during the series. Although Philadelphia would finish in sixth place in 1923, it was the beginning of Mack's resurgence back to respectability.

The Yankees' nine-game winning streak ended before 20,000 fans at Shibe Park when the Philadelphia Athletics pushed across a run in the bottom of the ninth to win a hard-fought contest, 1–0. Eddie Rommel, the ace of Connie Mack's staff, pitched a courageous game. He allowed seven singles and walked six, Babe Ruth four times. Joe Bush pitched an even better game, giving up five hits and three walks. It was a tough loss for Bush and the Yankees. Their first-place lead slipped to four games ahead of the surprising A's. There was one bright spot of the day. Wally Pipp went 1-for-4, extending his hitting streak to 14 games.

The Yankees lost their second straight game to the Athletics, 4–2, cutting their first-place lead to three games. Rollie Naylor recorded his fifth straight victory. He allowed 11 hits but was tough in the clutch as the Yankees continued to miss scoring opportunities with runners on base. Bob Shawkey pitched a complete game for the Yankees but was hurt by the long ball. Three of the four runs by the A's were the result of home runs. Wally Pipp went 1-for-3, running his hitting streak to 15 consecutive games.

The Yankees salvaged the last game of the series, defeating Philadelphia, 10–8, in 11 innings. Center fielder Whitey Witt drove in the winning runs with a sharp single to center with the bases full. It was Witt's fifth hit of the day.

It was an exciting game right from the start. Philadelphia used three pitchers: Bob Hasty, Freddie Heimach and Rommel. The trio gave up 20 hits, 6 walks and 10 runs. The Yankees pitchers, Carl Mays, Waite Hoyt and Pennock, were not much better. The three accounted for 15 hits, 6 walks and 8 runs. It was an ugly victory but still counted in the standings. On the bright side, Babe Ruth hit his ninth home run, and Wally Pipp had a 2-for-6 day, extending his hitting streak to 16 games.

The hero of the day was the 28-year-old center fielder Whitey Witt. He was born Ladislaw Waldemar Wittkowski on September 28, 1895, in Orange, Massachusetts. Happily for sportswriters and announcers, someone changed the young man's name to Walter Lawton Witt early in his life.

Witt had no minor league experience when he joined the Philadelphia A's in 1916. As he told author Rich Westcott in an interview for his book *Diamond Greats*, " I went right from high school to the A's. I was going to a boarding school in Barre, Vermont, and playing in the White Mountain League. That was a summer league with teams sponsored by the big resort hotels in New Hampshire and Vermont. Most of the teams were made up of college boys from places like Harvard, Yale and Dartmouth who had summer jobs at the hotels," he explained. "I was hitting over .400 while playing for St. Johnsbury. A scout was following me. One day, I got a telegram from Connie Mack asking me to meet him in Boston."[15]

Witt jumped at the opportunity and met Mack, who offered the young man a two-year contract. It was generous too, calling for a $5,000 bonus and a $1,800 salary. Needless to say, Witt signed on the dotted line and reported to the A's the following season as their regular shortstop. Remember, after the A's lost the World Series to the Braves in 1914, Mack began selling off his star players and stocking his club with college kids. It was a case of Witt being at the right place at the right time.

Witt was a diminutive 5'7" and 150 pounds, a slap hitter and skilled bunter, and he was lightning fast. He also had a keen eye at the plate. In his rookie season, Witt had the ominous distinction of leading American League shortstops with 78 errors. By his own admission, he was not a very good infielder. But he was a versatile player for Mack, who used him at second, third and the outfield.

After the first two seasons with the A's, where he batted .245 and .252, Witt was drafted into the Army as the United States became involved in World War I. After Witt returned in 1919, Mack began using him in the outfield more often. His hitting continued to improve as he batted .267 his first year back, but then the following year, 1920, he put together a solid season, batting .321 in 65 games. The A's finished last again, for the sixth year in a row. Living in baseball's basement was not fun for Witt or any of the Philadelphia players and it began to wear on him, which probably led to his falling out with Mack.

In 1921, Witt turned in a career year. He played in all 154 games in the outfield, batted .315, collected 198 hits, including 31 doubles and 11 triples, and scored 100 runs. The A's finished last for the seventh straight year with an embarrassing 53–100 record.

Over the winter, Mack offered the young outfielder a chintzy $500 raise, which angered Witt, who believed that after five years with the club and an outstanding season, he should have received considerably more. Witt took the money, but was not happy. During spring training in 1922,

Whitey Witt, the diminutive center fielder for the Yankees, turned in a career high year in 1923. He batted .314, scored 113 runs and led the league with a .974 fielding average. He also helped win Game Four of the World Series, going 3-for-4 and driving in two runs. (Courtesy National Baseball Hall of Fame Library, Cooperstown, New York.)

Witt's frustration boiled over. The A's were playing the Cardinals in a spring exhibition game in Eagle Pass, Texas, a week before the season opened. Witt was in right field, and it was pouring rain. He was standing in an ankle-deep puddle thinking about the money Mack should have given him. Witt picks up the story from here. "The winning run's on base, and the ball comes to me. Instead of throwing it to third, I just threw it over the catcher's head into the grandstand. The run scored, and we lost the game."[16]

After the game, Mack told Witt he was getting rid of him and he did. He sold him to the Yankees in April for a reported $16,000. It turned out to be a bargain for the Yankees.

Witt's first three years in center field for the Yankees were solid. In 1922, he batted .297, led the American League in walks with 89 and helped the Yankees win their second pennant. Like the rest of the team, he didn't perform well in the World Series, hitting an anemic .222. In 1923, Witt batted .314, scored 113 runs and this time led the league with a .979 fielding average. Although the Yankees won their first World Series in 1923, overall Witt turned in a mediocre performance. He did, however, help win Game Four, going 3-for-4 and driving in two runs.

Witt followed up with another solid season in 1924. He hit .297 and scored 88 runs. But during the season, the Yankees acquired a young outfielder by the name of Earle Combs from the minor league Louisville Colonels. The Yankees paid $50,000 plus two players. That purchase was the beginning of the end for Whitey Witt as a Yankee. In 1924, Combs batted .400 in limited playing time, but Huggins could clearly see the potential. The following year, Combs took over in center field and performed superbly. He batted .342, collected 203 hits and scored 117 runs in 150 games. Witt played in only 31 games and batted .200. The following year he finished out his major league career with Brooklyn in the National League.

"Babe Ruth always considered me one of his best friends," opined Witt years later. "I loved the guy. There was a lot of jealousy on our club. Some guys were always knocking Ruth, calling him a big bum and so forth. Wally Pipp was one of them, and they had a helluva fist fight once. I always said to those guys, 'Why do you knock him? He's our meal-ticket.' We would have been nowhere without him."[17]

Few Yankee fans or baseball buffs remember the name Whitey Witt. He doesn't have the name recognition the likes of Ruth, Meusel, Dugan, Bush, Hoyt or Pennock. But the pesky hitter and speedy outfielder did make significant contributions to two of the Yankees' first three pennants and, of course, their first World Series.

Oddly and maybe even sadly, Witt is remembered for an unusual incident that happened September 16, 1922. Let's set the stage. The Yankees arrived at Sportsman's Park in St. Louis for an important series with the second-place Browns, hanging on to a half-game lead in the pennant race. During the first game of the crucial series, over 30,000 screaming fans were cheering their hometown favorites and jeering the Yankees, particularly the Babe. The fans were rowdy. The atmosphere was ripe for mischief. The Yankees were leading, 2–1 (and would win by that score), in the bottom of the ninth when a fly ball was hit between Witt and Meusel. As they converged on the ball, a bottle came flying out of the stands and hit Witt on the forehead. "Bleeding, he fell unconscious, and three players carried him to the bench. As Meusel looked up at the silenced stands, a raucous voice shouted,

'We'll get you too, Meusel.'"[18] A doctor revived Witt and examined the gash. It was serious but not disabling. Whitey played the next day with a bandage around his forehead.

But the story doesn't end there. Ban Johnson offered a $1,000 reward for identification of the bottle thrower. Some say the culprit was a young boy. One popular story floating around St. Louis at the time was that the bottle was already on the field and Witt inadvertently stepped on it, the bottle flipping up and hitting him in the forehead. That version was hard to believe and it's doubtful anyone did. This incident and others over the years would eventually lead to the introduction of the paper cup at all ballparks. Perhaps that's the legacy of Ladislaw Waldemar Wittkowski.

After leaving Brooklyn, Witt kicked around the minor leagues for three more seasons, finally retiring to his home in South Jersey where he owned and operated a tavern for 38 years. He also spent his winters in Florida after selling his tavern and generally led a leisurely lifestyle until his death in 1988 at the age of 92. Whitey Witt is buried in Saint Joseph's Roman Catholic Church Cemetery in Woodstown, New Jersey.

On May 25, two interesting stories surfaced in the press. First, the Baseball Writers' Association of America sent a strongly worded telegram to Commissioner Landis, National League president John Heydler and American League president Ban Johnson, saying that they were vehemently opposed to broadcasting baseball games from major league parks throughout the country. Apparently, the BBWAA discovered that permission to broadcast had been granted to a radio corporation. The writers sincerely believed it would destroy the circulation of afternoon newspapers and result in less publicity for baseball. In hindsight, it was clearly an over-reaction. Eventually afternoon papers would disappear but not because of broadcasting games. With respect to less publicity for baseball, on the contrary, radio gave the game more exposure to fans than newspapers alone. Today there is baseball coverage 24–7. Television, radio, newspapers, magazines and the internet reach millions of fans hungry for the latest information about their team and favorite players, and attendance is still on the rise.

Second, Detroit Tigers immortal Ty Cobb, not noted as a slugger, hit a home run on May 25 against the Chicago White Sox in a losing cause. The home run in itself wasn't notable. It was the run he scored. It gave the Georgia Peach 1,742 career runs, one more than Honus Wagner for the most runs scored in major league history at the time. At least that's what was reported in the *New York Times*. Over the years, however, baseball stats have been revised when new information has been uncovered. Apparently, this was the case with Wagner's lifetime runs scored. It was not 1,741. A check of several baseball encyclopedias and the internet reveals the "Flying Dutchman" scored 1,736 or as high as 1,739, whichever source you choose. In other words, Cobb had passed Wagner earlier than May 25, 1923. At the time no one knew it. It's all academic anyway since Cobb went on to record 2,246 runs in his illustrious career, which total, by the way, was eclipsed by Hall of Famer Rickey Henderson at 2,295.

The New York Yankees continued their long road trip, which began way back on May 8 against Cleveland, arriving in Washington to play the Senators in a four-game series. Bad weather in Cleveland, tiring and endless train travel and a demanding schedule could not stop the Yankees juggernaut. They swept the series. Once again, the great pitching staff shared the glory. Jones (5–3), Hoyt (3–0), Pennock (6–0) and Bush (7–4) won games.

In the second game of the series, Wally Pipp's 17-game hitting streak was in serious jeopardy. Entering the top of the ninth, he was 0-for-4 and might not have gotten another chance to hit. Waite Hoyt, Whitey Witt, Joe Dugan and Babe Ruth were ahead of Pipp in the batting order. Both Hoyt and Witt grounded out to Roger Peckinpaugh at short. The situation looked bleak with Dugan coming to the plate. Paul Zahniser was on the mound for Washington, and he induced Dugan to hit a slow roller to Bucky Harris at second. Harris juggled the ball, then threw wild to first, allowing Dugan to advance to second, but more importantly, keeping the inning alive with Ruth coming to the plate. Zahniser, not wanting another run to score, pitched carefully to Ruth and wound up walking him. Pipp now had his opportunity to keep the streak going. But all he could do was slap a ground ball to short, an easy chance for Roger Peckinpaugh. But before the shortstop could field the ball, it hit Dugan going from second to third. Dugan was declared out and Pipp given a hit according to baseball rules.

The question is: was it divine intervention or Dugan chicanery? Regardless of the answer, Pipp's streak had reached 18. Blame it all on Bucky Harris' error, giving Pipp another at bat. For the record, Harris was considered a slick fielder, but he did lead the league in errors in 1923, probably none more important than Dugan's boot, at least to Pipp. This is the same Bucky Harris who would become player/manager the next year for the Senators and immediately became known as the "Boy Manager" at 27. He led the Senators to the pennant in 1924 and beat the New York Giants in the World Series. Living up to his name, he repeated in 1925 but lost out to the Pittsburgh Pirates in seven games in the World Series. In addition to Washington, Bucky Harris managed the Detroit Tigers, Boston Red Sox, Philadelphia Phillies and the New York Yankees. In 29 years of managing, he won three pennants, two World Series and finished with a 2,157–2,218 record. Bucky Harris was inducted into the Hall of Fame in 1975.

During the Memorial Day doubleheader, Ruth hit two home runs, bringing his league-leading total to 11. Pipp extended his hitting streak to 20 consecutive games. He was 1-for-4 in the morning and 2-for-5 in the afternoon. The only downside to the entire holiday doubleheader was the injury to catcher Wally Schang. It occurred in the morning game. In the second inning, Schang was running out a grounder and tripped over his own bat. Trainer Al Wood examined Schang and immediately sent him to New York on the afternoon train. Back home, the team physician examined Schang, and his diagnosis was a groin injury that would keep the catcher sidelined for several weeks. Benny Bengough took over the catching duties while Schang was disabled, which turned out to be considerably longer than expected.

The road trip had begun on May 8 in Cleveland with the Yankees in first place by one game over the Detroit Tigers. It ended on May 30 in Washington, D.C., with New York in front of Philadelphia by seven games. The Yankees won 17 of 20 games and at one point ran off nine straight victories. Although no one knew it at the time, the Yankees' successful road trip set the tone for the rest of the season. The Yankees would experience peaks and valleys in the months ahead, but they would continue to play inspired baseball, build an insurmountable lead and make a mockery of the American League pennant race.

4

Out in Front by Nine

New York returned to Yankee Stadium to open a 19-game home stand with a seven-game lead over Philadelphia. It was an opportunity for the Yankees to fatten up on the weaker eastern clubs. It didn't work out as expected. After their triumphant road trip, the Yankees played surprisingly poor baseball. More specifically, Huggins' club won eight, lost ten with one rainout and watched their comfortable seven-game lead drop to four. The home stand began on a chilly day before a small crowd of 12,000 with the Yankees easily beating the Red Sox, 8–1. Shawkey earned the victory, his fifth of the season. But New York lost the next two games. The first was to Boston starter Jack Quinn, who pitched a masterful game, blanking the Yankees on seven hits for a 5–0 victory. The right-hander stopped two streaks with his shutout. He halted the Yankees' six-game winning streak and put an end to Wally Pipp's 21-game consecutive hitting gem. Over that span Pipp batted a laudatory .351.

Quinn did not just beat the Yankees, he dominated them. Only two runners reached as far as third base. He relied mostly on a good curve and fastball with an occasional spitter to keep the hitters guessing. Babe Ruth and Everett Scott had five of the seven hits. The rest of the Yankees were helpless. Sam Jones took the loss for New York.

Medical reports concerning Wally Schang's groin injury continued to be vague and contradictory. Doctor's re-examined the catcher and decided that Schang did not have a rupture, but there was a threat of an "abscess complication" that may require surgery. They claimed the next few days were critical. It all seemed quite mysterious.

The next day, before 20,000, the Yankees lost again to the Red Sox, this time 7–3 behind the fine pitching of Howard Ehmke. Waite Hoyt started for the Yankees and was handed a 3–0 lead after five innings but couldn't hold it. The Red Sox scored two in the sixth, four in the seventh and an insurance run in the eighth. After the fourth inning, Ehmke blanked the Yankees the rest of the way for the victory.

After the game, many of the fans, including Babe Ruth and Joe Bush, rushed to their old home, the Polo Grounds, to witness the world's featherweight championship bout between Eugene Criqui of France and the champion, Johnny Kilbane. Consistent with their celebrity status, Ruth and Bush had ringside seats. They were greeted by Benny Leonard, the great world's lightweight champion. Ruth's persona was like a huge magnet. No matter where he went, the Babe attracted the greats, near greats and the average citizen. They all wanted to meet and greet the bigger-than-life baseball immortal.

Kilbane, who had held the title for 11 years, was showing signs of aging, his hair was streaked with gray and his face drawn from the rigors of training. In Criqui, he was facing an aggressive, tough challenger, a veteran of World War I. For the first five rounds, Kilbane boxed cautiously, preserving his strength and stamina. Then in round six, Kilbane's long cherished dream of retiring undefeated was crushed by the younger man. Criqui knocked out Kilbane after one minute and fifty-four seconds of the sixth round to win the crown. The end came so suddenly the crowd of 20,000 were spellbound. They were stunned. There were no warning signs. Eugene Criqui was now the world's featherweight champ.

The final game of the four-game series between the New York Yankees and the Boston Red Sox was rained out, disappointing nearly 30,000 fans. The rain began just before game time, and it poured for about an hour-and-a-half before the game was called.

An oddity of the schedule had the Yankees traveling to Washington for a single game against the Senators (which they lost, 5–2, for their third consecutive defeat), returning the next day to the Bronx to open their first home stand against the western clubs that they recently demolished. The Chicago White Sox was the first to arrive at Yankee Stadium, followed by the Cleveland Indians, the St. Louis Browns and the Detroit Tigers. Pre-season analysis had Ty Cobb's Tigers as the Yankees' toughest opponents. Even with Harry Heilmann leading the league in hitting, the Tigers were not even playing .500 ball and were entrenched in fourth place.

Before opening the series with the White Sox, New York received a positive report regarding Wally Schang's mysterious groin injury. Surgeons at St. Vincent's Hospital announced that Schang would be ready to play within a week. Surgery was not needed. That was encouraging news for Miller Huggins since both Benny Bengough and Fred Hofmann, filling in for Schang, were not hitting.

In what was expected to be a dull game, the Yankees hosted the last-place Chicago White Sox, which turned out to be one of the most exciting games of the season. New York won, 7–6, in 10 innings, but that doesn't begin to tell the real story. Fast forward to the top of the ninth inning. The Yankees were holding on to a slim 4–2 lead with Bob Shawkey on the mound. John Mostil led off for the White Sox with a triple to deep left-center. Earl Sheely singled, scoring Mostil. The score was now 4–3. Miller Huggins couldn't get to the mound fast enough to remove Shawkey and replace him with Sam Jones. Chicago manager Kid Gleason countered by yanking Sheely for the speedy Roy Elsh (who would steal 16 bases in 1923). With Wally Schang recuperating from a groin injury and Benny Bengough benched because he wasn't hitting, Miller Huggins had to play Fred Hofmann, who committed a passed ball allowing Elsh to go to second base with the tying run. The 18,000 fans were in a state of shock. The next batter, Bibb Falk, sacrificed, Elsh taking third with only one out. Willie Kamm, up next, hit a sizzling grounder to Joe Dugan at third, who back-handed it and quickly tagged Elsh, who had started for home. With two out and Kamm at first, it looked like the Yankees would escape the threat as many of the fans headed for the exits. Not so fast. The next batter, Ray Schalk, walked, moving Kamm into scoring position. Amos Strunk, batting for pitcher Charlie Robertson, lined a single over short, tying the score. The next batter, Harry Hooper, was out on a sterling play by Wally Pipp, robbing him of a base hit.

The Yankees went out meekly in the bottom of the ninth. In the top of the 10th Harvey McClellan homered to right-center off Jones' first pitch. The inning went downhill from there. Two doubles and a single later, Jones was finished for the day, and the White Sox had a 6–4 lead. Carl Mays came in and stopped the bleeding. Once again, the fans that remained headed for the nearest exit. Not so fast.

Babe Ruth grounded out to start the bottom of the 10th. Pipp hit a grounder to Eddie Collins, who let the ball bounce off his chest for an error. Bob Meusel doubled to right-center, sending Pipp to third. Aaron Ward, who had previously homered, singled to left, driving in both Pipp and Meusel to tie the score once again. The next batter, Everett Scott, hit three long foul balls that, if fair, would have been home runs. A nervous manager, Gleason, had seen enough of Ted Blankenship and replaced him with John Thurston. Hard to say, but, it might have been the first time a pitcher was taken out because of long foul balls. Back to the game. Scott tapped a weak grounder to Amos Strunk at first, who tossed to McClellan at short for the attempted force but threw the ball into center field with Ward racing to third. Benny Bengough walked, loading the bases. Mays popped up for the second out. Whitey Witt saved the day when he singled between first and second to finally end the game and send the remaining thousands of fans home to a late dinner, but exceedingly happy.

Actually, the game should have been over after the ninth. It was Ruth's bonehead play that resulted in extra innings. It happened in the eighth with the Yankees ahead, 4–2. Ruth was on second with nobody out and a 3–0 count on Pipp. Ruth tried to steal third and was thrown out! This cost the Yankees a run because after Pipp made out, Meusel singled and Ward hit a sacrifice fly. It wouldn't be the last time Ruth's brain froze on the ball field. One of his most famous blunders happened in the 1926 World Series against the St. Louis Cardinals. It was the seventh game and the Cardinals were leading, 3–2, in the ninth inning. Grover Cleveland Alexander had just walked Ruth with two out, which wasn't terribly surprising since the Babe had hit four home runs in the Series. With Bob Meusel up next and Lou Gehrig on deck, Ruth inexplicably took off for second. He was out by the proverbial mile. Game over. Series over.

Before a modest crowd of 12,000 at Yankee Stadium, the Chicago White Sox, behind the brilliant pitching of Urban "Red" Faber, defeated the New York Yankees, 4–1. Faber allowed five hits, all singles except for Joe Dugan's double. Faber controlled the game from beginning to end, and his spitball made the Yankees batters look helpless, striking out seven throughout the game. Faber would win only 14 games for Chicago in 1923, but in the three previous years, he won 23, 25, 21 games, respectively. Somewhat unique, he pitched only for Chicago for 20 years, compiling a lifetime record of 254–213 with an ERA of 3.15. Faber would be elected to the Hall of Fame in 1964.

Herb Pennock, who pitched well enough to win, if given more run support, lost his first game of the season. His record now stood at an impressive 6–1. In January 1923 when the Yankees acquired Pennock, his career with the A's and Red Sox was less than spectacular. Few knew this left-hander would be one of the Yankees greats, especially in World Series play.

In 1912, at the tender age of 18, Pennock signed with the Philadelphia Athletics directly out of Wenonnah Military Academy. Supposedly, he fanned 22 college players in one game. The tall, slender lefty had a graceful motion, but his fastball left a lot to be desired, so he relied on an assortment of curve balls. Connie Mack used the young lefty sparingly his first two years with the A's. Then in 1914, he was given more of an opportunity to pitch and posted a respectable 11–4 record in over 151 innings. But a slow start in 1915 prompted Connie Mack to trade him to the Boston Red Sox. Mack was not impressed with Pennock's fastball or lack there of, or his control. Mack was not alone in his impression of Pennock's fastball. A Detroit Tiger outfielder once commented, "The only comforting thing about hitting against him [Pennock] is that you don't have to be afraid of getting hurt. Even if he hits you on the head with his fastball he won't knock your hat off."[1]

The Red Sox used Pennock mostly in relief his first two full seasons with the club. Then in 1919, after a year out of baseball due to a stint in the Navy, he led the Red Sox rotation with a 16–8 record and an ERA of 2.71. Pennock's pitching partners that summer were Sam Jones, Carl Mays, Waite Hoyt and Babe Ruth, all later to be reunited as members of the Yankees pitching rotation. This would be Pennock's best year with Boston. The next three years, he was less than mediocre with a 39–44 record. Two of the years his ERA climbed over 4.00. Boston finished last in 1922 and with few quality players remaining, the team unloaded "The Knight of Kennett Square."

He was given this unusual nickname because he raised thoroughbreds and hosted fox hunts in his affluent home town of Kennett Square, Pennsylvania.

When Pennock joined the Yankees, a transformation took place. It was no secret the left-hander was not blessed with a blazing fastball, but he did have effective weapons that he continued to hone. "Besides his excellent curve ball, he possessed masterful control and a baffling change of pace. In many games, he would not throw over one dozen fastballs."[2] Apparently, Connie Mack didn't have the patience when Pennock was young and had problems with his control.

Herb Pennock, the only left-hander on the 1923 Yankees, won 19 and lost 6 for a team-leading .760 winning percentage. He won two of the Yankees' four games in the World Series, leading them to their first championship. He was elected to the Hall of Fame in 1948. (Courtesy National Baseball Hall of Fame Library, Cooperstown, New York.)

In his first six years with the Yankees, Pennock won 115 games and lost only 57 for a .668 winning percentage. However, if you eliminate 1925, an off-year when he posted a 16–17 record, his winning percentage jumps to an incredible .712. At one point during this span, Jack Conway of the *New York Daily Mirror* claimed, "The Yankees can get along without Herb Pennock like an automobile without its gasoline, like a hunk of liver without its rasher of bacon, like a mud-turtle without its shell. Pennock is the best left-hander in the business."[3] Huggins thought so, too. He loved Pennock and thought he was the best in the league.

Pennock made major contributions to three of four Yankee pennants: 1923, 1926 and 1927. In 1932, he took on a lesser role, pitching in a little more than 146 innings, giving way to stars Lefty Gomez, Red Ruffing, George Pipgras and Johnny Allen. In his 11 years with the Yankees, he had a 162–90 (.642) record. Lifetime it was 241–162 and an ERA of 3.60.

Pennock's star shone brightest during the pressure-packed World Series. He had an unbeatable 5–0 record. In 1923, he was 2–0 with a 3.63 ERA against the New York Giants, leading the Yankees to their first World Series title. In 1926, he was again 2–0, this time against the St. Louis Cardinals. Pennock won the opener in a masterful performance, limiting the Cardinals to three hits and one run. He also won Game Five and finished the Series with a minuscule earned run average of 1.23. With the 1927 Yankees, often called the greatest team ever, he beat the Pittsburgh Pirates in Game Three as the Yankees swept the Series. By 1932, Pennock was nearing the end of his career, so manager Joe McCarthy used his left-hander twice in relief.

The following year, the Yankees released Pennock, who returned to the Red Sox in a limited role, mostly in relief, but managed to tack on two more victories to his lifetime record. After his playing days ended, Pennock coached for the Red Sox and supervised the team's farm system. In 1944, he was named general manager of the Philadelphia Phillies by owner Bob Carpenter. As general manager of the Phillies, Pennock had a difficult time, as many others did, accepting Jackie Robinson into major league baseball. Prior to a visit by the Dodgers to Philadelphia in May, 1947, Pennock made it known to his counterpart, Branch Rickey, that Robinson was not welcome. Rickey stood his ground and Robinson played. It was not one of Pennock's finest moments. To his credit Pennock was instrumental in building a pennant winner in Philadelphia in 1950. They were nicknamed the "Whiz Kids." The average age was 26. He signed two key players to that club: pitcher Curt Simmons and infielder Willie "Puddin' Head" Jones. Unfortunately, Herb Pennock never got to see the fruits of his labor. On January 30, 1948, attending a National League meeting at the Waldorf-Astoria, Pennock collapsed in the lobby from a cerebral hemorrhage. He died hours later. He was 53 years old. There is little doubt Herb Pennock turned a so-so career into Hall of Fame stature when he put on the pinstripes. He was elected to the Hall of Fame in 1948 (the year he died) along with Pie Traynor of the Pittsburgh Pirates.

The third game of the series was rained out, but Chicago won the final, 7–3, behind the fine pitching of Mike Cvengros, the same left-hander that John McGraw dumped the previous year. Perhaps manager Kid Gleason saw something in Cvengros that McGraw missed. Not to diminish Cvengros' performance, but the way the Yankees were playing lately just about any decent pitcher could beat them. The defeat pointed out Ruth's tremendous hold on the game. The *New York Times* ran this sub-headline, "Babe Strikes Out Twice." Those four words reveal the enormous influence Ruth possessed during his playing days. Every move he made was analyzed and chronicled.

Since their six-game winning streak ended, the Yankees were 1–5. They lost two to Boston, one to Washington and two games to Chicago. In spite of Ruth's 12th home run, the team was in a slump. On top of this, the A's, behind the outstanding relief pitching of Rube Walberg, beat the St. Louis Browns, 6–5, to narrow the Yankees' lead to only four games.

John McGraw, not satisfied with the way his club was playing (6½-game lead) and with the June 15 trading deadline closing in, made a deal with Judge Emil Fuchs, owner and vice president of the Boston Braves. McGraw sent pitcher Jess Barnes and catcher Earl Smith to Boston for pitcher John Watson and veteran catcher Hank Gowdy. No money was involved in the transaction. It turned out to be a wise move by McGraw. Both players helped the club down the stretch. Watson was 8–5 with a 3.41 ERA, and Gowdy batted .328 (a lifetime .270 hitter) in 53 games. The shrewd McGraw was clearly looking ahead to the Fall Classic and a rematch with the Yankees.

The Cleveland Indians, led by player/manager Tris Speaker, moved into Yankee Stadium for a four-game series. Speaker demonstrated why he was elected to the Hall of Fame in 1937 in the second year of the Hall's balloting. The man known as both "The Grey Eagle" and "Spoke" led the Indians in a 13–3 drubbing of the Yankees. It was the Tris Speaker show. He hit a grand slam in the sixth inning, walked twice, scored three times and was responsible for three other runs. The Yankees were in a serious slump and Speaker made it official. They had lost six games in the last seven.

Entering the top half of the sixth, Cleveland had a slim 3–2 lead. The Yankees were obviously still in the game. But that changed in a hurry. Cleveland scored two runs on a double, two singles, two walks and a sacrifice fly, and Joe Bush left the game with the bases loaded. Carl Mays replaced Bush and added to the disaster. He walked Bill Wambsganss, forcing in the third run of the inning. The bases were still full with the dangerous Speaker coming to the plate. The count went to 1–1, then Speaker launched the next pitch into the right field bleachers. Ruth didn't move. He simply turned his head and watched the ball sail gracefully into the crowd. The seven runs took the crowd (estimated at 20,000) out of the game. The Indians tacked on three more in the ninth, but the game was over in the sixth. It was an ugly, ugly game, one that Miller Huggins and the team wanted to quickly forget. Philadelphia lost, so the Yankees maintained their four-game lead.

Second baseman Bill Wambsganss, a hard name to forget, scored the third run in Cleveland's seven-run outburst. He will always be remembered for making baseball history in 1920. It happened in the World Series pitting the Cleveland Indians against the Brooklyn Robins. It was in the fifth inning of Game Five. Otto Miller was on first for Brooklyn. Pete Kilduff was on second. Clarence Mitchell was the batter, and he hit a line drive caught by Wambsganss, who stepped on second before Kilduff could get back and then tagged Miller, running from first on the pitch. It was the first and only unassisted triple play in World Series history. Also, in that memorable game, two other Cleveland players made history. Elmer Smith hit the first World Series grand slam, and Jim Bagby hit the first home run by a pitcher. Quite a day for Cleveland fans. The Indians won the game, 8–1, and the Series.

The next day the Yankees ended their three-game losing streak before 55,000 screaming fans by edging the Cleveland Indians, 8–7, in an exciting game. It was the third largest crowd at new Yankees Stadium. "As late as the second and third innings people were still filing into the park, and the athletes were almost completely surrounded by a ring of humanity."[4] Waite Hoyt started for the Yankees, Stanley Coveleski for the Indians. It was a see-saw battle with the lead changing several times.

With the game tied 7–7 in the last half of the ninth, Coveleski found himself with runners at first and third with two out. Not wanting to face the dangerous Bob Meusel, Coveleski walked him on four straight balls, an unintentional intentional walk, loading the bases for the weak hitting Aaron Ward, who was 0-for-4 for the day. As so often happens in these situations, you walk one batter to face another and it backfires. That's exactly what happened. Ward lined a single to left and the game was over.

Aaron Lee Ward, the hero of the game, was born in Booneville, Arkansas. He received his middle name from the great Confederate general, Robert E. Lee. Ward's early years were spent in Little Rock, Arkansas, where he was a page boy and later sergeant-at-arms in the state legislature. He learned to play baseball in the local parks for the home team.

He attended Ouachita Baptist College in Arkadelphia, Arkansas, and graduated with a BA degree. He was the shortstop for the baseball team but also played quarterback on the football squad. His career goal was to become a lawyer, but baseball intervened.

In 1916, he joined the Montgomery Rebels in the South Atlantic League, also known as the Sally League, which was designated Class C. In 1917, Ward played for the Charleston Sea Gulls, also of the Sally League. He played well and attracted the attention of the Yankees, joining the club as a shortstop in 1917 at the age of 21. In his first three years with the team he was mainly used as a utility infielder. He played all four positions, including first base. Up to that point, the most games he played in was 27, and that was in 1919. He spent most of the 1918 season in the Army. Young Ward found it difficult to break into a veteran lineup that consisted of Wally Pipp at first, Roger Peckinpaugh at short, Frank "Home Run" Baker at third and Del Pratt at second. Sadly, in 1920 Ward was the beneficiary of a tragic story. Baker's wife, Ottilie, contracted scarlet fever and passed away on February 17. Devastated, he told a reporter, "The death of Mrs. Baker has killed all chances of my playing baseball again. There have been more or less talk throughout the country about my playing this year with the Yankees. But there is no possible chance of me wearing a uniform. Since the death of my wife I have lost interest in the game and feel I could not do justice to the club or myself under the circumstances."[5] Christy Mathewson voiced his sentiments, "It is a sad ending to a brilliant career. Baker was one of the coolest, steadiest men in the game. Like Eddie Collins, he always played better in a World Series than he did in any other games during the season."[6] Baker, along with his mother, took care of his children, Ottilie and Janise, in 1920, and he returned the following year, but at age 35 his skills had diminished. His best years were behind him. He retired after the 1922 season.

Ward took over third base full time in Baker's absence in 1920. Miller Huggins had a fondness for Ward, saying, "I just have to get that aggressive kid, Ward, into my lineup."[7] He turned in a mediocre season, batting only .256. Surprisingly, he hit 11 home runs, which would turn out to be his career high. In 1921 Huggins shifted the young infielder to second base, the manager's old position during his playing days with Cincinnati and St. Louis in the National League. Ward responded well to his new position. He batted .306 and drove in 75 runs, a significant improvement over the previous year, and helped the Yankees win their first pennant. Ward took great pride in his defensive skills. Years later, in an interview with *Baseball Magazine*, he said, "The backbone of the infield is undoubtedly at second base. For one thing, that's where most double plays originate." He went on to say, "Weakness in a club anywhere is bound to show, but weakness around second base is likely to be fatal." He concluded, "In the average season since I have been with the club, I do not believe five ball games a year have been lost by the Yankees infield."[8]

Ward had such a good year, he felt he deserved a considerable raise over his current salary, which was $5,000. The Yankees offered $6,500. Ward wanted $10,000 and refused to sign. Not coincidentally, Ward's name was beginning to surface among the trade rumors. Finally, in early March, Huggins happily announced that Ward had agreed to sign a contract for $7,500. According to one source, Yankees records indicate Ward settled for $7,000.

The Yankees lost to the New York Giants in the World Series. Ward had a respectable Series, especially compared to his teammates. He batted .231 and drove in four runs. Bob Meusel batted .200, Roger Peckinpaugh .179 and Wally Pipp .154.

The Yankees won their second consecutive pennant in 1922 but not before some tense moments. With spring training in New Orleans, Huggins had his hands full trying to control his players. Carl Mays and Waite Hoyt, in particular, gave him fits. Then Landis suspended Ruth, Meusel and Bill Piercy for the beginning of the season for disobeying barnstorming rules. The craziness carried into the season and peaked in July when fists started flying in the dugout. Pipp punched Ruth for criticizing his fielding. The next day Ward and Braggo Roth went at it; Al De-Vormer wrestled with Mays and

Aaron Ward, a favorite of Miller Huggins, was an outstanding second baseman who took pride in his defensive skills. He finished 1923 batting .284 with 82 RBIs and 79 runs scored, the last two stats career highs. The hero of the 1923 World Series, he led the Yankees with a .417 batting average while scoring four runs and driving in two. (Courtesy National Baseball Hall of Fame Library, Cooperstown, New York.)

later with Fred Hofmann. Meusel and Schang also participated. Was it time to call in Tex Rickard to promote a fight night? In spite of the many distractions, the Yankees still won the pennant. Ward had a disappointing year. His average dropped from .306 to .267, his doubles from 30 to 19. But Ward's game really fell apart in the World Series as the New York Giants swept the Yankees. It was an awful Series for the entire Yankee team. Meusel and Pipp had a half-way decent Series. The rest of the team was pathetic. Dugan batted .250, Witt .222, Ruth .118 with no home runs, Schang .188 and Scott .143. Ward batted .154 but hit two home runs and drove in three.

In 1923, Ward bounced back, helping the Yankees win their third consecutive American League pennant. He finished the year with a respectable .284 average, 82 RBIs and 79 runs scored, the last two stats career highs. He also led the league in fielding with a .980 percentage.

Finally, the Yankees won a World Series, defeating the New York Giants, 4 games to 2. Ward had an outstanding Series, leading the position players with a phenomenal .417 average, scoring four runs and driving in two. At a dinner celebrating the Yankees' first World Series championship, Ruppert singled out Ward for his outstanding play. The Colonel said, "Babe Root (Ruppert's pronunciation of Ruth) was great, but then we expect Root to be great. Bob Meusel had a good Series, and Herb Pennock pitched two great games. But let us give credit where credit is due, and give most of the credit to 'Wardie,' who hit .417 and to 'little Hug,' the fine manager of this fine team."[9]

Aaron Ward's numbers declined over the next two years, so in spite of Huggins' admiration for the second baseman, it was time for a change. In 1926 the Yankees purchased a 23-year-old phenom by the name of Tony Lazzeri for $50,000 and five players. Playing for Salt Lake City in the Pacific Coast League the previous season, Lazzeri hit .355 with 60 home runs and an unheard of 222 RBIs. Keep in mind, the PCL season consisted of 200 games and with the light air in Salt Lake City, baseballs flew out of the park with regularity. Still, the numbers were impressive. The kid also played second base. Ward's days as a Yankee were numbered.

The end came quickly. On January 17, 1927, the Yankees traded Ward to the Chicago White Sox for two players—catcher Johnny Grabowski and infielder Ray Morehart. It was a trade where both teams benefited. Chicago was eager to get Ward to replace the fading future Hall of Famer, Eddie Collins. The Yankees needed a catcher to help Benny Bengough. However, the timing of the trade was bad for Ward. He missed playing for one of the greatest baseball teams in the history of the game—the 1927 Yankees. He had to settle for a fifth-place club with a record of 70–83. Quite a disparity. The following March, the Cleveland Indians picked up Ward for the waiver price of $4,000. He played in only six games for the Indians and then called it quits. He played in the minor leagues for several years, and in 1946 he managed the New Iberia Cardinals in the Evangeline League (Class D) in Louisiana. After baseball, Ward dabbled in both oil leases and the real estate business.

Aaron Ward, never gifted with extraordinary talent, made the most of his abilities. Over a 12-year career, he batted a respectable .268, played fine defense and had the distinction of being an integral part of the New York Yankees' first World Series championship. He died in 1961 in New Orleans at the age of 64.

The Yankees lost the next two games to Cleveland, extending their slump to a 2–8 record over the last 10 games. During the series, Ruth connected for his 13th home run. It was the second series in a row they lost, as Chicago had taken two out of three the previous week. The Yankees' comfortable 6½-game lead was now down to three games.

Although the team was not playing well, it did not affect the activity in the front office. The Yankees managed to sign Lou Gehrig, one of the all-time greats of the game, off the Columbia campus. There was high praise for the 20-year-old. Some called him the best college player since George Sisler. Others compared him to the Babe. Heady stuff for a young sophomore. As a pitcher, he was 6–3, but the Yankees were intrigued by his bat, not his pitching. He hit .440 for the 1923 school season along with seven home runs. Several of the home runs were monster shots—the longest ever seen at South Field. One of the home runs Gehrig hit (out to 116th Street and Broadway) attracted the attention of Yankees super-scout Paul Krichell. After the Gehrig blast, Krichell introduced himself to the young man and set up an appointment at the Yankees' office the next morning. At the meeting general manager Ed Barrow and Krichell offered Gehrig $2,000 for the remaining four months of the season and a signing bonus of $1,500. At the time, Gehrig's dominating mother was ill with pneumonia and his father was in poor health. Gehrig sought advice from

Lou Gehrig was signed by the Yankees right off the Columbia campus in 1923. After a slow start, the "Iron Horse" was sent to Hartford in the Eastern League. He returned in late September and in six games went 10-for-21 (.476) with one home run. Huggins was so impressed, he appealed to Giants' manager John McGraw to allow Gehrig to play in the World Series, even through he was ineligible. McGraw quickly and firmly nixed the idea. (Courtesy National Baseball Hall of Fame Library, Cooperstown, New York.)

Archibald Stockder, a professor at Columbia. He told Stockder about the money the Yankees offered but said that his parents always wanted him to graduate college and pursue a profession. He was in a quandary. When the professor heard Gehrig's story, he calmly said, "You've been in my class for almost a year. ... I think you better play ball."[10]

When Gehrig showed up at Yankee Stadium for his first batting practice session, he was accompanied by Huggins. The two standing together were quite a sight. Gehrig, a giant of a man, along side Huggins, who now, in our politically correct society would be described as vertically challenged, reminded one of the old cartoon characters, Mutt and Jeff. Gehrig, the typical Rube out of a Ring Lardner story, took batting practice along with Scott, Ward and Pipp. Legend has it that Huggins beckoned Pipp to let the kid hit a few. Pipp obliged.

At the batting rack, Gehrig accidentally picked Ruth's favorite bat, a 48-ounce piece of lumber. Very few hitters were strong enough to use that heavy a bat successfully. Initially Gehrig struggled, probably from nerves, but then he began to park some balls into the right field bleachers. A group from Columbia had come to the Stadium to watch their idol, and they began to cheer the young kid, giving him the encouragement he needed. Earlier, Gehrig was introduced to Ruth, who knew the rookie had selected his bat but said nothing of the incident except the Babe's usually greeting of "Hiya, keed." It was a rare display of kindness by Ruth, who was often self-centered around other ballplayers, including teammates.

Hoyt and some of the other Yankees saw Gehrig as a diamond in the rough. Granted, he was a raw, inexperienced and shy young man, but the potential for future greatness was obvious. The kid from Columbia would fulfill that potential and then some.

On June 13, the St. Louis Browns visited Yankee Stadium for the first time to open a four-game series. It was just what the doctor ordered. Joe Bush pitched a magnificent game, blanking the St. Louis Browns on four singles, one a fluke bunt, as the Yankees won, 5–0. Bush was in complete command.

The second game of the series proved what seemed like an undeniable fact: all a left-hander had to do was throw his glove on the mound and the Yankees would fold. Cleveland's Sherrod Smith and Chicago's Mike Cvengros were living proof, handily beating the Yankees in previous games. No surprise then, when the St. Louis Browns sent Hub Pruett, a left-hander who couldn't crack an egg with his fastball, to the mound, and the results were the same. The Browns defeated the Yankees, 3–1. Since the Yankees' six-game winning streak ended June 1, their record was an abysmal 3–9! The once formidable lead sunk to a mere two games, the closest Connie Mack's A's had been to anything but last place in nine years.

Let's digress for the moment and take a look at the mysterious hold Pruett had over the Babe. It's a fascinating story and hard to believe if it didn't actually happen. First, a quick review of Ruth's hitting prowess to set the stage. Babe Ruth's lifetime batting average is .342, placing him ninth on the all-time list. He hit .300 or better 17 of his 22 years in the major leagues. He led the American League once in 1924 with a .378 average. His best year was 1923 with a mark of .393. Remember this, the Babe's reputation was built on his ability to hit home runs— 714 to be exact. But Ruth was not only a home run hitter. There was much more to the Babe than the long ball. So it's no small feat when a pitcher could legitimately claim he "owned" the Babe. That unique distinction belongs to an unknown left-hander named Hub Pruett. He pitched in the major leagues for seven years with, to be brutally honest, an awful 29–48 record. His ERA was an inflated 4.63, and the most wins he had in one season was seven. There's more. With the St. Louis Browns, he pitched against Ruth for three years (1922–24) because he spent the other four years in the National League.

The great New York Giants pitcher Christy Mathewson was the inspiration left-hander Hub Pruett needed to develop his fadeaway pitch, later known as a screwball. It was the pitch Pruett used to dominate Babe Ruth, who batted a pathetic .190 in 30 at-bats against him. "I got to thinking if a righty pitcher like Matty could throw it, why couldn't a lefty like myself do it?" explained Pruett. (Courtesy Miller Library, Keystone Junior College, LaPlume, Pennsylvania.)

This raises the obvious question. How could a pitcher of no distinction (other than getting Ruth out) with a lousy record, dominate one of the greatest hitters of all time? In fact, if you combine average and home runs, Ruth is probably the greatest overall hitter of all time. But that's a discussion for another day.

Back to Pruett and the million dollar question. The answer is that Pruett had developed a fadeaway pitch, like the great Christy Mathewson before him. It later became known as a screwball. Thrown by a lefty to a left-handed hitter, the ball curves towards the batter. In Wayne Stewart's marvelous article in *Baseball History*, Pruett explains how he came to throw the pitch. "When I was a small boy, my baseball idol was Chirsty Mathewson. Matty's most famous pitch was the fadeaway. When he threw it, the ball would break in on a right-handed hitter and away from a lefty. I got to thinking if a righty pitcher like Matty could throw it, why couldn't a lefty like myself do it?"[11]

Although it's a highly effective pitch, it puts a tremendous strain on your arm. The pitch is thrown in a very unusual inward twist of the arm and wrist. Mathewson was well aware of the damage the pitch could do to your arm. In his book, *Pitching in a Pinch*, he said, "Many people have asked me why I do not use my fadeaway more often when it is so effective. It is a very hard pitch to deliver. Pitching it ten or twelve times a game kills my arm, so I save it for the pinches."[12]

Carl Hubbell, the great left-hander for the New York Giants, owed his Hall of Fame election to the fadeaway. Unlike Matty, Hubbell used his screwball throughout the game, not just in critical situations. He paid the price in later years with a deformed arm and wrist.

Pruett's mastery over Ruth is one of the great oddities of baseball. Author Stewart points out that the first time Pruett faced Ruth on April 22, 1922, he fanned the Bambino on three pitches. According to Stewart, Pruett faced Ruth a total of 30 times. The Babe "...managed only four hits in 21 official at-bats, which translates to a microscopic .190 average. Ruth grounded out twice, hit one sacrifice fly, coaxed eight walks, hit one homer, and whiffed 15 times, exactly half the times they battled."[13]

It's simply amazing. If not for Pruett's childhood idol, Mathewson, and his famed fadeaway, Hub would be just another name in a 20-pound baseball encyclopedia. Unlike many other ballplayers of the 1920's, Pruett had a rich life after baseball. In 1932, he earned his MD degree from St. Louis University and practiced for over 40 years in the St. Louis area.

The end to the Pruett/Ruth story is fascinating. Pruett spoke only once to Ruth, and that was in 1948, two months before the Babe's death from throat cancer. It was at a baseball dinner at the Chase Hotel in St. Louis. Pruett explains, "I went up and introduced myself and said, 'Thanks, Babe, for putting me through medical school. If it hadn't been for you, nobody would ever have heard of me.'" Ruth replied in a hoarse and raspy voice, "That's all right, Kid, but I'm glad there weren't many more like you or no one would have heard of me."[14]

The Yankees won the last two games from St. Louis, 10–0 and 9–4, restoring a modicum of respectability to the home stand. Two interesting events occurred that are noteworthy. First, Aaron Ward in a close play at home slid into Pat Collins, spikes high, and caught the catcher above the eye, opening a small gash. After some emergency first aid, he was replaced by Hank Billings. It was a serious enough injury to disable Collins for several games. Understandably, the St. Louis fans were irate over the incident, but they might have carried their displeasure to extreme. They sent telegrams to Miller Huggins denouncing him, also to Ward, Jacob Ruppert, Ed Barrow and the groundskeeper. Yes, the groundskeeper. Blaming Ruppert and Barrow is hard to fathom, but the groundskeeper is simply ludicrous. No doubt emotions were quite fragile in St. Louis.

Second, Lou Gehrig made his major league debut (June 15) in the ninth inning, replacing Wally Pipp at first base. It was uneventful. He had one chance, a routine grounder that Gehrig fielded cleanly and stepped on first for the out.

As an interesting aside, the major league batting averages were released through June 14. Harry Heilmann of the Tigers was leading the American League with a lofty .436. Brooklyn's Zack Wheat was leading the National League with an impressive .495. Babe Ruth's average was .355, and he was leading the league with 47 runs scored.

Ty Cobb and the Detroit Tigers moved into the Stadium to complete the Yankees' 19-game home stand. New York split the series, winning the first and third games. In the first game, the Yankees mauled the Tigers, 9–0, before a huge crowd of 52,000. Ruth hit his 14th home run, a monster shot half-way up into the right field bleachers. With a safe 9–0 lead, Huggins sent in Gehrig, like he did against the Browns, to replace Pipp in the ninth inning. Lou made two routine putouts.

Gehrig's historic replacement for Pipp wouldn't come until June 2, 1925. That was the day he took over the first base job for good. It would be the second day of his record 2,130 consecutive games played in a New York Yankee uniform. Technically, Gehrig's streak began on June 1 when he hit for Pee Wee Wanninger in the bottom of the eighth against Walter Johnson. Gehrig swung late on Johnson's fast ball and lofted a fly ball to left. As most baseball fans know, the record has since been broken by Cal Ripken when he played in an unbelievable 2,632 consecutive games.

A day later on July 18, it was another historic moment in the immortal career of Lou Gehrig, or at least a great future trivia question. In a hopeless situation (the Tigers were winning, 11–3), Miller Huggins called on Gehrig to bat for Aaron Ward in the ninth. It was Gehrig's first official at-bat for the New York Yankees. He faced right-hander Ken Holloway. Gehrig managed to get the disappointed crowd excited (what was left of it) when he ripped a foul down the first base line. Eventually, Gehrig struck out.

Wally Pipp was the hero in the third game of the series. The first baseman blasted a home run with Ruth on first, which turned out to be the margin of victory as the Yankees won, 6–5. Pipp was born on February 17, 1893, in Chicago. His parents, William and Pauline (nee Stauffer), were Irish-Catholics. Pipp spent his early years in Grand Rapids, Michigan. He attended Catholic University in Washington, D.C., and studied architecture. Pipp never finished his studies, turning to professional baseball in 1912 when he signed a contract to play for Kalamazoo (Class D) in the Southern Michigan League. The lefty-batting first baseman played in 68 games and batted .270 for Kalamazoo. Impressed with this performance, the Detroit Tigers bought his contract. The 19-year-old Pipp, way ahead of his time, had the nerve to challenge the transaction by demanding a share of the purchase price. In those days, that argument fell on deaf ears. The holdout lasted until the end of June when the young slugger caved in to the lords of baseball.

It was an inauspicious start for the 6' 2", 180-pound first baseman. He played in only 12 games for the Tigers in 1913 and batted a miserable .161. Surprisingly, three of his five hits were triples. With a .161 batting average, Pipp did not impress Tigers manager Hugh Jennings, so he was sent back to the minors to play for the Providence Grays (Class AA) of the International League. His fielding was so poor in only 14 games that he was sent down further, this time to Scranton (Class B) of the New York State League. In 1914, playing for the Rochester Hustlers (Class AA) of the International League, the 21-year-old turned in an exceptional year. "He batted .314 and led the International League with 15 home runs, 290 total bases, and a .526 slugging percentage."[15]

Based on this performance, Pipp probably believed he was going to get another call from the Tigers. Not so. Detroit had another 21-year-old at first by the name of George Burns, who had a solid year as a rookie. Apparently, Detroit decided Burns was their future first baseman. Prior to the 1915 season, Pipp and outfielder Hugh High were sent to the Yankees for the waiver price.

Pipp became the Yankees' starting first baseman for the next 11 years, taking over for Charlie Mullin, a .250 hitter with no power. In his rookie season with New York, Pipp hit only.246 but played a marvelous first base, leading the league with a .992 fielding average. In 1916, he defied baseball's so-called sophomore jinx by batting .262 while leading the league in home runs with 12 and driving in 93 runs. The following year Pipp led the league again in home runs with nine. Keep in mind this was the deadball era where home runs were scarce. To put Pipp's accomplishments in perspective, Frank Baker, who was nicknamed "Home Run," never hit more than 12 in a season during his 13-year career. Of course, Babe Ruth would come along and bury (no pun intended) the deadball era in one season.

From 1918–1924, Wally Pipp matured as a hitter. During that seven-year span, his batting average was a solid .297. His best years were 1923 and 1924. During the former, he batted .304 and drove in 108 runs. The following year he batted .295 and drove in 114 runs, led the league in triples (19) and fielding with a .994 average.

Pipp was a solid defensive player. He was tall, agile, had soft hands and a wide range at first. He anchored the Yankees infield during their three consecutive pennants (1921–23) and their first World Series in 1923.

In spite of Pipp's fine performance in 1924, the Yankees failed to duplicate their historic World Series championship of the previous year. The Washington Senators nosed out the Yankees by two games. It was Pipp's last year as the starting first baseman. Lou Gehrig, who had been up with the Yankees at the tale end of 1923 and 1924 seasons, finally took over the first base job on June 2, 1925. He began his streak the day before when Huggins sent him in to pinch hit for Pee Wee Wanninger. Gehrig flied out to left.

There has been much written about how Gehrig replaced Pipp in the lineup. One story has Pipp claiming a headache and Miller Huggins suggesting an aspirin and offering to let Gehrig take his place at first. There are variations on the aspirin tale, but basically the theme is the same. This myth was perpetuated for years until another version surfaced, which was that Pipp was beaned on June 1 in batting practice by pitcher Charlie Caldwell. Pipp was groggy and semi-conscious and spent the next two weeks in the hospital. Another long-held myth. What really happened is not as romantic as the legend. It's quite mundane, actually. It happens every season in professional baseball. Here's the true story. At the start of the season, Ruth was having all kinds problems off the field and some of the other players were out of control. By June 2, the Yankees were 13½ games out of first with a miserable 15–26 record. Pipp, among others, was in a huge slump, hitting .181 the last three weeks of May. Faced with this unacceptable situation, Huggins did what managers have done since Abner Doubleday invented baseball (yet another myth that has been dispelled). Huggins benched Pipp as well as Aaron Ward and Wally Schang in order to shake up the lineup and get the team moving again. Not as exciting a story as the headache or beaning, but at least the truth.

Pipp accepted his new role graciously but still had hopes of returning one day to the starting lineup. On July 2 (not June 1, according to the myth) those hopes were dashed when he was beaned during batting practice. He spent a week in the hospital with a fractured skull and played sparingly the rest of the season. It was clear at this point Gehrig was the Yankees first baseman of the future and Pipp was no longer needed. Although discouraged, Pipp did not let the situation destroy his sense of fairness and duty. He worked hard with Gehrig, showing him the finer points of playing first base. It was a gracious gesture by the fading star. "Lou didn't learn quickly," recalled Pipp, "but he learned thoroughly. He sweated out each detail, step by step, until he had mastered it."[16]

Barrow wasted no time. After clearing waivers on Pipp, he sold him to the Cincinnati Reds for $20,000. Maybe it was a wake-up call, but Pipp had a good year with the Reds. He batted .291 and drove in 99 runs for second-place Cincinnati. But at age 34, his skills began to decline and his next two years with Cincinnati were unremarkable. He was released by the Reds and in 1929 played for the Newark Bears in the International League where he made a deal with management that he would get a percentage of the gate. According to his son, Pipp made $40,000 that year, more than he ever made playing for the Yankees. Pipp retired from baseball after the season. It was the beginning of the Depression and jobs were scarce and, if you could get one, paid little. Pipp was willing to try his hand at several tasks. Initially, he played the stock market and penned a book entitled *Buying Cheap and Selling Dear*. "...he organized baseball programs for the National Youth Administration, tried his hand at publishing, worked as an announcer on a pre-game baseball broadcast, and even wrote scripts for a Detroit radio announcer."[17]

During World War II, Pipp worked for the war effort by helping to make B-24 bombers. After the war, he turned to a career in sales, calling on automobile companies in the Detroit area and peddling such mundane but essential items as screws and bolts. He loved his job, was energetic and a great talker. He was a very successful salesman.

Pipp's interest in baseball never waned. He continued to love the sport and would attend many Detroit Tigers games. He never missed an Old Timers' game at the Stadium. "Pipp's passion for sports did not end with baseball. He was an avid golfer, playing several times a week for many years and shooting regularly in the high 70's."[18] On January 11, 1965, Wally Pipp died of a heart attack at the age of 72.

After the Tigers left town, New York had a day off while Chicago beat Philadelphia, 6–1, increasing the Yankees' lead to 4½ games. Actually, the Yankees weren't idle. They traveled to Albany, New York, to play their spring training opponents, the Brooklyn Robins. A record crowd witnessed the Robins defeat the Yankees, 9–4. Manager Wilbert Robinson played his regulars while Huggins went with a make shift lineup.

From Albany, the Yankees traveled to Boston to play a four-game series at fan-friendly Fenway Park. The Yankees won the first three games. Shawkey (7–4), Bush (10–7) and Jones (8–5) all pitched well. Bush, in particular, hurled a dandy, blanking Boston on six hits. He dominated the Red Sox lineup from top to bottom. While Bush was tossing his third straight shutout in the month of June, American League president Ban Johnson went on record reminding the press that he was keenly interested in supporting the development of baseball in Mexico and would do everything in his power to promote the game for his neighboring country. Even though Johnson's intentions were sincere towards Mexican baseball, the real reason for the announcement was to prevent players of questionable character from becoming established in this new market. And he was "taking steps" towards that goal. Johnson's comments were clearly aimed at Hal Chase, former major league first baseman, who had been hired to manage the Nogales team in Mexico.

Hal Chase, an accomplished hitter, batted .291 over a 15-year career in the major leagues. He even won a batting title towards the end of his career when he hit .339 in 1916 with Cincinnati. But Chase didn't build his reputation at

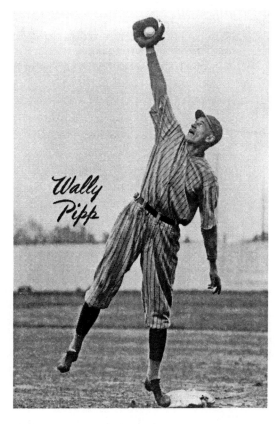

Noted for being the man Lou Gehrig replaced at first base, Wally Pipp enjoyed a solid 11-year career with the New York Yankees. His most productive seasons were 1923 (.304, 108 RBIs) and 1924 (.295, 114 RBIs). Pipp unselfishly taught Gehrig the finer points of playing first base. (Courtesy National Baseball Hall of Fame Library, Cooperstown, New York.)

the plate. It was formed by two undeniable facts. He was one of the premier fielding first basemen in the game and one of the most notorious villains.

He was nicknamed "Prince Hal" for his exceptional skill with the glove and adept footwork at first base. According to old timers, his range was incredible and he was deadly charging bunts, a huge part of the game in the early 1900's. His grace and dexterity as a defensive genius was well known around the league.

Chase was also an unrepentant scoundrel. For many years, it was rumored he was throwing games. In 1913, Frank Chance, the manager of the Yankees, even told a few sportswriters of his suspicions. However, the accusation never found its way into print simply because it was almost impossible to prove, and Prince Hal was a big draw and a fan favorite. Eventually, Chase wound up playing in Cincinnati in the National League for manager Christy Mathewson, a paragon of honesty and integrity and a champion of clean living. In 1918, the rumors and whispers that Chase was crooked all came to a head when Mathewson went to the press and National League president John Heydler and told them that Chase had thrown some games. Heydler immediately began a full-scale investigation, but with Matty in the army (he had joined late in the season) and unavailable to support him, the National League president could not make the charges stick.

Like a cat with nine lives, Prince Hal moved to the New York Giants in 1919, managed by the legendary John McGraw. McGraw's acquisition of Chase was puzzling, especially considering his close personal relationship with Mathewson. Nevertheless, by the middle of August, McGraw was on to Chase and suspended him and Heinie Zimmerman. Heydler made the suspension permanent and Chase finally got what he deserved for so many years. Sportswriter Fred Lieb in his book *Baseball As I Have Known It*, relates what Heydler told him about new evidence of Chase's guilt. "I never was satisfied with my earlier acquittal of Chase," he said. "I was unconvinced. Eventually I got a signed affidavit from the Boston gambler and a photographic copy of Chase's canceled check for five hundred dollars given him by a gambler as pay for throwing a game in 1918."[19] Is it any wonder Ban Johnson sent out warning signals to the Mexican government to beware of Prince Hal?

In yet another scheduling quirk, New York had a day off in the middle of the four games in Boston. Idleness is the mother of all sin, so the team traveled to Connecticut to play the New Haven club of the Eastern League in an exhibition game. The Yankees were embarrassed, 9–5. In their defense, most of the regulars did not play. The loss, however, was not the problem. It was the Babe's failure to appear. That *faux pas* caused major problems on and off the field. There were approximately 10,000 disappointed and outraged fans who came to see Ruth play and, of course, hit a home run. When New Haven president George Weiss (future Yankee general manager), discovered that Ruth would be a no-show, he demanded the fans be reimbursed. It cost the Yankees a cool $1,000, the difference between the admission price of a regular New Haven game and the increased price to see the Yankees and the Babe. It was a painful but wise move by the Yankees management because it clearly avoided a possible riot.

Where was Babe Ruth? That was the unanswered question circulating throughout the stands that even Yankee management couldn't answer. Miller

Huggins received reports that Ruth was injured in an auto accident which made headlines in the *New York Times*. Details of the accident were non-existent, including the type or seriousness of Ruth's injuries. The story went like this: the team left Boston in the morning bound for New Haven. Ruth overslept, missed the train and started for New Haven in his automobile. Phone calls to his farm in Sudbury, a short distance from Boston, provided more vague but ominous information. Ruth's chauffeur claimed the Babe hurt his foot but hung up after being pressed for details. Ruth's wife Helen wasn't even aware of what happened until informed by the press.

The great mystery was solved the next day. The auto accident and the injured foot were all a fabrication. How these rumors started and spread, well, that's another mystery. Ruth cleared up the mess when he spoke to the press. He simply overslept, decided to drive to New Haven because he had done it before and it was faster than going by train. On the way, he was unexpectedly delayed by traffic. He explained his next decision, "I then decided that I could not get to New Haven in time for the game, so I turned around and went to my farm in Sudbury, Mass., for the night. I came to Boston early this morning and spent the morning at the ball park tinkering with my car."[20]

Back in New York, word was that Ruppert and Barrow were discussing the episode and what action should be taken, if any. Barrow denied the rumors and said that any fine, suspension or reprimand would have to come from the manager. Huggins didn't take any action, so the incident was quickly forgotten. The joys of managing the Babe.

The stories surrounding Ruth are numerous, chronicled in the many biographies of his life. Some are believable, others are legend and still others raise questions. The one thing everyone agreed on is that he was a complex man. Bob Shawkey explained the uniqueness of the Babe. "He was special, any way you look at him. You can't believe the publicity and attention that man got and how little impression it made on him. He'd hardly ever look at his mail. He would dump stacks of it into his locker and now and then ask me or one of the other fellows to look at it for him to see if there was anything interesting. I'd go through it and find lots of opportunities for him to make money, by endorsing cigarettes or bubble gum and things like that. I'd show them to him and he'd say 'okay, okay,' and then forget about it. But on the other hand, he'd almost never turn away somebody who wanted a handout, and he'd never say no to a kid asking for his signature. He would stand in the middle of a crowd of kids and sign for every one of them."[21] At age 70, Waite Hoyt, who played with Ruth for many years, had this to say about the big guy, "there was buried in Ruth humanitarianism beyond belief, an intelligence he was never given credit for, a childish desire to be over-virile, living up to credits given his home run power—and yet a need for intimate affection and respect, and a feverish desire to play baseball, perform, act and live a life he didn't and couldn't take time to understand."[22]

The Red Sox salvaged the last game of the series by beating Waite Hoyt and the Yankees, 3–1. The day belonged to right-hander Jack Quinn. At 40 years of age, the veteran held the mighty Yankees bats in check until the ninth inning when New York pushed across a run on Aaron Ward's double. He would later score on a fielder's choice. Although Quinn gave up 11 hits, seven between Ward (4-for-4) and Witt (3-for-5), he was outstanding with runners on base.

Quinn had a long and interesting career. He pitched in three different leagues—American, National and Federal—on eight teams in three decades for 23 years. His performance during this period was somewhat erratic, probably due to his involvement with weak teams. In 1914, pitching for Baltimore in the Federal League, Quinn won 26 games. The following year—same league, same team—he lost 22 games. He pitched in three World Series without distinction—in 1921 with the Yankees when they lost to the Giants and again in 1929 and 1930 with Philadelphia. The A's had a powerful club and won both World Series led by Jimmy Foxx, Al Simmons, Jimmy Dykes and Mickey Cochrane and pitchers Lefty Grove, George Earnshaw, Eddie Rommel and Rube Walberg.

Quinn pitched seven years for the Yankees on two separate occasions, finishing with a respectable 81–65 record. No question Quinn was a workhorse. Pitching in over 3,920 innings, his lifetime record was 247–218 with a 3.29 ERA. Quinn's pitching gem against the Yankees sliced a game off their first-place lead. Philadelphia clobbered the Senators, 16–7, and now trailed New York by five games.

Before traveling to Yankee Stadium at the conclusion of the Boston series, New York stopped at Haverhill to play an exhibition game against an all-collegians team. The Yankees won, 12–5. Ruth delighted the fans when he shared the pitching duties with George Pipgras. After the exhibition tune-up, the Yankees headed back to the Bronx in preparation for the arrival of Connie Mack's second-place Philadelphia A's. It was an important series for both teams, but more so for the A's. The Yankees had a comfortable five-game lead, and a sweep of the four games would be a crushing and demoralizing blow to the A's. Conversely, if Mack's club could win the series or better yet, take all four games, they would make a positive statement that they were serious challengers, not to be taken lightly. Philadelphia entered the series at a disadvantage with three players on the injured list—first baseman Joe Hauser, outfielder Bing Miller and third baseman Sammy Hale. Also, the ace of their pitching staff, Rollie Naylor, pulled a tendon in his right leg, so he wasn't available either. The Yankees, on the other hand, were at full strength except for catcher Wally Schang, who was still not one hundred percent.

What Connie Mack and Philadelphia feared most became a reality. The Yankees swept the series and dealt a devastating blow that all but eliminated the A's from contention. The Yankees won the opener, 4–2, in a fine pitching match-up between Bob Shawkey and Eddie Rommel. Shawkey allowed six hits and two runs as he went the distance for his eighth victory of the season. Pipp had another splendid day, going 2-for-3, driving in two runs and scoring one.

In a wild and nerve wracking afternoon, New York won the second game, 10–9. Unlike the first game, this was a slugfest. Joe Bush, who had pitched three shutouts in June, was simply awful. The A's Rube Walberg, McGraw's castoff, was even worse. Neither pitcher finished the game, which mercifully ended in the bottom of the ninth. With the score tied, 9–9, Ward led off by drawing a walk on four straight balls. Huggins sent Elmer Smith to bat for Everett Scott. Al Kellett continued to have trouble finding the plate and ran the count to 3–0 on Smith. Seven straight balls without a strike. Mack had seen enough and wouldn't let Kellett finish pitching to Smith. He called on veteran Ed Rommel, who pitched the day before and lost, to salvage the inning. Poor Rommel, he didn't even have time to warm up. He entered the game directly from the dugout. Rommel's first pitch to Smith was called a strike, soliciting scattered applause. On the 3–1 pitch, Smith topped a grounder to first baseman Fred Heimach, who had plenty of time to force Ward at second but threw the ball over shortstop Chick Galloway's head, advancing the runners to second and third. Mack and Huggins were now in a chess match to see who could outwit whom. Mack ordered Rommel to walk Fred Hofmann to load the bases and then brought the infield in for a play at the plate. Huggins countered by sending Ernie Johnson to hit for Hoyt. Johnson smacked a pitch past Galloway at short and the game was over.

The next day, New York made it three straight over Philadelphia by a score of 6–1 behind the brilliant pitching of Herb Pennock. The left-hander scattered seven hits, and if not for Frank Welch's fluke home run, he would have had a shutout. Pennock was 8–2. The Yankees had an eight-game lead over the demoralized Philadelphia A's with one more game remaining in the series.

Sam Jones put the icing on the cake. He blanked the A's, 4–0, giving up five hits to complete the four-game sweep and extend the Yankees' first-place lead to nine games. Eddie Rommel took the loss. The A's workhorse pitched in three of the four games, totaling 17 innings. Jones pitched a marvelous game and was in trouble only twice. In the sixth the A's had runners at second and third with one out. The Yankees were leading, 4–0, so a clutch hit would have put the A's back in the game. Jones rose to the occasion and struck out clean-up hitter Heimach. Frank Welch walked, loading the bases, but Jones came right back and fanned Galloway to end the threat.

In the eighth, Jones wiggled out of a similar jam. The A's had runners at the corners with one out. Jones bore down and got Heimach to pop out and Welsh to fly to Meusel in left. Jones was so dominating that in five of the innings, he retired the A's in order. His record was 9–5.

Manager Huggins was given a scare in the seventh inning. Ruth, running hard, beat out a throw to first but came up limping and was taken out of the game for precautionary reasons. It turned out to be nothing serious and Ruth played the next day.

The smallest Sunday crowd of the season, 30,000, witnessed the final humiliation of Connie Mack's club. Perhaps the game at Ebbetts Field between the Giants and Brooklyn, which drew 26,000, one of the largest crowds of the season, had a lot to do with the disappointing low attendance at the Stadium. For the record, Brooklyn edged the Giants, 2–1. Irrespective of the defeat, McGraw's club still led Pittsburgh by 4½ games and was playing excellent baseball.

The New York Yankees were making a mockery of the American League pennant race with a record of 43–22 (.662) and a nine-game lead. This was just the beginning. In the months ahead, as the season unfolded, the Yankees' lead would widen, and the only challenge facing Huggins and the club was to figure out how to beat McGraw and the Giants in the fall.

5

Yankee Pitching Dominates

After the four-game humiliation in New York, Connie Mack couldn't wait to get out of town and travel to Boston to play the last-place Red Sox and let the Washington Senators deal with the red hot Yankees. The A's, still reeling from the beating at the Stadium, fared no better at Fenway. They lost, 7–4, while the Yankees continued a deadly combination of hard hitting and excellent pitching, defeating Washington in the opener for their fifth consecutive victory, 13–1. The Yankees pounded out 19 hits against three Washington pitchers while Bob Shawkey held the Senators to eight hits.

From the Yankees' standpoint, the game was pure fun and an easy victory on their quest for another pennant. From the Senators' view, it was an embarrassing loss and one they wanted to quickly forget. From the fans' perspective, it was an ugly game to watch but a win nevertheless. Attesting to its ugliness and not surprisingly, many fans left before the final out.

By the third inning, the Yankees led, 9–0. When they scored four more runs in the fifth, Huggins emptied his bench. Lou Gehrig was one of the replacements, taking over first base for Pipp. In the seventh, what was left of the crowd gave Gehrig a huge ovation, only to be disappointed when he wiffed on three pitches. Ruth missed hitting for the cycle by the easiest of the four hits, a measly single. The Babe whacked a double, triple and his 15th homer. The round tripper was a long time coming. The last home run Ruth hit was on June 17 against George Dauss of the Detroit Tigers. Wally Pipp also had a fine game, going 3-for-5, including a home run. Shawkey even helped his own cause with a 3-for-5 day. The Yankees' lead climbed to 10 full games.

Shawkey won his ninth game against four losses, and it was one of his easiest. Bob Shawkey was born on December 4, 1890, in Sigel, a small town in western Pennsylvania near the Ohio border, to John and Sarah Shawkey. He was the second of four children.

Bob Shawkey, nicknamed "Bob the Gob" for his stint in the Navy during World War I, was one of the mainstays on the New York Yankees pitching staff for 12 seasons. During one six-year span, he won 110 and lost 70, including three 20-win seasons. The right-hander won the opening day game at Yankee Stadium in 1923 and Game Four of the World Series. (Courtesy National Baseball Hall of Fame Library, Cooperstown, New York.)

After a meager education, young Shawkey worked for a logging company gang at age 15, twelve hours a day for a $1.25. He toiled for three years swinging an ax before he landed a less strenuous job as a tool dresser in the oil and gas fields of Pennsylvania. After a year and a half, a friend persuaded him to continue his education, which he did at Slippery Rock Normal School where he was mentioned as a pitcher for the team in the 1910 school yearbook.

Shawkey knew little about pitching, but his natural athletic ability plus the strength and endurance he developed working at hard labor attracted the attention of the coach, who hooked him up with Bloomsburg, a semi-pro club in the Mountain League. The following year (1911), the tall lanky, unassuming, self-confident young man moved on to his first professional baseball job with Harrisburg in the Tri-State League.

After the 1911 season, word got back to Connie Mack that Shawkey was a solid prospect, so the A's manager signed him to a contract for the 1912 season. An agreement between the A's and Baltimore kept Shawkey pitching with the Orioles until mid-season of 1913 when he joined the Philadelphia Athletics with their $100,000 infield of Eddie Collins, Frank "Home Run" Baker, Jack Barry and Stuffy McInnis, along with such greats as Chief Bender, Joe Bush and Eddie Plank. He was also introduced to Wally Schang, his catcher for many years to come.

Philadelphia won the pennant that year by 6½ games over the Senators. Shawkey made a small contribution, pitching in 18 games with a record of 6–5 and a low earned run average of 2.34. The A's went on to trounce the New York Giants in the World Series in five games using only three pitchers: Bender, Bush and Plank. As Shawkey matured and gained experience facing hitters throughout the league, he began studying the opposition—their strengths and weaknesses. This attention to detail would reap benefits in later years.

The following year Shawkey blossomed and helped lead the A's to their second consecutive pennant with a 15–8 record. The young right-hander attributed much of his early development to Chief Bender. "And I can't praise Chief Bender enough. He was a veteran and a great star, and I was just a kid, but he took time to work with me on improving my delivery. I was throwing too much with my arm, and he showed me how to get my body into it more and how to be better balanced on my follow-through so I could field a bunt."[1]

Connie Mack had seven pitchers, including Shawkey, with 10 or more victories in 1914, and the A's were heavily favored to beat the Boston Braves in the World Series. These were the "Miracle Braves" who rallied from last place on July 19 to win the National League pennant by 10½ games. After the A's lost the first three games, a stunned Mack called on Shawkey to salvage Game Four. He pitched five innings and gave up two earned runs and lost, 3–1, as the Braves completed the shocking sweep.

In 1915, after being embarrassed by the Braves, Mack decided to break up his championship club for financial reasons and because he believed his team quit on him during the World Series. Shawkey was one of the players caught in the fire sale. He went to the Yankees for a reported $18,000 on July 7 and finished the season with a combined 10–13 record and a 3.68 ERA.

For the next 12 years, Shawkey was one of the mainstays on the New York Yankees pitching staff. His first full season, 1916, he posted a 24–14 record and a 2.21 ERA for a club that barely played .500 ball. The following year Shawkey won 13 and lost 15 with a low 2.44 earned run average, the best record on a team that finished 28½ games out of first place. In 1918,

Shawkey pitched in only three games before entering the Navy. "I was assigned to the battleship *Arkansas* and sent to the North Sea. There we cooperated with a part of the British Fleet during the final year of the war. It was an interesting experience," said Shawkey. "Although I admit I wouldn't like to go through it again. Some things happened, however, that I shall always remember. I was present at the surrender of the German Navy, which was a most impressive sight. I was also present when President Wilson arrived for his famous conference in Europe."[2] In the Navy, Shawkey was tagged with the sobriquet "Bob the Gob," which stuck with him throughout his career.

After Shawkey's tour of duty in the Navy, he returned to the Yankees and for the next six years was one of the premier pitchers in the American League. During this span, he won 110 games and lost 70, with three 20-game seasons, helping the Yankees to three pennants and their first World Series in 1923. The Yankees won another pennant in 1926, but by then Shawkey was 35 and his skills had diminished to the point where he pitched in a little more than 104 innings. He still managed an 8–7 record and a 3.62 ERA. He was also a member of the great 1927 club but never pitched in the World Series.

Shawkey's pitching performance in World Series play was less than spectacular at 1–3. In the 1921 World Series, he was hit hard in Game Three and took the loss. In the second game of the 1922 Series, after he allowed three runs in the first inning, he settled down and blanked the Giants the rest of the way. This was the controversial game that was called because of darkness tied at 3–3, which resulted in an unhappy crowd throwing seat cushions and bottles from the stands. Then in 1923, Shawkey won his only World Series game but needed help from Pennock. His final World Series appearance was in 1926 against the St. Louis Cardinals. Huggins used Shawkey in relief in Games Two and Three and as a starter in Game Six, which he lost to the veteran and future Hall of Famer Grover Cleveland Alexander.

The 1927 Yankees, still widely regarded by many as the game's greatest team, was Shawkey's last club in the major leagues. As Shawkey closed in on 37 years of age, Huggins used the right-hander sparingly and mostly in relief. Shawkey finished the season with a 2–3 record in a little over 43 innings. Sailor Bob saw no action in the World Series as the Yankees swept the Pittsburgh Pirates using four pitchers: Waite Hoyt, Wilcy Moore, Herb Pennock and George Pipgras. Shawkey's final major league stat line after 15 years was 195–150 with a 3.09 ERA.

During the off-season, the Yankees released Shawkey, but the right-hander was not ready to call it quits. He swallowed his pride and signed with the Montreal Royals in the International League, finally retiring as an active player after the 1928 season. The following year the Yankees hired Shawkey as their pitching coach. Huggins was pleased with the job he did, but the rejuvenated Philadelphia A's were much too powerful and ran away with the pennant in 1929. The real shock came just before the season's end. Miller Huggins suddenly passed away on September 25. He had developed a carbuncle below his left eye, which was later diagnosed as erysipelas, a rare skin disease. The infection rapidly spread throughout his body. He died days later. Ruppert, Barrow and the baseball world mourned the sudden loss of the "Mighty Mite."

The search began for a replacement. Several names were bandied about, the most prominent being Babe Ruth, who desperately wanted the job. Ruth never had a chance at being appointed manager of the Yankees. Ruppert and Barrow firmly believed Ruth lacked maturity for the position. Actually, Barrow offered the job to Art Fletcher, the Yankees third base coach. Fletcher, a quiet and reserved man off the field, but a tyrant on the diamond, had previous experience managing the Phillies from 1923 to 1926. He also filled in during Huggins' short illness. But Fletcher refused the job, claiming he had enough of managing with the Phillies. Barrow settled on Shawkey, explaining to Ruppert, "I don't know why I didn't think of him at first. I guess he's been around so long and I've gotten so used to looking at him, I just couldn't see him."[3] Shawkey, whether he knew it or not, was walking into a buzz saw. Ruth wanted the job badly. He saw fellow ballplayers Ty Cobb, Tris Speaker, Rogers Hornsby, Eddie Collins and George Sisler all become managers. He couldn't understand or didn't accept that the Yankees didn't want him managing a team when he couldn't manage himself. Rumors circulated that Ruth resented Shawkey's getting the job. Another problem facing Shawkey was that he recently played with many of the players and was now their boss, which made for an awkward arrangement.

Shawkey dealt with the situation as best he could and guided the 1930 Yankees to an 86–68 record and a third-place finish, 16 games back of the pennant-winning Philadelphia Athletics. Ruppert and Barrow were not happy campers in spite of telling Shawkey they were pleased with the attendance figures and his performance even though the Yankees finished third. After the season, they stalled signing Shawkey to another contract until the winter. In the meantime, the Chicago Cubs fired their authoritative manager, Joe McCarthy, whom Barrow had long admired. When Barrow found out McCarthy was interested in managing the Yankees, Shawkey's fate was sealed. In fact, McCarthy signed with the Yankees before Shawkey even knew about it. Years later Shawkey said, "One day after the season had closed, I went up to the office to talk over some business. I was heading for Barrow's office when the door opened and Joe McCarthy came walking out. I took one look and turned around and got out of there. I knew what had happened."[4] He was not the only one unhappy. Once again Ruth felt he should have gotten the

job and was miffed the Yankees turned him down for the second time and had
to go to the National League for a replacement.

Over the next five years, Bob Shawkey managed minor league clubs in
Jersey City, Scranton, Newark, Watertown and Tallahassee. He also took
turns as a pitching coach in the Pittsburgh Pirates and Detroit Tigers farm
systems. Shawkey even tried his hand at college baseball, coaching Dartmouth
from 1952 to 1956. His teams went 44-71-1, not a record you want on your
resume.

Twenty years later, on April 15, 1976, Bob Shawkey was given the honor
of throwing out the first ball at refurbished Yankee Stadium on opening day
before 52,613 fans. Joining him from the 1923 opening day club were Whitey
Witt, Waite Hoyt, Joe Dugan, Hinkey Haines and Oscar Roettger, plus a
galaxy of past stars from professional baseball, football and boxing along
with numerous celebrities. It was a grand day and a heartwarming tribute to
Bob Shawkey, the winner of the first game ever played at Yankee Stadium.
Shawkey died on New Year's Eve at the Veterans Administration hospital in
Syracuse, New York, at the advanced age of 90 after a long illness.

The Yankees won the next three games from the Senators, running their
winning streak to eight in a row. Their lead in the American League pennant
race increased to 11½ games. The second game of the Washington series was
a complete reversal of the 13–1 blowout. The Yankees beat Washington, 2–1
in 15 innings. It was a classic pitchers' duel between Joe Bush and southpaw George Mogridge. Both pitchers dominated right from the start, matching each other pitch for pitch. In the bottom of the eighth, Bush put the
Yankees ahead when he hit a Mogridge mistake for a home run into the left
field stands for a 1–0 lead. In the top of the ninth, the Senators were down to
their last out and had Patsy Gharrity on first. The small Tuesday afternoon
crowd of only 5,000 was slowly making its way to the exits when Steve Evans
drove the ball between Witt and Ruth in right center. Gharrity raced all the
way home with the tying run as Evans rounded third not far behind. It was
an anxious moment for the fans, but Witt recovered the ball quickly and
threw to Ruth, who fired to Hofmann at the plate to nail Evans. It was a perfectly executed relay from Witt to Ruth to Hofmann and turned out to be the
game saver.

Mogridge retired the Yankees in the bottom of the ninth, and the game
went into extra innings. During the next four innings, both teams had opportunities to win the game but either failed to hit in the clutch or a sensational
catch ended a threat. The game entered the top of the 14th with second baseman Stan Harris leading off with a booming fly to left which hugged the foul
line and was about to drop into the stands for a home run when Bob Meusel

reached back over the edge of the stands and snatched the ball away from a bunch of eager fans. It was another game saver.

In the bottom of the 15th, Ruth ended it all when he sent a Mogridge fastball on a line into the right field stands, a few feet inside the foul line, for his 16th home run of the season. It was a laser, and as soon as it left his bat, the small crowd jumped onto the field as Ruth was rounding the bases. The Babe had to elbow his way to reach and touch home plate with the winning run.

The Yankees and Senators played the last two games as a July 4th holiday doubleheader before a loud and boisterous crowd of 45,000. The Yankees clobbered the Senators, 12–6, in the first game and 12–2 in the nightcap to sweep the series and extend their winning streak to eight. It was a wonderful day if you were a Yankees fan, not so for the loyal followers of the Senators.

In the first game, New York pounded Washington right-hander Paul Zahniser. By the end of the third inning, the score was 9–0. The durable shortstop, Everett Scott, not noted for his power, went 3-for-4, including two home runs and four RBIs. Interestingly, in his 13-year career, Scott hit a total of 20 home runs. In all, the Yankees collected 14 hits, giving Herb Pennock his ninth win against only two losses.

The Yankees continued their hard hitting in the second game in an even more impressive fashion by chasing the immortal Walter Johnson after $1\frac{1}{3}$ innings. Clearly, Johnson's fastball wasn't moving on this Fourth of July. While the Yankees were fattening their batting averages with a 17-hit attack, Sam Jones quietly and methodically checked the Senators on eight hits and two runs. His record was an impressive 10–5. To the north of the Stadium at Fenway Park in Boston, the A's split a doubleheader with the Red Sox, enabling the Yankees to enjoy an $11\frac{1}{2}$ game lead.

Almost half way through the season, the Yankees could do no wrong. With eight victories in a row, everything was going their way. They even picked up another half game following the fourth of July doubleheader. The Yankees were not scheduled while the A's lost to Boston, 7–5. The lead was now 12 games as the team headed to St. Louis to open its second long road trip. It would be hard to imagine the Yankees duplicating the first one when they won 17 of 20 games, including nine straight, while increasing their first place lead by six games.

The second western swing started the same way as the first with the Yankees beating the St. Louis Browns, 5–2, behind the superb pitching of right-hander Waite Hoyt. Urban Shocker, the Browns' ace, took the loss. It was the Yankees' ninth consecutive victory and extended their first place lead to $12\frac{1}{2}$ games over Philadelphia as the A's were rained out in Detroit.

The injury list, however, continued to swell as Everett Scott suffered a cramp in his left leg running the bases. He was replaced later in the game by Mike McNally. Scott's streak was now at an incredible 1,056 games. Miller Huggins was also concerned about two other ailing Yankees. Bob Meusel was suffering with a lame arm, and reserve player Ernie Johnson injured his hand and would be unavailable for at least a week. It was Hoyt's fifth win of the season, but the 24-year-old phenom would accelerate the pace in the months ahead to help the Yankees make the American League pennant race a joke.

Waite Hoyt was born September 9, 1899, in Brooklyn, New York. He attended the local public schools where he began playing baseball. He learned to pitch on the sandlots of Flatbush. He attended Erasmus Hall High School and failed to make the baseball team not because of a lack of talent but because of his poor grades. When his grades improved, Hoyt made the team. William A. Cook, Hoyt's biographer claimed, "Pitching for Erasmus Hall, Hoyt was overpowering with his fastball, curve and control. His high school coach, Dick Allen, rounded out his pitching repertoire by teaching him to throw a palm ball that would become an insurance policy for Hoyt in the late stages of his major league career."[5]

At 15 years old, Hoyt declined several opportunities to play professional baseball. His father, Addison, felt the young man would be better served if he gained experience playing locally. It didn't take long for the word to spread that Hoyt had the potential to be a major leaguer. A month shy of Hoyt's sixteenth birthday, John McGraw, New York Giants manager, signed him to an optional contract, but he continued to play with the local semi-pro team. In 1916, Hoyt returned to Erasmus and pitched outstanding baseball, including two no-hitters. In May, Hoyt left high school to pitch for the Mt. Carmel club in the Pennsylvania State League. His record was 5–1. Shortly after the league disbanded (not an uncommon occurrence in the financial shaky minor leagues), Hoyt returned to Brooklyn and hooked up with a semi-pro team, which didn't last long because the Giants sent the youngster first to Hartford and then to Lynn, both in the Eastern League, where he finished the season with a 4–5 record. In 1917, Hoyt was invited to the Giants' spring training camp. He didn't stick with the big club but was sent to play for the Memphis Chicks in the Southern League. In spite of Hoyt's 3–9 record with the Chicks, he received rave reviews from his manager and others. It earned him a spot with Montreal in the International League where his record was a misleading 7–17 with an ERA of 2.51.

Hoyt went to spring training with the Giants in 1918 in Marlin, Texas, for the second time but ended up pitching for Nashville in the Southern

Association. But not for long. Due to the country's involvement in World War I, many ballplayers were lost to the military. Thus, Nashville ended its season abruptly. In a sense, it was a break for Hoyt. McGraw called up the young man to pitch for the Giants. On July 24, 1918, Hoyt made his major league debut against the St. Louis Cardinals. He pitched one inning and fanned two batters and received plaudits from the *New York Times.*

McGraw felt the kid needed more experience, so he sent him to Newark in the International League. Hoyt, who always had a short fuse, protested his demotion, but went to Newark and finished the 1918 season with a 2–3 record and a 2.09 ERA. In the spring of 1919, McGraw added fuel to the fire when he sent Hoyt back to the International League, this time to Rochester. The kid refused to report. Once Rochester realized they couldn't sign Hoyt, they traded his contract to New

Brooklyn-born Waite Hoyt won 17 and lost 9 in 1923 to help the Yankees clinch their third consecutive pennant. During his almost-ten full seasons with the Yankees, Hoyt pitched in six World Series, posting a 6–3 record with an amazing 1.63 ERA. After baseball, Hoyt spent 24 years broadcasting Cincinnati Reds games and was elected to the Hall of Fame in 1969. (Courtesy National Baseball Hall of Fame Library, Cooperstown, New York.)

Orleans. Once again, Hoyt refused to report. While all this confusion was going on, Hoyt was still pitching for an independent team called the Baltimore Drydocks. Eventually, word got back to Boston manager Ed Barrow that Hoyt was major league material. Barrow invited him to pitch batting practice for the Red Sox. He liked what he saw and signed Hoyt to a major league contract.

On July 31, 1919, Waite Hoyt made his first start for the Boston Red Sox. He beat Ty Cobb and the Detroit Tigers, 2–1, in 12 innings for his first major league victory. Hoyt was used sparingly the rest of the season, finishing with a losing record of 4–6 with an ERA of 3.25. The following year he improved to 6–6, but his earned run average ballooned to 4.38. Half of the 22 games he appeared in were in relief. Although Hoyt's experience with the Red Sox was ordinary at best, he did make the acquaintance of Babe Ruth, which began a long and sometimes rocky friendship. After the 1920 season, in late October, Barrow left the Red Sox to join the New York Yankees in their front office. One of the first trades he made was on December 15, 1920. He sent Muddy Ruel, Del Pratt, Sammy Vick and Hank Thormalen to Boston for Hoyt, Wally Schang, Harry Harper and Mike McNally.

The following morning after the trade, Addison Hoyt went into his son's room where he was sleeping, woke him and said, "Waite, you've received a wonderful Christmas present—you've been traded to the Yankees!"[6]

Hoyt had his finest years pitching for the Yankees. In 1921, he, along with Carl Mays and Bob Shawkey, led the Yankees to their first pennant. He had a marvelous season, winning 19 and losing 13 with a 3.09 earned run average. In spite of the Giants beating the Yankees in the World Series, Hoyt pitched brilliantly. His record was 2–1, and he didn't allow an earned run in 27 innings. He pitched three complete games! Unquestionably, Hoyt was the most outstanding pitcher in the World Series.

In 1922, the Yankees won their second straight pennant, and Hoyt had another outstanding season with a record of 19–12 and an ERA of 3.43. Once again, the Yankees lost to the Giants, this time in humiliating fashion, four games to none (one tie). Hoyt relieved in the first game and pitched only one inning. He started Game Three and lost 3–0. His ERA for eight innings was a mere 1.13.

The Yankees won their third straight pennant in 1923. Hoyt had another fine year, winning 17 and losing nine with a 3.02 ERA. The Yankees finally beat McGraw and his Giants for their first World Series championship. Based on his previous clutch pitching in World Series play, Miller Huggins selected Hoyt to pitch the opener. He was given a 3–0 lead but couldn't hold it, lasting only 2⅓ innings before he was replaced by Joe Bush. Surprisingly, Hoyt didn't pitch again in the Series. In spite of this, he had the greatest respect and admiration for Huggins. In an article in the *Saturday Evening Post*, Hoyt said, "...I unhesitatingly nominate Miller Huggins of the Yankees as the greatest manager who ever lived. I rate Huggins at the top, followed by Mack and then McGraw, and, as far as I know, I am the only player who worked for all three."[7]

For the next five years with the Yankees, Hoyt had a 90–53 record for a winning percentage of .629. During this period, his most outstanding years were 1927 and 1928. Pitching for arguably the greatest team ever, the 1927 club known as Murderers' Row, he led the league with a 22–7 record. The following year he was even better with a 23–7 mark. His eight saves were also tops in the league. In all, Hoyt pitched in six World Series with the Yankees, won six games, lost three and recorded a fabulous earned run average of 1.63.

Although at this point in his career, Hoyt was earning a decent paycheck, he buttressed his salary by singing and dancing in vaudeville shows. Appealing to his darker side, Hoyt also went into business as a mortician in the off-season. Clearly, Waite Hoyt was more than one dimensional.

By 1930, Hoyt's pitching effectiveness had slipped. In addition, a confrontation with new manager Bob Shawkey resulted in a trade to the Detroit Tigers. He and Mark Koenig were shipped to Detroit for three players: pitcher Ownie Carroll, shortstop Yats Wuestling and outfielder Harry Rice. For the next two years, Hoyt bounced around playing for the Athletics, Dodgers, Giants and Pirates, remaining with Pittsburgh until 1937. The following year he found himself with Brooklyn where it all began at age 15. After he appeared in six games with an 0–3 record, the Dodgers released him. It was the end of his career. "Outside the ballpark after receiving his unconditional release, he looked up at the flags flying atop Ebbets and remembered watching them building the park when he was a kid, he cried."[8]

After baseball, Waite Hoyt enjoyed a full and active career in broadcasting. Actually, Hoyt had laid the groundwork for his new career back in 1927. The Yankees had won the pennant early and Hoyt found himself with a lot of free time. NBC offered him a job with radio station WEAF. Every Monday night for 15 minutes, he would talk about the Yankees and the 1927 season, which was an enjoyable experience and one he wouldn't forget.

Ten years later, in 1937, the articulate and witty Hoyt hosted his own 15-minute radio program on WNEW, telling baseball stories and commenting on the game in general. But it wasn't until 1941 when Hoyt got his big break. He signed with radio station WKRC in Cincinnati to do play-by-play for the Reds, which began with the 1942 baseball season. Twenty-four years later, then considered the "Voice of the Reds," Hoyt called his last baseball game.

Russ Hodges, the well-known baseball announcer for the New York Giants, had high praise for his colleague: "Waite Hoyt is authoritative. When he makes a statement there is no doubt as to its accuracy. When Hoyt says it's so, the Cincinnati public goes by what he says. He gives a clean-cut description of the game, drawing a clear, positive picture for his listeners. His voice is really very fine. During the occasional lulls he dips into a vast store of baseball knowledge. His stories of associations with such immortals as Babe Ruth, Lou Gehrig, John McGraw and countless others are a delight for Waite's fans. One thing I'm positive about is the fact that he is just as fine an announcer as he was a player."[9]

Waite Hoyt pitched in the major leagues for 21 years with a record of

237–182 and an earned run average of 3.59. He participated in seven World Series (six with the Yankees and one with the A's) and was on three championship teams. Hoyt was elected to the Hall of Fame in 1969 and has been credited with the now famous phrase, "It's great to be young and a Yankee." He died in Cincinnati on August 25, 1984, 15 days before his 85th birthday. He was buried at Spring Grove Cemetery in Cincinnati, the same site as his favorite manager, Miller Huggins.

After winning the series opener against St. Louis, the following day the Yankees' nine-game winning streak came to a screeching halt when the Browns trounced New York, 13–3. To put it succinctly, Bob Shawkey was horrible. By the sixth inning, the Browns had a commanding 6–2 lead. Oscar Roettger relieved Shawkey, and that's when the fun really began. The Browns lit up Roettger, scoring seven runs and driving the official scorekeeper nuts. It all added up to a laugher for St. Louis at the Yankees' expense.

The one bright spot for New York was Ruth. The Babe went 3-for-3, including two home runs, bringing his total for the season to 18. Another noteworthy event, or more accurately, an historic moment, was when Miller Huggins, realizing the game was lost, cleared his bench and sent in his reserves. One of the replacements was Henry Louis Gehrig, who batted for Roettger in the ninth. Gehrig smacked a line drive single to right field off of Elam VanGilder for the first of 2,721 hits in his 17-year career. It was an historic hit. The date was July 7 and another great trivia question.

The American League pennant race changed significantly on this warm Sunday in July. The Detroit Tigers took both ends of a doubleheader from the slumping Philadelphia A's, while the Cleveland Indians won their twin bill over the last place Red Sox. Cleveland's first game against the Red Sox was a dandy. The Indians set an American League record by scoring 27 runs. The previous record was 24, set by Philadelphia against Detroit on May 18, 1912. Cleveland also tied a record by scoring in every inning. Since they were the home team, the Indians only batted eight times. The scoring in each inning went like this: 3, 2, 3, 1, 2, 13, 1, 2. Boston used three pitchers. This enabled Cleveland to climb into second place, 11 games back of the first-place Yankees. The A's were rapidly heading south on their way to a sixth-place finish.

The Yankees won the next two games from the Browns, 6–4 and 9–3. Over the last 17 games, including the 9–3 mauling of the Browns, the Yankees had won 15 and lost 2. Huggins again had the team playing outstanding baseball in spite of the long list of injuries. Bush won the 6–4 game even with a sore shoulder, which caught up with him in the ninth inning when Huggins sent in Sam Jones to save the game. Witt didn't play because of a sprained ankle, so Huggins moved Ruth to center, Meusel to right. He stationed Hinkey Haines, former Penn State football and baseball star, in left field. This was one of the concessions Huggins made to Ruth who didn't like to play the field where he had to look directly into the sun on fly balls.

In the 9–3 game, Ruth was back patrolling center field because Witt was still out with his ankle injury. He hit his 19th home run, a two-run shot into the left field stands. Huggins called on two of his bench players to fill in for the walking wounded. Elmer Smith played right, and the super sub went 3-for-4, including an eighth inning homer, and scored three runs. Bob Meusel tried to play left but couldn't do it, so after one inning, Huggins replaced him with Harvey Hendrick, who played brilliantly in the field and drove in two runs in the five-run fourth. Pennock went the distance, registering his 10th win against only two losses. While the Yankees were winning, Cleveland lost to Boston, 4–1, so the lead climbed to 12 games.

The Browns used four pitchers trying to stop the hot bats of the Yankees in the 9–3 loss. One of the four was Charlie Root, a name linked with the Babe in one of the great all-time baseball tales that over the years has morphed into legendary status. Fast forward to the 1932 World Series—New York Yankees versus the Chicago Cubs. The Yankees had won the first two games at the Stadium, so Game Three was played at Wrigley Field. On the mound for the Cubs was the same Charlie Root, who as a rookie pitched for the Browns in 1923. Now he was a seven-year veteran and one of the aces of the Cubs' staff.

In the first inning, Ruth tagged Root for a home run with two men on base. Root won the next encounter, getting the Babe to fly to deep right center. Up to this point, both teams were razzing each other unmercifully from the bench. The catcalls started when the Yankees commented on how cheap the Cubs were for voting shortstop Mark Koenig a half-share of World Series money. Koenig, a former Yankee, had joined the Cubs late in the season and played magnificently. He batted .353 in 33 games and helped the Cubs win the pennant. The bench jockeys, led by Ruth, continued their relentless attack, variations on Chicago's cheapness. From the Chicago side, the name calling turned personal, mostly aimed at Ruth. He was an old man, fat and washed up. Even the "N" word was used.

This was the atmosphere when Ruth came to bat in the fifth with the score tied, 4–4. Root delivered his first pitch. Strike one. Ruth looked to the Cubs' dugout and put up a finger, indicating one strike. The next two pitches were balls followed by a strike to even the count at 2–2. Ruth held up two fingers to the Chicago dugout as if to say that's only two strikes.

At the moment Ruth pointed is where the story becomes clouded. Was he pointing to center indicating a home run? Was he saying it only takes one to hit? Was he indicating he was going to smash the ball down Root's throat? Was he simply pointing at the Cubs' bench? Eyewitnesses even saw it differently. So that's how the legend of the "called shot" began and continues to this day.

What happened next is pure fact. Ruth blasted a Root slow curve into the right field bleachers. He circled the bases with a huge smile and raised four fingers to the Cubs' bench. It was a moment in baseball history that will live forever.

What happened after that, surprisingly, has received little attention in the years since the "called shot." The next batter, Gehrig, stepped to the plate and clobbered Root's first pitch deep into the right field bleachers for a 7–5 lead and eventual victory. The Yankees won the following day, 13–6, to wrap up the World Series in four games.

After the Yankees took three of four games from the St. Louis Browns, they boarded a train and headed for Chicago to play the White Sox in another four-game series. The train was three hours late. Why? It lay wrecked about 30 miles south of Chicago in a middle of a corn field. A broken axle resulted in a tender, a small car, two baggage cars, a mail car and a day coach leaving the track. All three cars were ahead of the sleepers that were carrying the team. Fortunately, no one was hurt and only a few players knew they were in a train wreck.

This incident didn't phase the Yankees one bit. They opened the series on time at Comiskey Park by defeating the White Sox, 3–2. Sam Jones pitched another marvelous game, spreading six hits, all but one a single, over nine innings to record his 11th victory.

The Yankees won the second game, 3–1, behind the excellent pitching of Waite Hoyt. The young man from Brooklyn scattered eight hits. It was a solid performance by the right-hander, who notched his sixth win of the season.

The offensive star of the day was Babe Ruth. In an out-of-character performance at the plate, Ruth had no extra base hits. Off of the deliveries of Urban Faber and Hollis Thurston, the Babe went 4-for-4 (all singles), scored two runs and drove in another. For the second game in a row, Elmer Smith, filling in for the injured Bob Meusel, delivered a key hit—an RBI single in the eighth.

The latest addition to the injured list was catcher Fred Hofmann. In the third inning, a foul tip off Earl Sheely's bat smashed the nail of Hofmann's index finger on his throwing hand. Gamely, he shook off the mishap and continued to play. The next inning, however, he aggravated an old injury to his right leg and had to be replaced by Benny Bengough, the Yankees' third-string catcher. With Schang still not able to play, Huggins found himself with only one catcher. Huggins' walking wounded list now looked like this: "Meusel has a lame arm. Witt a sprained ankle. Ward and Pipp swollen glands. Scott a charley horse, Ruth a pair of lame legs. Bush a sore arm and Shawkey a wrenched stomach muscle."[10] Huggins wasn't overly concerned. With a substantial 12-game lead, he could still relax and look forward to his key players returning to the lineup.

In the third game of the series, Bob Shawkey was a one-man wrecking crew. On the mound, he pitched the Yankees to a 10–6 victory and at the plate, he went 2-for-4 (double and triple), scoring a run and driving in three. Ruth hit his 20th home run. It came off Ted Lyons in the sixth inning with Dugan on base. The Babe unleashed his ferocious swing on a 2–2 fastball and drove it into the right field bleachers. Even with lame legs, Ruth was swinging a hot bat. His average was up to a lofty .378, second to Harry Heilmann of the Detroit Tigers, who was batting an out-of-sight .404.

Ted Lyons, the 22-year-old rookie who gave up Ruth's 20th home run, was fresh from the campus of Baylor University. His intention was to become a lawyer, but his pitching was so good, he attracted the attention of major league clubs. "An important reason he signed with the White Sox rather than Cleveland or the Philadelphia A's, both of whom were also courting him, was because Chicago owner Charlie Comiskey pledged that Lyons would not be demoted to the minors until he'd spent at least one full year in the majors."[11]

Comiskey was true to his word. Lyons made his major league debut on July 2 and spent the rest of the season with Chicago and 20 more years racking up 260 wins against 230 losses with an ERA of 3.67. He accomplished this while playing for consistently poor White Sox teams. Over his long career, Lyons had three exceptional years: in 1925 he tied Eddie Rommel with 21 victories for the American League lead and turned in the most shutouts (5); in 1927 he led the league in victories (22), complete games (30) and innings pitched (over 307); in 1930 he again led the league in complete games (29) and innings pitched (over 297) while winning 22 games. At the tail end of his career in 1942 at the age of 41, he posted a 14–6 record with a league leading 2.10 earned run average and 20 complete games in 20 starts.

In 1931, Lyons injured his arm in a spring training game, which forced him to resurrect his knuckleball that he had abandoned earlier in his career. As testimony to his determination and competitive spirit, he remained in the major leagues for another 13 years, using his effective knuckler sparingly, but wisely.

During World War II, Lyons served three years with the Marines. When the war ended, he returned to the White Sox and pitched five complete games, winning one and losing four. He retired as an active player on May 25, 1946, when he was named White Sox manager, replacing Jimmy Dykes, who left with a 10–20 record. Lyons guided Chicago to a fifth-place finish. The following year, the team dropped to sixth with a 70–84 record. In 1948, when the White Sox finished last, Lyons was fired and replaced by Tony Lupien.

Lyons spent the next five years as a pitching coach for the Detroit Tigers, then a year as a coach for the Brooklyn Dodgers. Lyons eventually returned to the White Sox where he scouted for 12 years before retiring to his 750-acre rice farm in Vinton, Louisiana. He was elected to the Hall of Fame in 1955. It is interesting to note that during his career, Ted Lyons gave up 223 home runs. His first in the major leagues was Ruth's two-run shot.

The Yankees lost the closing game of the series, 4–3, in extra innings when White Sox pitcher Ted Blankenship singled down the third-base line, driving in Johnny Mostil with the winning run. The Chicago victory snapped the Yankees' five-game winning streak and sliced a game off their lead, which stood at 10. Bush was charged with the loss. His record was 12–8.

During the Chicago series, National League president John A. Heydler announced that attendance was over 300,000 ahead of the like period the previous year. It was solid proof that the popularity of baseball was soaring. Heydler confidently predicted 1923 would be a record year for attendance in his league. Earlier Ban Johnson, American League president, had announced that attendance in the junior circuit was close to 450,000 more than in the same period in 1922. Much of the increase in the American League was due to the opening of Yankee Stadium and the record crowds plus the surprising early play of the Philadelphia Athletics, which attracted thousands of fans.

Speaking of record crowds, at Boyle's Thirty Acres in Jersey City, 100,000 people witnessed Luis Angel Firpo knock out Jess Willard in the eighth round. It was a bruising battle of heavyweights and ended when Firpo, after a succession of rights and lefts to the head, landed a swift right to Willard's jaw, decking the Kansas giant and ending the fight. Face bruised and puffed, Willard made a valiant effort to get up, but he just didn't have the strength. The blows he endured to the head and body during the previous seven rounds took their toll. When referee Harry Lewis reached the ten count, Willard was still on his hands and knees.

The fight attracted the largest crowd in the history of boxing, even more than the historic battle between Jack Dempsey and George Carpentier in the same arena two years earlier. Every seat was filled, the aisles were jammed and thousands were unable to gain admission. Boxing promoter Tex Rickard estimated that 25,000 were turned away and that gate receipts were $600,000, a lucrative night's work in 1923. Willard received $210,000 and Firpo $120,000 for their efforts.

As soon as the match ended, speculation began to circulate about a

Firpo-Dempsey fight for the heavyweight championship. Firpo, fresh off his convincing victory, claimed he was ready for Dempsey and boasted he would beat him just like he did Willard. Firpo did show remarkable strength and stamina, but a shot at Dempsey was something else. However, some believed the Argentinian needed more seasoning and that his win over Willard was not that impressive. They claimed he was not a boxer, had no agility and virtually no fancy footwork. He would be a stationery target for the likes of Dempsey.

The *New York Times* concluded, "Firpo only accomplished the downfall of Willard. He did not, by any stretch of the imagination, demonstrate that he would prove a dangerous opponent for the destructive, crushing Dempsey."[12]

A word about Jersey City and its contribution to the world of professional boxing in the 1920's. It was the site of many of the great fights during the decade, and it all began when Jack Dempsey fought Georges Carpentier of France on July 2, 1921. Actually, it began months before when the famous promoter, Tex Rickard, signed the two heavyweights to the match and needed an arena to hold what was later to be called "The Fight of the Century."

Rickard had his eye on the Polo Grounds, which at the time was the home of the New York Giants and New York Yankees. But it was not to be. Governor Nathan L. Miller, who opposed boxing, did not want the fight held in New York. He even threatened to repeal the Walker Boxing Law, which made boxing legal in the state, if Rickard continued his plans to hold the match at the Polo Grounds.

Never one to be easily discouraged, Rickard looked across the Hudson River to New Jersey for a possible location. The master promoter then met with New Jersey Governor Edward I. Edwards and the powerful and autocratic Democrat mayor of Jersey City, Frank Hague, who during his long tenure in office was called "I am the law," and later in his career had connections with Franklin Delano Roosevelt when he was president. Edwards and Hague were close friends. Newark and Atlantic City were considered as possible locations, but that was probably for public show. It's hard to conceive of Hague letting a spectacle of this magnitude slip away from his beloved Jersey City.

Not surprisingly, Hague recommended a property owned by John F. Boyle as the site of the fight. Boyle just happened to be the brother of Hague's fire chief, Roger Boyle. Clearly there was some political chicanery going on, which was confirmed or at least brought to the public's attention. "George Mecurio, of the *Jersey City Reporter*, writes that years later Dempsey's manager Jack (Doc) Kearns claimed Hague received $80,000 under the table for the deal."[13]

Once Boyle's Thirty Acres, located near Montgomery Street and Cornelison Avenue, was chosen (technically it was 34 acres) construction began in earnest. In fact, it was built in two months by 600 carpenters and 400 work-ers using 2,250,000 feet of lumber and 60 tons of nails. It was an eight-sided, all-wooden structure that held approximately 80,000 people. It cost about $325,000.

Rickard, Dempsey and Carpentier made huge sums of money for the times. Spectators might have been disappointed since the fight lasted less than four rounds. Dempsey knocked the Frenchman out cold in one minute and sixteen seconds of the fourth round. After the Dempsey-Carpentier bout, Boyle's Thirty Acres was the home for a number of other boxing cards. There was the Benny Leonard-Lew Tendler bout on July 27, 1922; the Firpo-Willard fight on July 12, 1923; and the Firpo-Wills fight in 1924. There were other notable fighters that fought at Boyle's Thirty Acres, namely Tiger Flowers, Paul Berllenbach, Mike McTigue, James J. Braddock and Johnny Wilson.

It was a marvelous decade for Jersey City and professional boxing. By 1927, however, Yankee Stadium and the Polo Grounds were the main venues for important boxing events. Also, Governor Miller was no longer in office to prevent boxing in New York. Once the sport shifted to New York, Boyle's Thirty Acres became obsolete. In June, 1927, the wrecking ball demolished the once grand arena and its memories, putting an end to a short but exciting time in Jersey City history.

The Yankees continued on their long road trip with a swing into Cleve-land to play the second-place Indians six games, including two doublehead-ers, very strange scheduling indeed. It was an opportunity for Tris Speaker and his Indians to make serious inroads into the Yankees' 11-game lead. The best they could do, however, was to split the six games, so the lead remained the same.

During the second game of the first doubleheader, Babe Ruth connected for his 21st home run before a jam-packed Dunn Field. His batting average had climbed to .372, but was still 20 points behind Harry Heilmann at .392. Sam Jones went the distance in the 10–7 Yankees victory. It was his 12th win against only five losses.

The Yankees won the third game of the series, 4–2. Waite Hoyt, the young right-hander from Brooklyn, won his third game on the western tour. Earlier, he beat St. Louis and Chicago. His record was 7–4. Stan Coveleski, the Polish spitballer, as the press referred to him, was hammered hard early in the game. Before the second inning was over, the Yankees had six hits and four runs, and Coveleski was taking a shower. Ruth received two walks in the game, bringing his total for the season to an even 100.

The Yankees issued an update on two of their injured players—Bob Meusel and Wally Schang. Meusel, who was still out of the lineup, was sent to Youngstown, Ohio, to have his ailing arm examined by a specialist. Schang, who had not played in several weeks, announced he was ready to catch full-time. Huggins didn't agree. The manager had other plans for his catcher. "I am sending him home to Philadelphia tomorrow night. He may be as fit as he thinks he is, but we don't exactly need him, and an extra week of rest won't hurt him any. He will rejoin the club when we get to Philadelphia on July 24."[14]

With a 12-game lead over second-place Cleveland, Huggins had the luxury of giving his number one catcher more time to heal. It was a wise decision by the manager and would pay dividends later in the season and in the World Series.

Miller Huggins was born on March 27, 1879, in Cincinnati, Ohio, the third of four children. His father was a grocer and a strict Methodist who strongly objected to his son playing baseball on Sundays. Years later when Huggins was playing semi-professional baseball, he would use the name Proctor to hide his identity from his father. Huggins attended the local schools in Cincinnati. His neighborhood was one of the roughest in the city, which forced the diminutive lad to learn to fight his own battles. He was an excellent student who was encouraged by his father to study the law. To please his father, Huggins matriculated at the University of Cincinnati. He passed the bar exam in 1902 but never practiced. He preferred baseball, and when he discovered he could earn a living playing the game he loved, the profession of law was abandoned. Physically, Huggins was a small man. Some even described him as gnome-like. He was five feet, six-and-a-half inches tall and weighed 140 pounds. Both height and weight vary according to the source. Huggins' exact height and weight are irrelevant. He was a tiny man whose stature earned him the nickname the "Mighty Mite." Huggins did not allow his size to affect his overall play. He was a fair hitter with obviously no power, but was fast, aggressive, a skilled leadoff man and an excellent fielder. He also taught himself to become a switch-hitter.

He began his professional career at age 19 with the Mansfield, Ohio, club in the Inter-State League. The following year, as author Leonard Koppett noted, "...he played for a semi-pro team in the Catskill Mountain resort area for a hotel run by the Fleischmann brothers, Max and Julius, who would eventually buy the Cincinnati Club."[15] This would turn out to be an opportunistic summer for the young man. Four years later, after playing for St. Louis at the highest minor league level (AA) at the time, his contract was purchased by the Reds. He was made the regular second baseman by player/manager Joe Kelley, who starred for the legendary Ned Hanlon's Orioles early in his career.

Miller Huggins played 13 years in the National League. His lifetime batting average was an unimpressive .265. But he was a gutsy ballplayer. He excelled in drawing walks and by some was considered the perfect leadoff man. He was fast, could bunt and steal (41 in 1906) a base when his team needed it. He was an excellent defensive second baseman.

In retrospect, his years as a major league player were really all about learning how to manage. He spent six years with the Reds and seven with the St. Louis Cardinals. With the Reds, he played under Joe Kelley, who was greatly influenced by Ned Hanlon. After Kelley came the legend himself, Hanlon, the man who guided the rough-and-ready Baltimore Orioles of the 19th century. The third manager at Cincinnati was John Ganzel, who had played first base for the driven, take-no-prisoners John McGraw. Connect the dots and you can clearly see a pattern developing. But it didn't end with Ganzel and Cincinnati.

Huggins' on-the-job training continued when he was traded to the St. Louis Cardinals. His field boss with the Cardinals for three years was Hall of Famer Roger Bresnahan, who had spent eight years in Baltimore and New York as McGraw's catcher. Huggins was building a reputation as one of the smartest men in the game. Apparently, the Cardinals organization saw Huggins as a leader, too, and appointed him manager in 1913. At the time, Cardinals owner Helene Britton didn't like Bresnahan's loud and brash ways and was looking for a more cerebral, low-key, thinking manager. Huggins fit the bill. He continued to play second base as well as manage in 1913 but finished last after inheriting a mediocre club. The Cardinals improved in 1914, battling the Giants and the Boston Braves, the "miracle" club that won the pennant after residing in last place on July 19. Huggins led the Cardinals to a third-place finish on the shoulders of a pitching staff that led the league with an ERA of 2.38. Huggins was gaining recognition as a field leader and an effective manager of players. The following year the Cardinals dropped to sixth as the pitching wasn't as effective and not one player was capable of hitting .300. Still playing second base, Huggins batted a weak .241 and walked only 74 times, a far cry from the league-leading 105 free passes the previous year. It was a clear sign the days of Huggins as a player/manager were coming to a close. In 1916, the little guy played in 18 games and managed the team to a last-place tie with his former club, the Cincinnati Reds.

Huggins continued to manage St. Louis in 1917, and with little talent to work with, he led the club to a third-place finish, 15 games behind the New York Giants. In the meantime, Mrs. Britton sold the team, and the new owners hired Branch Rickey to run it. In fact, they wanted Rickey to manage in the dugout, which he eventually did in 1919. Huggins, an intelligent man, saw the proverbial hand writing on the wall and resigned.

For Huggins, the old cliché, "when one door closes, another opens," was never more true in 1918. The door slammed shut in St. Louis but opened wide in New York. New Yankees owners Jacob Ruppert and Tillinghast L'Hommedieu Huston were looking for a new manager to lead the Yankees, and they had their eyes on Huggins. Well, at least one of them did. The two owners fought bitterly over their choices. Ruppert favored Huggins, who came highly recommended by American League president Ban Johnson, who knew him well. Huston wanted Wilbert Robinson, former Brooklyn manager, and close friend. Ruppert won out and hired Huggins while Huston was in France building railroads. The battle wounds were deep between the two men and never healed. It eventually led to Ruppert buying out Huston and becoming the sole owner in 1923.

In 1918, Huggins faced some monumental hurdles to overcome. First, he had to accept the reality that John McGraw and his Giants ruled New York baseball, at least for the moment. Second, Huggins realized he had to build a strong club to compete with the ill-tempered, yet popular manager across the Hudson River. It would take time, patience and some shrewd moves by the front office. In his first year at the helm, the Yankees finished fourth, 13½ games behind the pennant-winning Boston Red Sox. The following year the Yankees improved, finishing third, 7½ games in back of the Chicago White Sox. It was also the year they traded for pitcher Carl Mays, an acquisition that would help the club immediately but end poorly. Early in 1920, with strong encouragement from Huggins, the Yankees made the purchase of the century, acquiring Babe Ruth from the Red Sox for $100,000. Shortly after, with considerably less fanfare, the Yankees made another key purchase, obtaining the contract of outfielder Bob Meusel. Even with these two outstanding additions to the club, the best Huggins could do was finish third in 1920 with a respectable 95–59 record, three games behind the pennant-winning Cleveland Indians. Bob Shawkey, Huggins' ace the previous two years, had high praise for his manager. "Huggins was a very fine person and a good baseball man. He knew the game and he knew how to get the most out of his ballplayers. Most of the boys liked him very much. He was a quiet man by nature."[16]

Prior to the 1921 season, the Yankees made one of the best front office acquisitions in the history of the game. They acquired Ed Barrow from the Boston Red Sox as their general manager. Huggins now had a buffer between him and the owners, an arrangement he appreciated. He worked well with Barrow and welcomed the long list of players Barrow would soon bring to the Yankees. Before the season started, Barrow brought in Waite Hoyt and Wally Schang, who helped New York win its first pennant in 1921. But the celebration was over quickly when the Yankees lost to the Giants in the World Series.

Huggins led the Yankees to another pennant in 1922 in spite of losing Ruth and Meusel to suspensions (until May 20) from the commissioner for barnstorming around the country after the 1921 World Series. Once again, Barrow helped Huggins by trading for Everett Scott, Joe Bush and Sam Jones—all three made important contributions to winning the pennant.

After losing to the Giants in the World Series for the second straight year, Huston saw an opportunity to convince Ruppert to get rid of Huggins. Ruppert would not hear of it. Huggins remained the manager, won another pennant in 1923 and the Yankees' first World Series. In the meantime, Huston sold out his half-interest in the Yankees to Ruppert.

After the 1923 season, at least in the eyes of the fans, Huggins and the Yankees were on top of the baseball world, not to mention New York City. But it was not without its downside. Over the years, the often acrimonious relationship between Miller Huggins and Babe Ruth, which has been widely and extensively written about, came to a head in 1925.

Ruth was a man-child. He never grew up, which was part of his charm. He was fun-loving, a hard drinker, a woman chaser, self-centered, yet he was good-natured and loved children. He was a complex man. Author Koppett explained Ruth's feelings towards Huggins. "He had no respect whatever for Huggins. How could he? The man was tiny and old (forty-four in 1924), spoke softly, used long words, couldn't punch anyone out. All the success the Yankees were having was his, Ruth's doing; what had Huggins ever done before he had Ruth?"[17]

From the time Ruth joined the Yankees in 1920, Huggins had problems controlling the slugger, mostly minor incidents that could be overlooked. That is until 1925 when the frustration Huggins was harboring, due to Ruth's behavior, finally came to a head. The fact that the Yankees lost the 1924 pennant to the Washington Senators didn't help matters either.

The buildup began early. During the 1925 spring training Ruth experienced the most famous and publicized stomach ache of the century. Whatever the cause, and there were many offered, it was serious enough for him to be hospitalized. He didn't return to the Yankees lineup until June 1 at the Stadium and then was too weak to be effective. On top of this problem, Huggins found that some of his key players had suddenly aged, others were having bad years and Ruth was partying all night. The result was seventh place and little hope to recover. Author Leigh Montville noted, "Huggins had become more and more distressed with his star. The manager's history of confrontations with Ruth was not good. They argued all the time, back and forth, semi-comical stuff, but Huggins seldom was able to voice his real thoughts. Every time he was ready to say something, to truly read out the Caliph of Clout, the caliph would unload another couple of clouts."[18]

One of the happier moments shared by Miller Huggins and Babe Ruth. Up until 1925, Huggins had problems controlling the great slugger. But in 1925, in St. Louis, the free-spirited Ruth showed up an hour before game time after carousing all night. The "Mighty Mite" had enough and slapped the Babe with a $5,000 fine and suspended him for the rest of the season. Six days later Huggins reinstated a contrite Ruth, and the big guy played well the rest of the season with Huggins in full control. (Courtesy National Baseball Hall of Fame Library, Cooperstown, New York.)

It all came to a head in St. Louis when Ruth arrived an hour before game time after carousing all night. Huggins told Ruth not to suit up, that he was suspended for the rest of the season and fined $5,000. Ruth went ballistic. He vowed to take up his case with Landis and Ruppert. He passed up Landis but did meet with Ruppert, who surprised him by backing his manager unconditionally. A contrite Ruth was left with no alternative but to meet Huggins, who told him the suspension stayed and he would keep in touch. Six days later, Huggins reinstated the Babe, who played well and with a purpose the rest of the season. The confrontation was over. Huggins had won and regained control of the New York Yankees.

With Huggins in full control and the inmates no longer running the asylum, the Yankees dominated baseball for the next three years. They won the pennant in 1926 but lost the World Series to Huggins' old club, the St. Louis Cardinals, in seven games. You could call it the Grover Cleveland Alexander Series. The 39-year-old right-hander, who everyone thought was washed up except manager Rogers Hornsby, won Games Two and Six. In the seventh game with the Cardinals clinging to a 3–2 lead, the Yankees loaded the bases with two outs. Hornsby brought in Alexander, who had pitched nine innings the day before, to face the dangerous Tony Lazzeri, who had driven in 114 runs during the season. Lazzeri whiffed on a 2–2 curve. Alexander retired the Yankees in the eighth and had two outs in the ninth when the Babe stepped to the plate. He walked Ruth, who had already hit four home runs during the Series. With Meusel the next batter and Gehrig on deck, Ruth inexplicably tried to steal second and was thrown out easily. The game and the Series were over just like that. Publicly to the press, Huggins defended Ruth's poor judgment. One can only conjecture what Huggins was really thinking privately.

The next two years, 1927 and 1928, would be Miller Huggins' and the Yankees' finest up to that point in their history. The 1927 team, featuring Meusel, Earl Combs, Dugan, Lazzeri, Ruth and Gehrig, played .714 ball (110–44) and ran away with the pennant by 19 games. They swept the Pittsburgh Pirates in the World Series. The following year, the Huggins-led Yankees made it three American League pennants in a row and easily swept the Cardinals in the World Series.

Now Huggins had six pennants and three world championships to his credit in eight years. It was an unprecedented achievement. Not even McGraw or Mack could match that record. Huggins and the Yankees were the toast of New York. After the 1924 World Series loss to the Senators, McGraw's effectiveness and popularity were on the decline. Mack's A's hadn't won anything since 1914 and in that World Series, they were embarrassed by the Braves. Mack's resurgence wouldn't begin again until 1929.

The little Mighty Mite was king of the hill. He had arrived in the big city and had fought off the legendary McGraw to capture the hearts and minds of the locals. He had tamed Ruth (as much as one could expect), the most difficult player in the game to manage. He was loved and respected by a team he and Barrow had put together and was now an efficient winning machine.

The Yankees were fully expected to repeat in 1929. They got off to a fast start, winning 13 of their first 17 games. By mid–August, they were 25 games over .500. It was not enough. The surging A's were 45 games over! Sluggers Jimmy Foxx and Al Simmons plus Lefty Grove and George Earnshaw on the mound proved too much for Huggins' club. But there was a more serious problem. Late in the season, Huggins became ill. He felt terrible most of the season and even developed a carbuncle under his left eye. One day Hoyt found him in the clubhouse under a heat lamp treating his carbuncle. This turned out later to be absolutely the wrong thing to do. His growth wasn't a carbuncle but a skin disease called erysipelas. Unfortunately, the heat lamp helped spread the disease and infected his entire body. Five days after he entered St. Vincent's Hospital at 5:15 P.M. on September 25, Miller Huggins died at age 50.

A shocked baseball world mourned the loss. Two days later, as a tribute to the little manager, all American League games were called off. His death brought messages of regret and sorrow from many walks of life—city executives, politicians, baseball owners and, of course, players.

"It is one of the keenest losses I have ever felt."—BABE RUTH

"He was like a father to me."—LOU GEHRIG

"He was the finest man to work for I ever knew."—BOB SHAWKEY

"He was the most loving man, an honest and true friend, a zealous worker. He was a genius in baseball...."—JACOB RUPPERT

"I feel a deep personal loss and the American League will miss Miller tremendously."—CONNIE MACK

"I always entertained the highest regard for Miller Huggins as an able leader and as a man."—JOHN McGRAW[19]

The funeral for Huggins was at the Little Church Around the Corner in Manhattan. Among the pallbearers were teammates Ruth, Gehrig, Lazzeri, Combs, Pennock and Shawkey. Huggins was buried next to his parents in Spring Grove Cemetery in Cincinnati.

On May 30, 1932, the first monument at Yankee Stadium was dedicated to Miller Huggins. In 1964 another honor was bestowed upon him when he was elected to the Hall of Fame in Cooperstown.

The Yankees played their second twin-bill in two days against the Cleveland Indians. It was another split. The Indians won the first game, 6–0. Coveleski, who had only lasted 1⅔ innings the day before, returned to blank the Yankees on six hits, vindicating his earlier poor performance. New York won the second game, 11–7, in a slugfest. Joe Bush was smacked by a wicked line drive off the bat of Tris Speaker. It fractured the finger of his left hand, and Bush wouldn't pitch for another two weeks. The injury to Bush didn't phase Huggins. He had five other solid starters who could pick up the slack. At the time of the injury, Bush's record was 13–8. When he returned to the rotation, he went 6–7, so the injury could have been a factor.

While the Yankees and Carl Mays were being humiliated by the Indians, 13–0, in the final game of the series, Jacob Ruppert was back in New York denying rumors that Harry Frazee, of all people, was about to buy into the Yankees. The gist of the rumors went like this: Ruppert was unable to handle both the New York club and his other business interests. Frazee was coming into the Yankees organization to run the baseball operations, freeing up Ruppert to concentrate on his non-baseball ventures. It was one whopping story that had the press abuzz. Ruppert vehemently and categorically denied the rumor and in strong and clear language told the press and Yankees fans he was not looking for a partner and reaffirmed for everyone he was still the sole owner of the New York Yankees franchise. How the rumor started and then made its way to the press remains a mystery.

In the 13–0 drubbing, Huggins allowed Mays to remain in the game for the full eight innings while he was being hammered for 20 hits. On the surface, the beating of Mays by the Indians looked like a typical case of a player being asked to take one for the team. It allowed Huggins to save the rest of the staff for the upcoming series with the Detroit Tigers. It made sense. Some considered it smart baseball. However, there is another side to this story. It has been well documented that Huggins despised Mays, dating back to the 1921 World Series and his two losses to the Giants. He believed Mays threw Game Four. From that point on, there was no love lost between the two. Letting Mays take the beating was payback for the unforgiving Huggins.

The Yankees moved on to Detroit for the final four games of the western portion of the second road trip. They took three of four games from the Tigers. New York started the road trip on July 6 in first place, 10½ games over the Philadelphia A's. It ended on July 22 with the Yankees 11 games ahead of the Cleveland Indians, who had replaced the A's in second place. It was another excellent trip with the Yankees winning 12 of the 18 games (.666) and coming away with only one minor injury, Bush's finger. Meusel was healed and back in the lineup.

In the opening game Ruth, Ward and Dugan hit home runs to pace the

Yankees to a 4–1 victory over the Tigers. It was Ruth's American League leading 22nd. Hoyt pitched another brilliant game, limiting the Tigers to seven singles while walking only two. His record was 8–4. The following day Sam Jones lost to the Tigers, 9–2. It was his first loss after winning seven in a row over a month-and-a-half span. Catcher Wally Schang returned to the lineup after a long absence. He batted for Scott in the ninth and was ready to resume his full-time duties.

In 1923, owners of baseball teams forced fans to return foul balls hit into the stands. Keeping that in mind, an interesting story occurred in the National League that's worthy of repeating. An 11-year-old boy by the name of Reuben Berman, who was attending a Philadelphia Phillies game at Baker Bowl, was lucky enough to grab a foul ball. The excited kid put the ball in his pocket, thrilled at his good fortune. Moments later he was taken by a police sergeant "to the house of detention" where he spent the night!!! The story, however, had a happy ending. A municipal court judge found the boy not guilty of larceny. The judge further noted that a boy who gets a baseball at a game is acting on the natural impulse of all boys to keep it as a souvenir. Although not revealed, one assumes the boy was allowed to finally keep the ball.

After an exhibition contest in Grand Rapids where Ruth hit two home runs, New York won the last two games from the Tigers, 3–2 and 7–4. On one day's rest, Jones came back to save the first game and preserve the victory for Shawkey. With two outs and the bases loaded in the eighth in a 3–2 game, Jones induced Bob Fothergill (a lifetime .325 average) to hit back to the box for an easy out. Jones retired the side in the ninth, and Shawkey had his 11th win. Young Hoyt recorded his fifth straight win on the road trip and ninth of the season in the closing game.

The western portion of the road trip over the Yankees boarded a train and headed for Philadelphia. Miller Huggins couldn't have been happier. New York's record was a phenomenal 59–28 (.678). They had a 12½-game lead over the Indians. The entire team was hitting, led by Ruth who was batting .376. Injured players were slowly returning and Meusel wasn't even missed. Elmer Smith was filling in beautifully and there was a new hero every day. The pitching staff was superb. More than halfway through the season, Shawkey, Bush, Jones and Pennock had 10 or more victories—and Hoyt had nine. Mays, who was in Huggins' dog house and seldom used, had a 4–1 record. The Yankees were a talented and confident club heading into the home stretch.

6

Ruth Wields a Hot Bat

The Yankees rolled into Philadelphia with a commanding 12½-game lead over the second-place Cleveland Indians. The last time New York faced the A's was June 28 when they opened a crucial four-game series that was billed as a golden opportunity for Connie Mack and his club to get back in the pennant race. The A's, at the time, were trailing the Yankees by only five games. The A's did not meet the challenge as the Yankees swept the series and went on a 20–6 tear while Philadelphia disassembled, winning nine and losing 18, which dropped the club to fifth place, a distant 17 games behind the front-runner. It had been a rough month for Mack and now the high-flying Yankees were back at Shibe Park for four games, much to Mack's dismay.

Prior to the start of the series, Yankee Stadium was the host for the world's lightweight boxing championship. It pitted the current champion, the ever popular Benny Leonard from Harlem, against the Philadelphia southpaw, Lew Tendler. It was a thrilling 15-round battle before 60,000 screaming fans. After the first round, which broke even on points, Leonard won every round. In the seventh, Leonard almost knocked Tendler through the ropes, and from the 12th round to the end of the fight, the challenger was staggering from blows to the head and body.

It was a one-sided bout fought gallantly by Tendler which the crowd loved and appreciated. But it was in vain. He was outclassed by a superior boxer. The *New York Times* described Leonard's boxing skills in flowery prose, "Leonard's victory was glorious. He showed himself still the wonderful boxer of old—a perfectly harmonious piece of fighting humanity with every nerve centre and muscle working in co-ordination and admirably concentrated."[1]

The Leonard-Tendler lightweight championship bout was the second major event held at Yankee Stadium. The first was the Tex Rickard extravaganza of heavyweight boxing for the benefit of the Free Milk Fund. These events and others throughout the year were the beginning of the Stadium's popularity. Over the years, it would grow into a venue as popular as any in the country, and it would host many of the great events in baseball and outside of the national pastime. Years later, the press would compare the Stadium to a cathedral, a palace and even to the Coliseum in Rome. True or not, Yankee Stadium had a rich and exciting history that ended after the 2008 baseball season, 85 years later.

The New York Yankees once again swept the Philadelphia A's in the four-game series. In the first game, Ruth hit a three-run homer, his 23rd, in the ninth inning, tying him with Cy Williams of the Philadelphia Phillies for the major league lead. Mays (5–1) pitched another fine game, allowing only six hits and two runs while gaining the 9–2 victory for the Yankees.

The second game of the series was a thriller. Trailing 4–0 entering the eighth, the Yankees scored four times to tie the game and another in the ninth to win, 5–4. Shawkey was now 12–6. The next day, the Yankees made it three straight, winning another squeaker, 4–3. At this point, Huggins had the Midas touch. Whatever move he made turned into pure gold. Ruth started the game, but after one at-bat left with a stiff neck. Huggins called on Harvey Hendrick to replace Ruth in left field. In the fifth inning, Hendrick doubled, driving in two runs and helping to win the game. Huggins' uncanny managing and the Yankees' performance on the field made the 1923 season look way too easy.

The Yankees completed the Philadelphia sweep behind the fine pitching of Herb Pennock, who hadn't pitched since the previous Cleveland series when he hurt himself warming up for a relief appearance. The Babe showed no ill effects from his stiff neck the previous day. He went 3-for-4, including his 24th homer in a 7–3 victory. It was the Yankees' ninth straight win over the A's, dating back to May 26. The Yankees' first-place lead over Cleveland jumped to 14½ games. As Waite Hoyt would say years later, "It's great to be young and a Yankee."

On a sad note, Mack's A's dropped to sixth place, a whopping 21 games behind New York. One can imagine the tall, stately, well-dressed Mack sitting in the dugout after losing the four games and drifting back to 1914 when he had an opportunity to obtain Ruth from Baltimore Orioles owner Jack Dunn for nothing! No, it's not a misprint. Back when Ruth was playing for the Orioles, Mack and Dunn were pretty chummy. In fact, Mack had loaned Dunn $10,000 to buy the Orioles.

In 1914, Dunn's Orioles were losing money. He became so desperate he decided the only way out of the fiscal mess was to sell his players. Mack recalled the situation to famed sportswriter Red Smith in a 1944 interview.

"I remember when Jack—it must have been about 1914—offered two pitchers, Ruth and Ernie Shore, and told me to take 'em for nothing. I said no."[2]

In all due respect to Smith, Mack's memory at 82 might have been a little fuzzy. It's hard to believe, as desperate as Dunn was, he would give away two great pitchers for nothing. Sell them, yes. Give them away, no. Truth be told, Mack was in a financial bind, too, so he really didn't have the cash even if they were for sale. Dunn eventually contacted Red Sox owner Joe Lannin, who had earlier loaned him $3,000 to make his payroll. Lannin bought Ruth, Shore and Ben Egan for $8,500 plus the cancellation of the loan, making the final price for the three $11,500. It's a fascinating story and inevitably leads one to play the "what if" game. Suppose Mack did buy Ruth from Dunn in 1914 and the Babe played for Philadelphia through the difficult years until the great 1929–31 A's Championship teams, what then? There might not have been a New York Yankee dynasty. Couple this with McGraw's signing of Gehrig and this book would never have been written. More likely the idea of the book would never have emerged.

The long road trip was finally over with the Yankees winning 16 of 22 games, a magnificent showing. Some in the press were so jubilant they were comparing the 1923 Yankees with the 1906 Chicago Cubs, a club that won 116 and lost only 36 (.763). This was the club that featured the famous double play combination of Tinkers to Evers to Chance. It was a flattering comparison but slightly off the mark. Solely examining stats and not taking into consideration the competition in the league and World Series, the clubs match up closely.

On the one hand, the Cubs set a record of 116 wins, 20 games ahead of the New York Giants, but lost the World Series to the Chicago White Sox, called the "Hitless Wonders" at the time. The Yankees won 98 games (.645) but beat the Giants in the World Series. The Cubs had the edge in pitching; the Yankees in hitting. Here are the comparisons:

Cubs (1906)				Yankees (1923)			
Player	W	L	Era	Player	W	L	ERA
Three-Finger Brown	26	6	1.04	Bob Shawkey	16	11	3.51
Jack Pfiester	20	8	1.51	Joe Bush	19	15	3.43
Ed Reulbach	19	4	1.65	Sam Jones	21	8	3.63
Carl Lundgren	17	6	2.21	Herb Pennock	19	6	3.13
Jack Taylor	12	3	1.83	Waite Hoyt	17	9	3.02
Orval Overall	12	3	1.88	Carl Mays	5	2	6.20

Player	Avg	HR	RBI	Player	Avg	HR	RBI
Frank Chance	.319	3	71	Babe Ruth	.393	41	131
Harry Steinfeldt	.327	3	83	Wally Pipp	.304	6	108

Player	Avg	HR	RBI	Player	Avg	HR	RBI
Frank Schulte	.281	7	60	Bob Meusel	.313	9	91
Johnny Evers	.255	1	51	Aaron Ward	.284	10	82

The Yankees offense also had major contributions from Joe Dugan (.283), Whitey Witt (.314) and Wally Schang (.276) plus utility players Fred Hofmann (.290) and Elmer Smith (.306), who filled in admirably when injuries were piling up. The comparison between the 1906 Cubs and the 1923 Yankees is interesting and like most baseball discussions, lots of fun, but ends with no final conclusion.

After the long road trip, the Yankees' triumphant return to the Stadium was marred by the Chicago White Sox, as the visiting club won the first game of the four-game series, 3–1. Charley Robertson outpitched Hoyt as the Yankee bats went cold in the clutch. Over 40,000 fans showed up the next day, a Sunday afternoon, to watch the Yankees and White Sox split a doubleheader. The Yankees lost the first, 3–2, on Everett Scott's error, a rarity for the sure-handed shortstop. In 1923, he would lead the league in fielding average (.961) for the eighth straight year, co-holder with Luis Aparicio of one of baseball's most impressive defensive records. Bush was the hard luck loser.

The Yankees came back in the nightcap to defeat Chicago, 8–2, behind the three-hit pitching of Bob Shawkey. But the day belonged to Babe Ruth. He had a magnificent afternoon. Counting both games, Ruth went 5-for-7 including a triple, three doubles and a single. He scored two runs, drove in one and made four great catches in the outfield. By the way, he also threw out a runner at second. The fans loved it, and why not? They were watching the greatest baseball player in the history of the game.

The Yankees won the final game of the series, 5–3. Jones pitched a six-hitter and led the pitching staff with 14 victories. The day's hero was Aaron Ward, who homered and tripled. Ruth went 1-for-3 and raised his average to a lofty .390. Heilmann, who was in a mild "slump," saw his average drop to .391. Ruth would eventually pull ahead of Heilmann, but at season's end the Tiger's outfielder prevailed.

The Cleveland Indians moved into Yankee Stadium for three games, hoping to cut into the Yankees' 13½-game lead. The pitching matchups for the three games featured Pennock versus Sherry Smith followed by Hoyt against Joe Shaute and ending with Shawkey and George Uhle. The Indians won two of three, shaving a full game off the lead, but still trailed by a 12½-game margin.

New York lost the opener to Cleveland, 5–3. Smith baffled the Yankees throughout the game, escaping from one jam after another until Ruth came up in the ninth with Witt on base and the score 5–1. Attesting to Ruth's popularity, not a fan left the Stadium. No one wanted to miss his last at-bat even though Ruth was hitless in his four previous trips to the plate, including two walks. The meager crowd wasn't disappointed.

Never missing an opportunity to entertain the fans, Ruth surprisingly jumped into the batter's box as if to hit right-handed. Taking him seriously, the Cleveland defense shifted to accommodate a right-handed batter. Ruth took the left-hander's first pitch, a called strike. The Babe then jumped to the other side of the plate, which forced the Cleveland defense to shift back. The defense was barely in place when Smith pitched. Ruth swung and launched a long drive that landed high up in the bleachers. It was his 25th of the season as the few remaining fans laughed and cheered in delight. Prior to the home run, in the eighth inning, Ruth took a shot at coaching third base. Huggins usually occupied the coach's box but didn't come out of the dugout in the eighth. No one thought much of it until Meusel reached second. That's when the Babe jumped out of the dugout and ran to the third base coach's box.

While Ruth was entertaining Yankee fans with his unorthodox antics, Huggins finally decided that Gehrig needed more playing time. The young first baseman had absorbed enough baseball strategy watching veterans perform from the bench. Huggins wanted Gehrig to play every day and to hone his skills that would eventually reap dividends down the line. After Gehrig appeared in only seven games and going 1-for-5, Huggins optioned him to Hartford in the Eastern League, which had a working agreement with the Yankees.

Initially, Gehrig struggled at Hartford, trying to live up to his advanced billing. He wasn't hitting and was playing poorly in the field. Word came back from Hartford manager Paddy O'Connor, a former coach under Huggins, that Gehrig was playing poorly and needed help. Barrow immediately sent super scout Paul Krichell to Hartford to straighten out the kid.

The wise and experienced Krichell probably had dealt with similar problems many times over the years. After talking with O'Connor and carefully assessing the situation, Krichell concluded the problem with Gehrig was two-fold. The first and the most easily corrected was that Gehrig, a decent, honest, shy kid was running around with the wrong crowd. Krichell minced no words in telling Gehrig he must stop hanging with those troublemakers on the club or else he would be in danger of ruining a very bright and lucrative career.

The second problem was much more difficult to solve, and Krichell knew it. The problem involved the head. It's called fear of failure. It can happen in all walks of life, but it is especially prevalent in baseball and not just with Gehrig. Simply explained, you cannot succeed at every at-bat. In fact, if a batter gets three hits every ten times up, he is a celebrated .300 hitter. Conversely, that means you have failed seven times. Even superior hitters who bat .400 for a season, which is a rarity (the last time was in 1941 when Ted Williams hit .406), fail six out of 10 times. Krichell made this point clear to Gehrig that he must overcome this fear of failure.

Gehrig bought into Krichell's lecture because his season at Hartford turned around in a hurry. He wound up batting .304, walloping 24 home runs, 13 doubles and eight triples. Author Ray Robinson points out that, "In one remarkable stretch Lou hit seven homers in seven days. In another seven-day span he hit five home runs, one each against Bridgeport, Waterbury and Pittsfield and two against Albany."[3]

Lou Gehrig would return to the Yankees at the end of the season after they clinched the pennant. The Iron Horse finished 1923 with a superb .427 average, albeit in only 26 at-bats. Although it wouldn't come for a few more years, Gehrig was on the path to greatness. Huggins, Barrow and Krichell deserve credit for recognizing a potentially serious problem and taking immediate action.

Waite Hoyt pitched the next day and spun a gem, limiting the Indians to six hits as the Yankees won, 4–2. The victory returned the lead to 13½ games.

That evening, the world was shocked to discover that President Warren Gamaliel Harding had died suddenly of a stroke in San Francisco. The date was August 2, the time of death 7:30 P.M. on the West Coast. Soon after Harding's death, a formal announcement was issued. It read: "The President died at 7:30 P.M. Mrs. Harding and the two nurses, Miss Ruth Powderly and Miss Sue Drusser, were in the room at the time. Mrs. Harding was reading to the President, when, utterly without warning, a slight shudder passed through his frame; he collapsed, and all recognized that the end had come. A stroke of apoplexy was the cause of his death."[4]

The beginning of the end for Harding began on June 20 when he and his entourage left Washington's Union Station for St. Louis, the first step of the President's 1,500-mile, two-month trip named the "Voyage of Understanding." Already, Harding had the appearance of a tired and fatigued man. The arduous trip would eventually take its toll. The long journey would take him across the United States, giving speeches, meeting dignitaries, greeting crowds of people and visiting historic and national sites. On July 4, at Tacoma, he embarked on a four-day voyage to Alaska where he visited Indian villages and met with Governor Scott Bone. Harding visited Alaska's capital, Juneau, and Skagway. Then he went through the Gulf of Alaska to Seward Harbor, then by train to Anchorage where he spent some time. Leaving Anchorage, the entourage headed for their two-and-a-half-day journey to

Fairbanks, the farthest northern point of the trip, and then back to Seward. The ship *Henderson* was waiting for the president for the next hop through the Prince William Sound to Valdez, a mining town. Re-embarking the *Henderson*, they sailed to Cordova, ending in Sitka on July 21. At Sitka, as in all the stops, Harding and his group were escorted by dignitaries to view churches, museums and relics. After leaving Sitka on a Sunday afternoon, the *Henderson* headed for Vancouver when the president was once again overwhelmed by enthusiastic Canadians. After leaving Canada for Seattle, the *Henderson*, in a heavy fog edged into the Puget Sound and struck the destroyer *Zeilen*. It was a minor collision. No one was hurt.

Delivering a speech at Seattle Stadium, Harding began slurring his words and accidentally called Alaska "Nebraska." Aides were alarmed and there were some anxious moments, but Harding finished the speech without further incident. He recovered enough to give another speech that evening. Immediately after, he was taken to the train and put to bed where he complained of violent cramps and indigestion. Further planned speeches were cancelled, and the train headed directly to San Francisco. After examining the president, the doctors were in disagreement as to the diagnosis. One physician said it was ptomaine, the other an enlarged heart. On Sunday, July 29, at the Palace Hotel in San Francisco, Harding began to feel better and insisted on giving the scheduled speech on Wednesday. By Monday, he had a temperature of 102 and a racing pulse. By Wednesday, the president was feeling much better and even sitting up in bed. Thursday evening still found Harding feeling good as Mrs. Harding was reading the *Saturday Evening Post* to him. After finishing the article, "A Calm View of a Calm Man," by Samuel Blythe, Mrs. Harding left his bedside to go to another room. At that point, President Harding experienced a massive stroke. He was 57 years old.

All major league baseball games and most other sporting events were cancelled the day after President Harding died. There were two exceptions: the races at Saratoga and the tennis tournament at Sea Bright, New Jersey. Both these organizations took the position that the day of the funeral was the day to suspend activity. From Chicago, Commissioner Landis issued the following statement: "It is the sentiment throughout baseball that no games be played either today or on the day of the funeral of the late president, and as a further mark of respect to his memory, flags at all parks will be displayed at half-mast until after the burial."[5]

When baseball resumed play after Landis' edict, the Yankees were soundly trounced by the Indians, 15–7, before a bewildered 30,000 fans at the Stadium. Shawkey was ineffective and left early in the game as his record went to 13–7 while the Yankees' lead dropped to 12½ games.

The St. Louis Browns followed on the heals of the Indians to take on the league leaders at the Stadium in a four-game series. The Yankees won the first two, 9–8 and 5–3, while the Browns won the last two by scores of 12–10 and 4–3. In the first game, Ruth hit two more home runs, one in the first inning and the other in the sixth. Both were off the deliveries of right-hander Ray Kolp. It brought the Babe's total to 27 for the season. Waite Hoyt picked up his 11th victory against five losses in relief of Sam Jones.

Ruth continued his hot hitting in the second game of the series. Urban Shocker, the ace of the Browns' staff, was pitching a masterful game, leading the Yankees, 3–1, entering the bottom of the eighth inning. Shocker, using an assortment of fastballs, changeups, curves and spitters, found himself in his first serious jam. The bases were loaded with one out and Ruth coming to the plate. Shocker was faced with a real conundrum. Intentionally walk Ruth (which the Browns bench was urging him to do) and force in a run, making the score 3–2. That would leave the bases full with Elmer Smith the next batter, who was playing for the injured Bob Meusel. Smith, utility player, was not a scary threat but far from an automatic out. He batted over .300 for the season. The other option was to pitch to the dangerous Ruth, who had hit two home runs the day before and was closing in on a .400 batting average. Shocker opted to face Ruth. Maybe it was an ego thing. It turned out to be a bad decision. The Babe drove a fastball on the outside of the plate into the gap in left center for a bases-clearing double, putting the Yankees ahead, 4–3. Ruth would score later in the inning for the 5–3 victory. Bush started the game and was touched for three runs after the first three innings. It looked like a long day for the right-hander but he settled down and blanked the Browns over the last six innings for his team-leading 14th victory.

The man with the ominous nickname of "Bullet Joe" had a fascinating 17-year career in the major leagues. Future teammate Eddie Collins tagged him with the nickname when he saw a letter in the club house addressed to "Joe Bullet" Bush. He had the good fortune to pitch for some great teams and the misfortune to pitch for some very poor clubs. It all started in 1911 when Bush was discovered by Cliff Blankenship, the catcher and manager for the Missoula Highlanders, a minor league team in the Union Association (Class D). Blankenship signed the young right-hander when he saw him pitch for the amateur Brainerd Baseball Club. On April 25, 1912, Bush made his professional debut in a relief role in a game the Highlanders won, 16–9. The next day the 19-year-old made his debut as a starter. He went the distance, allowing only five hits, as the Highlanders won the game, 6–1. Blessed with a mighty fastball and good curve, Bush had the locals calling him a phenom. He turned in a fabulous season with a 29–12 record in 54 appearances, which helped the Highlanders capture the Union Association pennant.

Toward the end of the season, Connie Mack got wind that there was a young pitching star in Missoula, so he called Blankenship and offered the manager $750 for Bush and another $750 if he made good with his A's. Blankenship agreed, and Bush was on the next train to Philadelphia. Bush made his major league debut on September 30 at Shibe Park. The A's won the game, 11–10, defeating the New York Highlanders (soon to become the Yankees), but Bush pitched poorly. Mack, however, wasn't discouraged over Bush's performance. Down the line, in his own mind, Mack was comparing him to his ace, Chief Bender.

When Jack Coombs became ill in 1913, Mack looked for another starter to replace his ace. Bush was chosen. In 1913, pitching in 39 games, Bush made Mack look like a genius. He won 15 and lost only six, helping the A's win the American League pennant and the right to meet the New York Giants in the World Series. Heady stuff for a 20-year-old who the previous year was pitching in Missoula. The A's won the first game of the Series behind their ace, Bender, 6–4. The Giants evened the Series as Christy Mathewson blanked the A's, 3–0. At this point, Mack could have chosen "Boardwalk" Brown (17–11) or Byron Houck (14–6) who had more experience, but he didn't. He tapped Bush for

"It's the greatest Christmas present imaginable," commented Joe Bush after he was traded to the Yankees in 1921. "Bullet Joe" won 19 games for the Yankees in 1923 and another one in the World Series. But Huggins still didn't like Bush because of his strong suspicions the right-hander, like Mays, threw games in the 1921 and 1922 World Series. (Courtesy National Baseball Hall of Fame Library, Cooperstown, New York.)

the third game. Why? Author Norman L. Macht explains Mack's reasoning, "He knew his pitchers' temperaments. The twenty-year-old Bush had no nerves, He was not the type to tighten up if he was told in advance when he would pitch."[6] As Mack anticipated, Bush pitched a great game, beating the Giants, 8–2, allowing only five hits. He became an instant hero. Bender and Eddie Plank won the next two, and the A's captured the World Series.

The A's won the pennant again in 1914, featuring seven pitchers with 10 or more victories. Bush's record was 17–13 with an ERA of 3.06. This time the outcome of the World Series was a lot different and led to the breakup of the A's. The Boston Braves, in last place on July 19, won 60 of their last 76 games to finish 10½ games ahead of the second-place New York Giants. The "Miracle Braves" came into the World Series a decisive underdog but swept Mack's A's in convincing fashion. Bush lost the third game in which he literally threw it away. The score was tied, 2–2, in the bottom of the 12th when Hank Gowdy doubled off Bush. Les Mann ran for him. Pinch hitter Larry Gilbert was intentionally walked to set up a double play. Herbie Moran bunted right back to Bush, who had plenty of time to force Mann but threw it past Frank Baker at third, allowing Mann to score the winning run. The next day the Braves completed the sweep. Young Joe Bush was devastated and could have easily fled the city when he was offered an opportunity to join the Federal League in 1914. He was offered a two-year contract for $18,000 to join the St. Louis club. He turned it down.

Not long after the embarrassing Series, Mack began to sell off his star players, including most of the $100,000 infield of Eddie Collins, Frank "Home Run" Baker, Stuffy McInnis and Jack Barry. Left with few accomplished players, it was no surprise the A's went from the penthouse to the outhouse. For the next three years, the A's finished dead last. Over that span, Bush turned in an ugly 31–56 record, reflecting the lack of talent on the club. There was at least one bright moment. It came on August 26, 1916, against the Cleveland Indians. Bush pitched a no-hitter, narrowly missing a perfect game by walking the first man he faced in the game. What made his performance even more extraordinary was that the day before he had pitched against the same Indians and was hit hard. It reminds one of the Yankees' Don Larsen in the 1956 World Series against the Brooklyn Dodgers. Larsen started Game Two and blew a 6–0 lead, only to return in Game Five to pitch the only perfect game in World Series history.

In December 1917, Mack sent Bush, Amos Strunk and Wally Schang to the Boston Red Sox for Vern Gregg, Merlin Kopp, Pinch Thomas and $60,000. In one swift trade, Bush's fortunes were reversed. He went from an abysmal, last-place club to the 1918 pennant-winning Red Sox managed by Ed Barrow. Bush (15–15), along with Carl Mays (21–13), (Sam Jones 16–5) and Babe Ruth

(13–7), led the Red Sox to the pennant. All four pitchers plus Barrow would become members of the New York Yankees in the near future and help the club win three pennants and a World Series in 1923.

Boston beat the Cubs in the World Series, but it took six games. Ruth pitched the opener and shut out the Cubs, 1–0, on six hits. Bush was out-pitched in Game Two by lefty Tyler, 3–1, but came back in Game Four to relieve Ruth in the ninth and shut down the Cubs for the 3–2 win. Who could have known it was the Red Sox' last world championship until 2004?

The following year, 1919, Barrow experienced some tough luck. Bush came down with shoulder problems that prevented him from throwing his curveball. He pitched a total of nine innings during the season. Twenty-one-game winner Mays, who was as unpredictable as the weather, left the club in July. That's not all. Jones, who was 16–5 the previous year, underperformed, winning 12 but losing 20 games. The team ERA fell to seventh, so it was no surprise that the club finished in sixth place.

In 1920, Bush reported to spring training in Hot Springs, Arkansas, three weeks early. The extra time in Hot Springs must have helped because he pitched over 243 innings. He posted a mediocre 15–15 record, but the bloated ERA of 4.24 was still a clear sign Bullet Joe was not completely healed. He also added a new pitch to his repertoire, the forkball, which enabled him to extend his career.

Bush bounced back in 1921, winning 16 and losing nine games. His ERA improved to 3.50 but was still not nearly as good as his first year with the Red Sox when his earned run average was a nifty 2.11. Former Red Sox out-fielder Hugh Duffy was now the Boston manager, having replaced Barrow, who went to the Yankees. Duffy, a former outfielder and future Hall of Famer, could do no better than another fifth-place finish. Once again, Lady Luck shined down on Joe Bush when Yankee general manager, Barrow, made a blockbuster trade in December 1921. He shipped Roger Peckinpaugh, Jack Quinn, Bill Piercy and Rip Collins to Boston for Everett Scott, Joe Bush and Sam Jones. Bush was thrilled with the trade. "It's the greatest Christmas present imaginable," he said. "Then another good point is that I will have Babe Ruth with me instead of against me. That always makes a pitcher's life a happier one."[7] Bush and Jones joined their former Boston teammates, Mays, Pennock and Hoyt, along with Bob Shawkey to form a devastating rotation that would win the 1922 American League pennant. Bush turned in a career year (26–7), leading the American League with a .788 winning percentage. He pitched in over 255 innings with a 3.31 ERA. Only Ed Rommel had more wins with 27. Shawkey won 20 and Hoyt 19 as the Yankees' strong staff brought them their second pennant under Huggins. No one on the club drove in 100 runs during the season, a testament to the excellent pitching.

The victory celebration was short-lived, replaced by embarrassment when the New York Giants swept the Yankees in the World Series. Bush got the call from Huggins in the first and fifth games (Game Two ended in a tie) and lost both. In the opener, with the Yankees ahead, 2–0, entering the bottom of the eighth, Bush gave up four straight hits and was replaced by Hoyt. The Giants scored three runs to win the game. Huggins was later criticized by Ruppert for staying with Bush too long. The Yankees lost the next two games and were one game away from elimination.

Huggins choose Bush for the deciding game, and again he was spooked in the last half of the eighth. The Yankees were leading, 3–2, when Bush found himself with runners on second and third with two outs. Huggins ordered Bush to walk Ross Youngs, a left-handed hitter, in order to face right-handed hitting George Kelly. The hot-headed Bush vehemently objected, cursing at Huggins in the dugout loud enough to be heard throughout the press box and by many fans in box seats. A brooding Bush walked Youngs but served up a fat pitch to Kelly, who singled driving in two runs. The Giants added another and won the game, 5–3, and the Series.

This incident infuriated Huggins. Years later, he confessed to famed sportswriter Fred Lieb his deep hatred for Bush. "Any ballplayers that played for me on either the Cardinals or Yankees could come to me if he were in need and I would give him a helping hand. I make only two exceptions, Carl Mays and Joe Bush. If they were in the gutter, I'd kick them."[8] Huggins' deep hatred for the two pitchers was based on his strong suspicions that they threw games in the 1921 and 1922 World Series. Even though Landis investigated the allegations against Mays, nothing was found to incriminate him. No allegations were made against Bush. No doubt Huggins' baseball instincts raised strong doubts about Mays and Bush and, thus, his hatred for the two.

Back at the Commodore Hotel, Cap Huston, who never wanted Huggins as manager, was enraged at losing the second straight World Series. At the hotel bar, he went ballistic, screaming and yelling, knocking drinks over and claiming that Huggins had managed his last game. Huston's childish ranting fell on deaf ears as Ruppert later supported his manager, who he believed had done a good job winning two pennants. This feud set the stage for Ruppert's complete takeover of the Yankees in 1923.

Bush was the workhorse of the 1923 team, pitching almost 276 innings. He won 19, lost 15 and along with Shawkey, Jones, Hoyt, Mays and the new addition, Pennock, pitched the Yankees to their third consecutive pennant. The Yankees' dominant pitching staff led the league with a 3.62 ERA. They had one of the all-time deepest rotations with five starters recording 16 or more victories, a record at the time and later matched by the 1998 Atlanta

Braves of Greg Maddux (18–9), Tom Glavine (20–6), Denny Nagle (16–11), Kevin Millwood (17–8) and John Smoltz (17–3).

For the third consecutive year, the people of New York City were treated to a World Series in their own backyard. But 1923 brought two significant differences. The Yankees finally defeated McGraw and his Giants, and half the games were played at Yankee Stadium. Young Waite Hoyt started the first game for the Yankees but was relieved by Bush in the third after allowing four runs. The Yankees tied the game in the seventh but lost in the ninth when Casey Stengel legged out an inside-the-park home run off Bush. Three days later in Game Five at Yankee Stadium, Bush redeemed himself by beating the Giants, 8–1. He pitched brilliantly, allowing three hits (all to Irish Meusel, Bob's brother) to give the Yankees a 3–2 edge in the Series, which they clinched the next day. It was the last time Joe Bush pitched in a World Series game.

The following year, the Yankees finished second to the Washington Senators. Bush's record slipped to 17–16 and a 3.57 ERA. This mediocre showing, plus Huggins' desire to get rid of Bush because he posed a serious challenge to his authority, set the stage for a trade. In December, Barrow sent Bush, Milt Gaston and Joe Giard, two young pitchers, to the St. Louis Browns for one-time ace spitballer Urban Shocker. Bush pitched for St. Louis without distinction, finishing the season with a 14–14 mark and a fat 5.09 ERA. St. Louis finished third, well ahead of the sixth-place Yankees.

Without sufficient reason to keep him, the Browns traded Bush. Off he went to the Washington Senators for pitchers Tom Zachary and Win Ballou. Manager Bucky Harris was counting heavily on Bush to help win another pennant. The trade turned out to be a flop. Bush was 1–8 with the Senators with a bloated 6.69 ERA. Not yet 35 years of age and pitching in over 1,487 innings since his arm injury, the work had finally taken its toll. In June, the Senators gave Bush his unconditional release. Shortly after, he signed with the Pittsburgh Pirates in the National League. He spent the rest of the 1926 season with the Pirates, going 6–6 with a 3.01 ERA as Pittsburgh finished third in the pennant race. The following year Bush returned to the Pirates, but he didn't stay long as new manager Donie Bush needed to bolster his pitching staff to win a pennant, which he did. Once again, Bush was given his unconditional release. This time he landed with the New York Giants. His stay with McGraw was even shorter. By July 19, after a 1–1 record in three games, McGraw had seen enough and Bush was given his third unconditional release. Bush finished the season helping the Toledo Mud Hens of the International League, managed by none other than Casey Stengel, win the pennant and the Little World Series over the Buffalo Bisons.

In December 1927, Connie Mack, in a nostalgic mood, signed Bush to a contract with the A's where his career began inauspiciously in 1912. He finished the season with a 2–1 record and an ERA of 5.09 in a little over 35 innings. It spelled the end of his long major league career. It was not, however, the end of baseball for Bush. For two years he was the player/manager for the Allentown team in the Eastern League, winning the championship in 1930 and finishing fifth the following year. Bush finally called it quits in 1932 after pitching for a semi-pro club in New York City.

The round trip had taken Bush 17 years to complete. On the journey, he won 196 games and lost 184 with a 3.51 earned run average in well over 3,000 innings. He helped win five pennants, two with the A's, one with the Red Sox and two with the Yankees. The 1913 A's, 1918 Red Sox and the 1923 Yankees were all world champions. Bush pitched in nine games in five different Series. Granted his 2–5 record is not noteworthy, but a 2.67 ERA is significant and may attest to poor run support. It was a respectable career, not Hall of Fame caliber, but one that was jam-packed with accomplishments and a myriad of memories. Joe Bush died in Fort Lauderdale, Florida, on November 1, 1974, at age 81.

The Browns won the next two games from the Yankees, 12–10 in a slugfest and 4–3 in a squeaker. Eight pitchers were used in the 12–10 fiasco, and 30 hits were collected in a game that lasted 2 hours and 27 minutes, a lifetime in 1923. It reminds one of Casey Stengel's famous line when he was managing the Mets—"Can't anyone here play this game?" In spite of the two losses, the Yankees still had a comfortable 12-game lead over the Indians.

In South Bend, Indiana, Notre Dame head football coach Knute Rockne made a shocking announcement that his coaching staff would include a dancing instructor. Yes, a dancing instructor. Each day the backfield would devote time to "aesthetic dancing," as it was called. Apparently, the purpose of the dance instruction was to develop a sense of rhythm that was important to some of the shift plays that Rockne was devising. Maybe there was something to the dancing. Notre Dame opened the season with a 74–0 trouncing of Kalamazoo ... or maybe it was the lack of competition. We will never know.

Ty Cobb brought his Tigers into Yankee Stadium for the second time and like the previous trip, split the series. Joe Bush and Waite Hoyt were responsible for all four decisions, each winning and losing a game. Ruth had a wonderful series, going 7-for-14 with two home runs, his 28th and 29th. He finally caught Cy Williams of the Philadelphia Phillies, tying him for the major league home run title. The two sluggers would battle all season and ironically end up at 41 home runs apiece. Ruth would eventually run away with the American League home run title, beating another Williams (Ken) from the St. Louis Browns, 41 to 29.

Ruth, wielding a hot bat all season, caught up with and actually passed Harry Heilmann during the race for the batting title. Heilmann was idle in the last game of the series with a "wrenched" arm, the result of trying to throw out a runner. It wasn't much of a lead at .0001. Ruth's average was .3939 and Heilmann's .3938.

Maybe the "Crawford Bat" had something to do with Ruth's hitting surge. American League president Ban Johnson might have had some suspicions because he ordered Ruth to stop using the specially constructed bat that was being manufactured by Sam Crawford, the former Detroit Tiger outfielder and future Hall of Fame member. Crawford was in the business of manufacturing baseball bats. Actually, Crawford had invented the bat called "the Betsy Bingle." The Crawford model consisted of four pieces of wood glued together. The normal bat was formed from one piece of wood using a lathe. Supposedly, the Crawford bat was stronger but more expensive, selling for eight dollars, four times the normal price.

Ruth was comfortable hitting with the Betsy Bingle and obviously successful. Like most ballplayers, he probably was superstitious and hated to give it up. Huggins quickly came to Ruth's defense, unfamiliar territory for the manager. Huggins filed an appeal claiming, "I can see no reason why Johnson should bar the Crawford model bat. The rules simply state that the bat must be sound, made entirely of hard wood and conform to certain dimensions. The new bat used by Ruth is made of hard wood and is perfectly round. The rules do not state that the bat be made out of one piece of wood. Ruth's bat is not a trick bat, but simply an improvement over the old style. A four-piece bat is much stronger than a one-piece affair and of course has more driving power."[9]

Johnson denied Huggins' appeal. The explanation was even sillier than the ruling. The problem, according to the league office, was with the glue. Supposedly, the velocity of the ball off the bat was enhanced by the glue. If allowed, then other substances would have to be permitted. According to Johnson, the bat was illegal, just like the emery or the shine ball. It was all much ado about nothing as Ruth continued his torrid pace and put more distance between himself and Heilmann for the batting crown. The entire brouhaha does raise an interesting question: how did Johnson and the league determine that the glue increased the velocity of the ball off the bat?

Major league baseball was put on hold for a day during the Tigers' series when the body of Harding was placed in a vault in the Marion Cemetery in Marion, Ohio. The funeral cortege was packed with dignitaries—President Calvin Coolidge, the Chief Justice, senators, representatives, governors, generals, admirals and many greats and near-greats were all in attendance. At Mrs. Harding's insistence, however, the requiem for her late husband was absent of any appearance of pomp and ostentation. She wanted a simple procession; no spectacle. The widow consented to only a small band of soldiers, sailors and marines to accompany the metal casket on its journey to the vault. Guns boomed and "Taps" was played in a parting salute to President Harding.

When the series ended, Cobb and his Tigers were still mired in fourth place behind the St. Louis Browns. Cobb, one of the all-time great players, a true immortal, never made it as a manager. He was too explosive, too demanding and fiercely competitive—traits that make an exceptional ballplayer but not necessarily a good field manager. In fairness to Cobb, he never wanted to manage the Detroit Tigers or any club for that matter. He didn't want the responsibility and thought it would hurt his hitting. But in 1921, he was pressured to take the job even after refusing several times. He even went so far as to recommend Kid Gleason. Tigers ownership nixed the suggestion and continued pressing Cobb to take the job. When Cobb heard that Pants Rowland might be the next manager, he had to reconsider. Cobb didn't like Rowland because he never played in the major leagues. Cobb felt he was a phony.

After continued pressure, Cobb relented and signed a contract to become a player/manager with the Tigers. His competitive nature was one of the big reasons Cobb finally decided to take the job. He had seen his longtime rival, Tris Speaker, lead his club as player/manager, to a championship in the 1920 World Series. He wanted to do the same.

Cobb's first year as a manager was a disappointment even as he rode his players hard. In spring training, he prohibited golf and ordered practices on Sunday, a move that was not very popular with his players. He singled out Bobby Veach, an exceptional ballplayer with a lifetime .310 batting average, for ridicule, claiming he had no guts and was a bush leaguer. By the end of the season, rumors were circulating that the team might strike. The Tigers finished with a 71–82 (.464) record and a sixth-place finish. In 1922, the Tigers improved to 79–75 (.513) and a third-place finish. His players were still an unhappy lot. The tongue lashings he handed out were tiring. His ranting was over the top. He even went so far as to imply the owners failed to supply him with quality talent. It was Ty Cobb being Ty Cobb.

The 1923 season was Cobb's best as a Detroit manager. His club finished second with a record of 83–71 (.539) but a distant 16 games back of the Yankees. One reason for the solid season was the acquisition of minor leaguer Heinie Manush, a .376 hitter with Omaha. Also, Cobb's aggressive play and crazy antics on the field and in the dugout finally got his club fired up. The aroused Tigers played well over .600 ball during the last third of the season.

Cobb biographer Al Stump commented, "The 1923 season went into the records as the Georgian's finest managerial accomplishment, the product of his willpower, seizing opportunities, goading his men, and playing tricks. He had no right whatever to second place."[10]

After the 1923 season, Ty Cobb's career as a Tiger manager headed south. The fights with owner Frank Navin became more bitter and acrimonious, often clashing over player needs. His health became an issue when he experienced stomach pains. His excessive drinking and smoking habits remained unchanged and finally caught up with him. The Tigers finished third in 1924.

In 1925, the Tigers were a virtual hitting machine, scoring 903 runs, the best in the league. Their pitching was a disaster with a team ERA of 4.61. Fans would often boo Cobb at Navin Field, a constant reminder he had yet to win a pennant. The Tigers finished fourth in 1925, 16½ games behind the pennant-winning Washington Senators. Dutch Leonard, a left-handed pitcher, who didn't get along with Cobb, couldn't take his abuse any longer and quit the team. An angry and revengeful Cobb sold Leonard to Vernon in the Pacific Coast League. A vindictive Leonard would later seek retaliation.

Cobb began 1926 as he had in previous years, taunting and riding his players unmercifully. Fans who were frustrated were calling for his firing. His ability to manage was widely questioned. The season ended once again without a Tiger pennant. The team finished in sixth place, the same position as in 1921 when Cobb first began managing.

In early November, shock waves reverberated within the Tiger's organization when Cobb handed in his resignation claiming he was "bone-tired." The truth was more complicated. Fingers were pointed. And the blame game began. Navin blamed Cobb for demoralizing the team. Cobb blamed Navin for not getting the talent he needed to win.

Whoever was to blame was a moot point. Cobb was out as the Detroit Tigers manager after six tumultuous years. His managerial record stood at 479–444 (.519), a mediocre showing at best, but not to Cobb, who defended his record to anyone who would listen. "In no way do I consider myself a failure as a manager. I took over a seventh-place club in 1921 and, with one exception, all my clubs won more games than they lost. We were in the first division four times."[11] All true, but what Navin and the Tigers fans wanted was a world championship, and that they didn't get.

Soon after Cobb's departure, Cleveland manager Tris Speaker abruptly resigned. Then the real thunderbolt hit when Landis revealed he had given both managers permission to resign because of accusations they fixed and bet on a game between the Tigers and Indians on September 25, 1919. The accusation was based on a letter made public by Dutch Leonard, the player Cobb had traded, claiming he met with Cobb, Speaker and Cleveland outfielder Smokey Joe Wood to fix the game so the Tigers would win and finish in third place to collect a share of the World Series money. It was payback time for the disgruntled Leonard. Landis, fully aware that baseball was still recovering from the 1919 World Series scandal, began his investigation. On December 20, he released a 100-page report to the press that acquitted both Cobb and Speaker. Since both men were back in the good graces of baseball, they were free to make any deal with another club. Cobb joined Connie Mack's Athletics and Speaker went to the Washington Senators.

It wasn't long after the Betsy Bingle episode when St. Louis Browns slugger Ken Williams (second to Ruth in home runs) was caught by umpire George Hildebrand using a plugged bat. Washington Senators manager Donie Bush was clearly upset, claiming he would protest every game the Browns won where Williams used the bat. Bush's argument was based on the fact that Williams' bat was made of more than one piece of wood, making it illegal.

Williams's explanation requires one giant leap of faith to accept. He claimed he had the bat custom-made, but when he received it, the bat felt a bit too heavy, so he bored a hole in the middle and plugged it up at the end. Somehow Bush got possession of the bat "accidentally" and that's how he knew about it. Shades of Sammy Sosa. President Harry Truman once said, "There is nothing new, just history you don't know," or something like that.

The Yankees' home stand against the western clubs was a disappointment. They played under .500, winning seven and losing eight. They split four games with the White Sox, lost two of three to Cleveland and split four each with the Browns and Tigers. At the start of the home stand, the Yankees had a 14½-game lead over the Indians. Now about to embark on their final swing out west, the Yankees lead had slipped to 12 games. Huggins wasn't overly concerned, but the pitching did get beat up in some of the games, especially Bob Shawkey. He was chased early in the 15–7 Cleveland win and then again in the 12–10 game against the Browns.

On the way to St. Louis, the Yankees stopped off at Cincinnati and played Indianapolis for two exhibition games. They lost both, but that was not important. The fans came to see the Yankees and the Babe. Ruth put on a one-man show for them, belting three home runs and pitching in one of the games. Eighty-six years later, it's hard to fathom why a team would play exhibition games and risk injury to valuable players. No doubt the answer is money, gate receipts. But why Huggins would allow Ruth to pitch and possibly injure his arm doesn't make much sense.

In St. Louis, the Yankees took two of three from the Browns. Ruth continued his hot hitting, sans the Betsy Bingle, with a 4-for-8 series, including his league-leading 30th and 31st home runs. He also widened his lead ever so slightly over Heilmann for the batting title. Ruth was now at .396 to

Heilmann's .394. Meusel and Dugan teamed up to win the second game of the series, 3–1. Meusel doubled in two runs in the fourth. Dugan went 2-for-4 and scored twice, one an insurance run after a one-out double in the ninth. The losing pitcher for the Browns was left-hander Dave Danforth. This was Danforth's first game since he was fined and suspended for tampering with the ball in a game against the Philadelphia Athletics. Home plate umpire Billy Evans watched Danforth's every pitch like a hawk, looking for something illegal. Nothing was found, but a total of 58 baseballs were tossed out of the game under the guise of being suspicious. Oh, and it cost the Browns $116 in baseballs to allow Danforth to pitch—and lose.

The Yankees moved on to the Windy City to face the White Sox, boasting a 12½-game lead over the Indians. Ruth was so zoned in at the plate, he could do nothing wrong. He was seeing the ball well, and everything he hit was right on the nose. In the first game, he went 3-for-3 to raise his league-leading average to a phenomenal .401, eight points ahead of Heilmann. But that wasn't the best part of his day. The Yankees were trailing 5–3 in the top of the ninth with two out, Dugan on first and Schang on third. Ruth strolled to the plate. On the first pitch Dugan stole second. White Sox manager Kid Gleason, instead of walking Ruth, elected to pitch to the hottest hitter in baseball. Hindsight is always 20–20, but this situation clearly called for an intentional walk. In fact, Huggins could have been criticized for allowing Dugan to steal, thus giving the opposition the chance to walk the Babe. Maybe Dugan stole on his own; if so, then Huggins should have reprimanded him. For whatever reason, Gleason elected to have Mike Cvengros pitch to Ruth. Both manager and pitcher must have short memories. Back on May 22, the Babe destroyed the little lefty in a similar situation. The Yankees and White Sox were tied at 1–1 in the 15th inning with Dugan on first. Ruth smashed a Cvengros delivery and parked it in the right-field bleachers for the victory.

Back to the game at hand. Cvengros got ahead of Ruth, one and two. On the next pitch, the Babe connected for his 32nd of the season. It was bye, bye baby, a 6–5 lead, and the Yankees held on to win. Earlier in the game, Ruth had doubled, driving in two runs, so for the day he contributed five RBIs.

Hoyt lost the second game to the White Sox, 4–3, but that was the least of Huggins's concerns. Hoyt was tossed out of the game in the eighth by umpire Brick Owens whom he tried to assault when he violently objected to a safe call at the plate. In his rage, Hoyt had to be restrained by Scott, Dugan and Schang. League president Ban Johnson came down hard on Hoyt and suspended him indefinitely. In the first inning, sloppy base running by Ruth cost the Yankees at least one run. He tried to make amends in the third by launching a long drive to deep right field that looked like a sure home run until the notorious Chicago winds swept in and dumped the ball into right fielder Harry Hooper's glove as he stood with his back against the bleacher wall. The Yankees won the last game trouncing the White Sox, 16–5. Pennock picked up the easy victory, his 13th of the season.

After Chicago, the Yankees headed to Detroit with a 13-game lead over the Indians. The two leading hitters in the American League were now matched against each other. When the series ended, the Tigers had taken two of three, but Ruth outhit his rival, going 3-for-9 while Heilmann went 3-for-11. The Babe was hitting at a torrid .400 clip. Heilmann was not far behind with a .388 mark. The Yankees lost the first two games, 6–3 and 2–1. Pennock saved New York from being swept by taming the Tigers 7–1 in the finale. His record stood at 14–6.

During the Detroit series, baseball fans around the country once again had their attention divided between rooting for their home teams and reading about shocking allegations of a new gambling scandal. Only four years since the notorious 1919 Black Sox scandal, and now another popped up, this time in the National League involving two Cincinnati players. It all began when *Collyer's Eye*, a weekly sporting newspaper, published an article claiming two Cincinnati players were approached by a gambling syndicate to throw games against the New York Giants. According to the article, third baseman Sammy Bohne and left-fielder Pat Duncan were offered $15,000 each. Supposedly, there was a third player involved, but his name was never revealed.

The article caused a huge stir in the press with the fans and between National League president John A. Heydler and Bert Collyer, publisher of the weekly. Heydler wasted little time gathering together the Cincinnati newspaper men covering the series with Bohne and Duncan to conduct a hearing. Both players denied the story; they were never approached directly or indirectly. After the hearing, Heydler declared the charges to be unfounded. He went further and advised the players and the Cincinnati club to take legal action against *Collyer's Eye*. The player's took Heydler's advice and filed a law suit in the United States District Court in Chicago for damages of $50,000 each against Collyer's Publishing Company.

This is when Bert Collyer jumped into action. He sent a telegram to Commissioner Landis calling for a full investigation. He further pointed out that his newspaper would not print a story such as this one without verification. Not backing down one iota, Collyer attacked Heydler personally, claiming he was "frantic" and hiding behind a group of reporters to give him "courage" to threaten him. Collyer also let it be known that Heydler was quick to dismiss his paper's charges in 1919 of the World Series scandal as "fake." Needless to say, his reporting proved true.

Collyer sent his lawyer, Barrett O'Hara, the former lieutenant governor of Illinois, to confer with Landis. The commissioner agreed to an investigation. A week later, he made his pronouncement. Landis found Bohne and Duncan beyond reproach. He cleared both men and even praised their hard work and integrity. He said he had no doubts right from the beginning of the investigation. He also urged the players to sue *Collyer's Eye* so as to vindicate their names and that of baseball. The commissioner further took a swipe at the newspaper, claiming the charges were made out of "malice" and with no foundation.

Five years later a Chicago jury heard the libel case, and it appeared to vindicate Bohne and Duncan. The operative word is appeared. Federal Judge Walter C. Lindley awarded each player $50 in damages against *Collyer's Eye*. Fifty dollars was a long way from $50,000. Counsel for the players made it clear Bohne and Duncan were not out to enrich themselves, just to clear their names. Of course, that raises the question, why sue for $50,000?

The Yankees ended their western road trip with a final stop at Cleveland. It was the last time Speaker and the Indians would face the Yankees at home and try to put a dent in their 13-game lead. The Indians made a valiant effort, winning the first two games, but took a genuine beating in the final contest. With less than a third of the season remaining, time was running out. It was an uphill battle, and Speaker and the players knew it.

The second game of the series was the most exciting. The Indians came from behind before an overflow crowd of 25,000 to edge the Yankees, 4–3. Entering the ninth, Joe Bush was holding on to a 3–1 lead when the Indians erupted for two runs on three singles and a double by Speaker that barely missed being a home run. Huggins took out Bush with runners on first and second and two out, replacing him with Herb Pennock. The left-hander walked Rube Lutzke to set up a force at any base or, with some luck, a double play. Joe Connolly hit for Frank Brower and grounded to Ward who threw home for the second out. Schang in turn fired to first to try and complete the double play, but the ball sailed over Pipp's head into right field. That was the ball game, a tough loss for the Yankees and an even more difficult defeat for Schang to accept since he was considered a great defensive catcher with a strong arm.

Wally Schang was born August 22, 1889, in South Wales, New York, to parents Frank and Mary. Wally was one of nine children who helped work the 170-acre dairy farm in upstate New York. The hours were long and the chores hard for Wally as it was for many farm boys of that era. These demands didn't discourage the young boy from his interest in baseball, or his brothers for that matter. In fact, the Schang family possessed a strong love for the game. Frank was a catcher for the local town team. Bob, Wally's older brother, caught for three years in the National League with Pittsburgh, New York and St. Louis. Unlike Wally, Bob was a weak hitter, attesting to his .188 career batting average. Another brother, Quiren, didn't make the major leagues but caught for 20 years as a semi-pro.

With a family of baseball players, it was not surprising that Schang was keenly interested in the game at an early age. Later in life he would recall, "From the moment I crawled out of bed my thoughts had to do with baseball, with the result that I raced the poor nag to the creamery every morning. I wanted to get my job over as early as possible so I could drive back home, walk the two miles to the school and get in forty-five minutes to an hour of baseball before the bell called us to our studies."[12]

During his high school days, Schang played semi-pro ball and developed a reputation as one of the area's best players. He could hit, was a solid catcher and was capable of playing other positions. Like his father and brothers, Schang favored catching. It wasn't long before someone with an eye for talent discovered Schang. That someone was none other than George Stallings, the future manager of the Boston Braves. In 1914, Stallings would take the Braves from last place in the middle of the season to win the pennant by 10½ games. In one of the greatest upsets in World Series history, his Braves swept Connie Mack's A's powerhouse club with the $100,000 infield. It earned Stallings the nickname "The Miracle Man."

At the time Stallings signed Schang, he was the manager of the Buffalo Bisons in the International League. After Schang had an excellent season at Buffalo, many of the major league teams courted the 23-year-old switch-hitter. Connie Mack landed him. In 1913, the inexperienced farm boy joined the A's and split the catching duties with Jack Lapp as the A's won the pennant. Schang batted .266, but more importantly, he handled the pitching staff that included two future Hall of Famers, Eddie Plank and Chief Bender, with aplomb, no small feat for a young kid. He also met up with Joe Bush and Bob Shawkey, which would serve him well in the future.

In the World Series against the New York Giants, which the A's won in five games, Schang was outstanding. He played like a seasoned veteran, batting .357 and driving in seven runs. His World Series paycheck was over $3,200, a tidy sum in 1913.

The A's won the pennant again in 1914 with a 99–53 record, making it three out of the previous four years. Schang continued to mature and improve his offensive numbers. He led all American League catchers with a .287 batting average, plus extra-base hits (22), home runs (3), a slugging percentage of .404 and 45 RBIs. He also committed 30 errors, but that was mostly the result of a broken thumb he struggled with most of the season.

The 1914 World Series against the Boston Braves was a huge disappointment for the A's as they lost in four games. Dick Rudolph and Bill James each had career years for the Braves during the season. Rudolph was 26–10 and James 26–7. Both continued their extraordinary pitching in the Series. Except for Chief Bender, who was manhandled in the first game, the rest of the A's pitching staff pitched admirably. It was the offense that performed poorly with a team batting average of .172. Schang, who had a great World Series the previous year, was a huge disappointment. He started all four games and batted a paltry .167. In fairness to Schang, he had a lot of company and some credit must go to the Braves pitching.

After the shocking World Series loss, Mack began dismantling his club. Eddie Plank, Chief Bender, Frank Baker and Eddie Collins all departed. They were the lucky ones. Schang remained with the A's for the next three years, playing on some of the worst teams in the game's history. Considering how difficult and demoralizing it must have been to perform at a high level every day behind the plate for a perennial last place club, Schang acquitted himself well. Over that span, his batting average was a respectable .266. On September 8, 1916, he became the first player to hit a home run from each side of the plate in the same game.

After the 1917 season, Schang's misery finally ended when he was traded to the Boston Red Sox along with Joe Bush and Amos Strunk. With the Red Sox, Schang shared the catching duties with Sam Agnew, a weak hitter who would be sold to the Senators the following year. It was Ed Barrow's first year at the helm of the Red Sox. He and Schang would later reunite with the Yankees.

Schang once again found himself in a World Series as the Red Sox won the pennant by 2½ games over the Cleveland Indians in a season cut short by World War I. It was an interesting and unusual Series. Boston beat the Chicago Cubs in six games. In order to reduce the use of trains for the war effort, the first three games were scheduled for Chicago, the next four in Boston. The Cubs also switched their games to Comiskey Park with a larger seating capacity than Wrigley Field.

In the opener, Babe Ruth defeated Hippo Vaughn, 1–0, adding nine more shutout innings to the 13 he completed in 1916. He would return in Game Four to hurl another 7⅔ innings for a total of 29⅔, a record that would stand until 1961 when New York Yankee great Whitey Ford passed the Babe's record in the third inning of the fourth game against the Cincinnati Reds. Ford's scoreless innings streak in World Series play ended at 33⅔ in 1962.

Schang had a marvelous Series, leading Boston with a .444 batting average. His real value, however, was in handling the pitching rotation of Ruth (2–0), Carl Mays (2–0), Joe Bush (0–1) and Sam Jones (0–1), a staff, except for Ruth, he would continue to catch in the near future with the Yankees. His skill in calling the game was especially important during this Series because all the games were close, and they required a battery that was in complete sync.

During the next two years, the Red Sox would finish well out of the pennant race even though Schang did an outstanding job behind the plate and showed consistency with the bat. In 1919, his average was .306 with a stellar .436 on-base percentage. In 1920, the switch-hitter almost duplicated the numbers, batting .305 with another high OBP of .413. Lady Luck touched Schang one more time when, in late December, he was traded to the New York Yankees along with Waite Hoyt, Harry Harper and Mike McNally for Muddy Ruel, Del Pratt, Sammy Vick and Hank Thormahlen. Ed Barrow, the Yankees general manager and former field manager for the Red Sox, was instrumental in putting together the trade. Schang, Hoyt and McNally all played for Barrow, who was a shrewd trader. Barrow was impressed with

Catcher Wally Schang, troubled most of the 1923 season with a nagging groin injury, still managed to bat .276. In the Fall Classic, however, he caught all six games and batted .318 to help the Yankees win their first World Series championship. During his 19-year career, Schang had the privilege of catching six Hall of Fame pitchers: Herb Pennock, Eddie Plank, Chief Bender, Babe Ruth, Waite Hoyt and Lefty Grove. (Courtesy National Baseball Hall of Fame Library, Cooperstown, New York.)

Schang's catching skills and physical strength. After a Boston victory, when he was the manager, a jubilant Schang picked up the two-hundred-pound Barrow and carried him around the clubhouse.

With Ruel now in Boston, Schang took over the catching duties for the Yankees as they won three consecutive pennants. In 1921 and 1922, Wally Schang was a consistent offensive threat in a star-studded lineup. In 1921, he batted .316 with 30 doubles and an OBP of .428. In 1922 he hit .319 with a .405 OBP. The Yankees lost both World Series to the Giants. In the '21 Series, catching all eight games, he batted a respectable .286. In the '22 Series, like the rest of the team, he batted a miserable .188. This was the Series Ruth hit an unbelievable .118 and Bush and Mays lost three of the four games, which Huggins would always hold against them.

In 1923, Schang was troubled most of the season with a nagging groin injury that accounted for his sub-par performance. He played in only 84 games and batted .276 with a .360 OBP, numbers considerably lower than his previous two seasons. But the sturdy catcher redeemed himself in the World Series, which the Yankees won in six games for their first championship. He caught all six games and batted .318 as New York finally defeated McGraw and the Giants. It would be the last time Schang appeared in a Fall Classic. In all. he took part in six World Series and was on the winning side three times. A model of consistency, Schang was 27-for-94 in the six World Series for a .287 average, three percentage points higher than his lifetime average of .284 over 19 years.

Schang remained with the Yankees for the next two years, but by 1925, his skills and production had slipped. Before the 1926 season began, Schang was traded to the St. Louis Browns for left-handed pitcher George Mogridge and cash. At age 37, Schang was determined to prove he could still be a productive player. Three of the four years he was with the Browns Schang proved he was the same player that contributed to three world championships in Philadelphia, Boston and New York.

In 1926, he enjoyed one of his best seasons, batting a career-high .330 with a .405 OBP and a .516 slugging percentage in 103 games. In 97 games in 1927, he hit .318 with a .414 OBP, and the following year his average dipped to .286, but he still had the knack of getting on base with a high .448 OBP. By 1929, Schang's age—he was now 40—and all the years of brutal beatings behind the plate were catching up to him. He batted a weak .237 but still managed to get on base (OBP .424) due to 74 walks. Surprisingly, Schang led all catchers with a .998 fielding average for the first and only time in his career.

Good fortune continued to follow Schang when at the end of the 1929 season, the Browns sold him to the A's, the team he started with in 1913. With the great Mickey Cochrane the full-time catcher for the A's, Schang logged very little playing time. He appeared in only 45 games, mainly to give Cochrane a rest. The A's won the pennant, but Schang did not appear in the World Series against the St. Louis Cardinals. The following year, he ended his long major league career with the Detroit Tigers in another part-time role.

Wally Schang enjoyed 19 years in the American League, played on seven pennant winners and caught in six different World Series. His lifetime batting average was a solid and consistent .284. He had the privilege of catching six Hall of Fame pitchers: Herb Pennock, Eddie Plank, Chief Bender, Babe

Ruth, Waite Hoyt and Lefty Grove. Not too shabby a rotation and not too many catchers can make that claim. Never a serious candidate for the Hall of Fame, nonetheless, he ranks as one of the best all-around backstops of his era.

In the 1920's and 30's, it was not uncommon for professional ballplayers who ended their major league careers to swallow their pride and continue playing ball in the minor leagues. In most cases, it was an economic necessity, especially during the Great Depression. They had few skills with which to earn a living. Baseball was all they knew, most coming from farms with little education. Playing baseball was their love and life. Schang was no different.

For the next 11 years, Wally bounced around the minor leagues with such colorfully named teams as the Chattanooga Lookouts, the Shreveport Sports and the Joplin Miners. By 1936 he was back in the major leagues as a coach for the Cleveland Indians, rooming with an 18-year-old rookie sensation named Bob Feller and instructing him in the fine points of the game. Schang finally left the baseball diamond for good in 1942 after playing for Owensboro in the Kitty League at age 52.

Wally Schang and his wife retired to Dixon, Missouri, to live in a modest house, enjoying the simple life. He would often regale the locals with stories of his playing days and teammates. One of the locals was a young boy named Skip Goforth. His father, Ralph, was the editor/publisher of the *Dixon Pilot*. Skip remembered Schang visiting his father at the printing office just to chat about old times. Skip recalls, "Wally was hyper and full of energy, balding, with a big toothy smile, and talked with a raspy voice in a short, gruff manner.... He would say 'I remember Ty Cobb.... Son of a bitch would sharpen his cleats so he could get me sliden' into home!' He had a peck of stories about 'the Babe,' usually featuring drinking, hot dogs, train rides, and whore houses. Mom usually sent me to the drugstore for a milkshake when Wally talked about 'the Babe.'"[13]

Wally Schang died in St. Louis, Missouri, at age 75. He was buried in Dixon Cemetery.

7

Third Straight Pennant

The Yankees were back home at the Stadium after a mediocre western road trip where they played .500 baseball, winning six and losing the same number. When New York left for St. Louis on August 13, they had been 12 games ahead of the Indians, and they maintained that lead after the four-city trip. With a month remaining in the season, time was now in the Yankees' favor. If the Indians were to have any hope of catching New York, they would have to play extraordinarily well, and at the same time have the Yankees collapse. Both were unlikely events.

The *New York Times* took it one step further, hinting that the pennant race was all but over and the current home stand was really to give the Yankees intensive workouts for the upcoming World Series. Maybe so, but who could ever forget the 1914 Boston Braves? As Yogi Berra would say years later, "It ain't over til it's over." Fan interest, however, had shifted to the pennant race in the National League where the Giants were battling Cincinnati and Pittsburgh. At the time, the Giants had a four-game lead over the Reds.

All the talk aside, the Yankees went out and won the first three games from the Senators at the Stadium but lost the finale at Washington (another quirk in the schedule). Ruth did it all in the first game with a perfect 3-for-3 day as the Yankees won, 4–3. Pennock picked up his 15th victory. Ruth's single in the first inning paved the way for the Yankees' first run. In the third, he doubled to right, tying the score. In the sixth, Meusel drove him home with the winning run. Ruth also threw out Joe Judge trying to stretch a single into a double. The only thing Ruth failed to do was hit a home run for the fans. It's interesting to note, the losing pitcher for the Senators, Tom Zachary, was the pitcher who coughed up Ruth's record 60th in 1927. Zachary kept the ball in the park this game.

Sam Jones notched his 16th win as the Yankees beat Washington, 4–2, in the second game. Poor Ruth. The man had set the bar so high he couldn't possibility live up to the fans' expectations. He went 0-for-3, striking out twice, which ignited the fans who hooted and howled at the Babe. The *New York Times* even ran the sub-head, "Ruth has off day at bat." Even DiMaggio, Mantle and Gehrig didn't get that much scrutiny. Every day it was a challenge for Ruth to try and satisfy the fans' high expectations. The man who was leading the league in both batting (.401) and home runs (32) goes hitless and the whole world knows about it. Ruth was so popular and loved (in spite of a few boos) by the fans throughout his fabulous career that, whatever he did, insignificant as it might be on or off the field, was magnified for all to see. But then again, he wallowed in the attention. He welcomed and adored the crowds, especially kids.

There are many stories about Babe Ruth visiting sick kids in hospitals, cheering them up and promising to hit a home run his next game. Some of the stories are true, many are not or are greatly exaggerated. The most famous of these stories is the one involving Johnny Sylvester, an 11-year-old living in Essex Fells, New Jersey, a wealthy suburban town a short distance from the author's home. Baseball stories, especially those that happened as far back as the early 1900's, have a tendency over the years to be embellished. The Sylvester story is one of them, that is, until author Brian Sobel interviewed the 70-year-old Sylvester in 1986 to get the facts.

It started during the summer of 1926 when Sylvester was injured riding a horse. The injury resulted in osteomyelitis that hospitalized the young boy. Sylvester's father was an executive at the National City Company of New York, a securities underwriting company. Through his connections, the Cardinals and Yankees, who were preparing for the World Series, were contacted and told of Johnny's plight. Each team sent autographed baseballs to the sick boy. The Yankees ball contained a message from the Babe that said he would hit a home run for the kid in Wednesday's game, the fourth game of the Series in St. Louis. True to his word, Ruth didn't just hit one round-tripper, he hit three, which was a record until Reggie Jackson accomplished the feat with three in 1977 on three consecutive pitches.

After the Series, which the Yankees lost, Sylvester was at home still recuperating when he recalled Ruth's unexpected visit. "I had no idea Ruth was going to come out to my house. I can remember his face most of all as he stooped to get his tremendous body through the door of my bedroom. The really amusing part of the story is at that time we had a maid, and she and my mother were in my room when we heard a knock on the front door. She went down to answer and came back up to say a man named Babe Ruth wanted to see me. She had no idea who Ruth was, and, of course, you can imagine my reaction"![1]

Ruth stayed for about a half-hour, and he and Sylvester talked mostly about baseball. The following year Johnny was invited to opening day at the Stadium and had his picture taken with Ruth, Gehrig and some of the other Yankees. This event and Ruth's visit to the boy's home created a vast amount of publicity in the United States and Europe.

Sylvester recuperated and the years passed as the young man grew into adulthood. Then in 1947, Ruth was dying of cancer when the *New York Daily News* arranged for the now 32-year-old Sylvester to visit the Babe at his home. It was payback time. When Sylvester arrived at Ruth's home, the Babe was in his pajamas and bathrobe, gaunt and a shell of himself when the two came face to face. They chatted for awhile and Sylvester thanked him one last time for his visit in 1926. Sylvester said goodbye, left Ruth's home and never saw the man again—a true story from the man who lived an unforgettable dream.

Waite Hoyt won game three, 6–1. It was his first start since his 10-day suspension by American League president Ban Johnson for attacking umpire Brick Owens. The long layoff helped Hoyt as he scattered three hits for his 13th win. The heart of the Yankees order—Ruth, Pipp and Meusel—went 6-for-12, including a double by Meusel, a triple by Ruth and a home run by Pipp. The Yankees increased their lead over Cleveland to 13½ games.

The last game of the series was played at Griffith Stadium in Washington D.C., where in 1910 William Howard Taft became the first president to throw out the ceremonial first pitch on opening day of the season. Perhaps Taft should have started the game for the Yankees because Joe Bush was smacked around for 10 hits and seven runs as the Senators broke their seven-game losing streak by a score of 7–2. It was only their fifth win against the Yankees in 21 games. This dominance over weak teams became a hallmark of future Yankee clubs—play even with the tougher teams and beat up on the weaklings. It was a formula that led to many pennants, which eventually led to all those World Series championships and ultimately the unparalleled Yankees dynasty.

Everett Scott had a good day at the plate, accounting for three of the Yankees' seven hits. He also drove in a run in the losing cause. Not known for his bat, Scott was a slick-fielding shortstop who combined with Aaron Ward at second to turn many a game-saving double play. Scott, nicknamed "Deacon" for a look that some claimed was not too friendly, enjoyed a 13-year career in the major leagues and is noted for two major accomplishments. He led all American League shortstops in fielding percentage for eight consecutive years, from 1916 with the Boston Red Sox, through 1923 with the New York Yankees. It is a record that stood for 43 years until Hall of Fame shortstop Luis Aparicio duplicated the feat from 1959–1966.

The other achievement was Scott's playing in 1,307 consecutive games. He began the streak on June 20, 1916, at Fenway Park as a member of the Red Sox. Any streak of this magnitude requires a gutsy ballplayer willing to play through injuries, illness and pain. A little luck doesn't hurt either. On one occasion, Scott was suffering from a boil that was so bad that it practically closed one eye. Years later, when playing for the Yankees, he related how he narrowly escaped breaking the streak. "Ed Barrow, who was managing the team, said that I was not to play that afternoon," Scott said. "I felt rotten so I didn't even go near the ballpark. And say, do you know what happened? It rained! Yes, sir—rained, and there was no ball game. That night the boil broke, and the next day I was back on the job with the record intact. Some luck, eh?"[2]

The streak ended nine years after it began, on May 6, 1925, when Scott, still healthy enough to play, was benched by New York Yankees manager Miller Huggins. The Yankees weren't playing well early in the 1925 season, and Scott, who had bad knees, was slowing down. Some speculated that the streak, which was so demanding, might have been the cause of his underperforming. Whatever the cause, Huggins replaced Scott with Pee Wee Wanninger. Ironically, less than a month later on June 1, Lou Gehrig hit for Wanninger which began the streak that would end 13 years later at 2,130, which earned Gehrig the nickname "Iron Horse." So Pee Wee has the distinction of being linked to ending one streak and beginning another.

For years, the baseball pundits pronounced with complete certainty that Gehrig's record would never be broken. It would last for all time. Apparently Cal Ripken wasn't listening to the experts. The durable shortstop for the Baltimore Orioles whizzed past Gehrig's streak, eventually ending his own on September 19, 1998, at an incredible 2,632 consecutive games played. Ripken, always a class act, unexpectedly asked manager Ray Miller to take him out of the lineup. He was healthy and capable of playing but felt the individual record was overshadowing team goals. Once again, for the trivia buffs the player who replaced Ripken was Ryan Minor.

Scott's streak of 1,307 seems puny when compared to Gehrig and Ripken, but in 1925 it was a major happening even in an era when personal records were hardly celebrated as they are today. Scott admitted it wasn't his bad legs that stopped the streak. It was the "lively ball" that did him in.

Everett Scott was born on November 19, 1892, in Bluffton, Indiana. After he graduated from Bluffton High School, the Scott family moved to Auburn, 30 miles further north, near the Ohio border. The young shortstop began his minor league career with Kokomo of the Northern State of Indiana League and for Fairmont in the Pennsylvania-West Virginia League. The following year he played for both teams again. In 1911, he moved on to

Youngstown in the Ohio-Pennsylvania League. In 1912 while Scott played for Youngstown, a minority owner of the Red Sox offered to purchase his contract. The Boston Braves and Washington Senators were also interested in the young shortstop. The Senators decided against Scott, believing he was too frail for the rigors of a long major league season. The Red Sox won out and signed Scott in late August. In 1913, Scott played for the St. Paul Saints in the American Association where he batted .269 among rave reviews for his fielding prowess.

In 1914, the 22-year-old sure-handed shortstop got the call from the Boston Red Sox, replacing fan favorite, Heinie Wagner. The veteran shortstop was out of baseball in 1914 but returned the following year and played second base. One of Heinie's main duties was to keep Babe Ruth out of trouble, a full-time job in itself. It's been written that when Ruth disappeared in July 1918, Wagner was instructed to travel to Baltimore, find him, and bring him back.

Everett "Deacon" Scott was one of the greatest defensive shortstops to play for the Yankees. The slick fielder led all American League shortstops in fielding percentage for eight consecutive years from 1916 with the Boston Red Sox through 1923 with the Yankees. Scott was also one of the most durable shortstops, playing in 1,307 consecutive games, an extraordinary record before Lou Gehrig and Cal Ripken established their monumental streaks. (Courtesy National Baseball Hall of Fame Library, Cooperstown, New York.)

Scott played in 144 games in his rookie year and batted .239. Throughout his 13-year career, Scott's value to whatever team he was playing for was not his bat. It was his glove in an era when baseball gloves were not much more than oversized mittens. It was his steady, sure-handed play at short that kept him in the lineup. He was consistent, reliable and, above all, durable. He had an accurate arm and a reputation for knowing where to play each hitter. All the manager had to do was pencil in Scott's name on the lineup card, and he knew exactly what to expect from him every day.

At five foot eight and 148 pounds, Scott was quick and agile at one of the most demanding positions in baseball. It's no wonder the Red Sox won three world championships during his eight years with the club. Playing with multiple second basemen, Scott was the glue that held the infield together.

Although Scott hit a miserable .201 in 1915, he did not let it affect his fielding, one of the reasons Boston advanced to the World Series, defeating the Philadelphia Phillies in five games. Scott was 1-for-18 in the Series, but the outstanding pitching of Rube Foster, Dutch Leonard and Ernie Shore plus the hitting of Harry Hooper, Duffy Lewis and Dick Hoblitzell was more than enough for the Red Sox to prevail.

In 1916, Scott turned in his typical season. He led the league in fielding with a .967 average but batted an anemic .232. The Red Sox were back in the World Series, however, this time beating the Brooklyn Robins in five games. Scott played his usual excellent defense, which prompted Brooklyn manager, Wilbert Robinson, to nickname him "Trolly Wire" for his accurate throws from short. But he had another poor Series at the plate, going 2-for-16.

Before the 1917 season began, Scott and the Red Sox had a contract dispute that was finally settled in the shortstop's favor. He received a substantial raise from $3,000 to $4,500. Although the Red Sox failed to win the pennant in 1917, Scott had a good year. He played in 157 games, batted .241 and led the league in fielding (.953) for the second year in a row.

In 1918, Boston returned to the World Series, defeating the Chicago Cubs, this time in six games. Scott had a fine season as author Ray Birch relates in the book *When Boston Still Had The Babe*. "During the shortened season, [due to World War I] which ended on September 2, Scott continued his consistent play, making only 17 errors and, despite hitting only .221 contributed 26 sacrifice hits and struck out only 11 times."[3]

Scott had one more horrendous offensive World Series, going 2-for-20 but was outstanding at short. The Cubs' Bob O'Farrell praised Scott's defense. "I pinch hit three times.... Every time I hit the ball hard through the box, and every time shortstop Everett Scott ran over, scooped the ball up and threw me out. I thought I had a hit each time."[4]

For the next three years, the Red Sox finished in the second division as Scott played every game and continued leading all American League shortstops in fielding. His batting steadily improved as he averaged .269 over the three-year span, including a career high of .278 in 1919. The following two years he drove in 61 and 62 runs, respectively, while establishing a new mark for consecutive games played. Scott's streak at the time, like Gehrig's later, was thought to be unbeatable. Credit for Scott's durability was given to an off-season conditioning program. He also wore padded shoes to protect his ankles from aggressive runners sliding into second base, spikes high.

With Boston mired in the second division, owner Harry Frazee contin-ued dismantling his club by trading Scott, pitchers Joe Bush and Sam Jones to the Yankees for shortstop Roger Peckinpaugh and pitchers Jack Quinn, Bill Piercy and Rip Collins. Scott was reunited with his old teammates Babe Ruth, Waite Hoyt and Wally Schang.

Peckinpaugh was the Yankees captain, which meant they needed a replacement. The team announced that Ruth would fill the vacancy, which pleased the big guy. But Commissioner Landis, in early December, suspended Ruth, Bob Meusel and Piercy until May 20 of the 1922 season. In the mean-time, the Yankees appointed newly-acquired Scott to be the captain, a logical choice and an honor he had held with the Red Sox. Supposedly, it was tem-porary until Ruth returned, but Scott remained captain until he was claimed by the Washington Senators on June 17, 1925.

Scott turned in a typical season in 1922 for the Yankees. He played in every game and batted a modest .269. Scott's streak continued, and when he reached his 900th consecutive game, the *Washington Post* named him the "Iron Man." However, on September 14, his streak almost came to an end. After some traveling problems on the way to Chicago to join the team (he had visited his home in Indiana) he arrived late and entered the game in the seventh inning, just in time to continue the streak. With Scott at short in 1922, the Yankees won another pennant and were matched against the New York Giants in the World Series for the second year in a row. Sadly, they lost to McGraw's club again, an embarrassing loss in four games (one tie). Scott played in all five games and batted .143, another terrible offensive perform-ance. This time he had plenty of company. Ruth batted .118, Schang .188 and Aaron Ward .154.

Days before the 1923 season opened, Scott injured his ankle in an exhi-bition game against the Brooklyn Robins. It happened in the second inning when he was running to second base. While sliding, he caught his spikes and twisted his ankle. It was serious enough that he was carried off the field. X-rays proved negative, but many feared he would not be in the lineup on open-ing day, including Huggins. Ice packs helped reduce the swelling, and the durable shortstop played in his 987th consecutive game on that historic open-ing of Yankee Stadium.

On May 2, at Washington's Griffith Stadium, Scott played in his 1000th consecutive game. Secretary of the Navy Edwin C. Denby presented the 31-year-old shortstop with a gold medal inscribed in "recognition of his remarkable achievement of playing 1,000 consecutive games at shortstop."

Scott continued the streak playing, in all 152 games while batting .246 and driving in 60 runs. Scott was the best-fielding shortstop in the American League for the eighth and last time. The Yankees ran away with the pennant by 16 games over the Detroit Tigers and for the third straight year faced the New York Giants in the World Series. The Yankees finally prevailed, winning the Series in six games. Scott had a wonderful Series, batting .318, driving in three runs and scoring two to help the Yankees to their first of 27 world championships. In Game Six, he produced a key hit and scored a run in the Yankees' five-run rally to help win the game and clinch the Series.

Over the winter, there were rumblings of Scott retiring or being traded. His age was creeping up and his knees were slowing him down. He spent the winter resting his aching legs. Despite the negative talk, Scott signed a Yankees contract for 1924. But the Yankees' three-year rein came to a halt when the Washington Senators, led by the 28-year-old player/manager, Bucky Harris, won the pennant. Scott had a good year. He played in every Yankees game, batted .250 (striking out only 15 times in 548 at bats) and drove in 64 runs, a career high.

In spite of a decent season by Scott, his value to the club was diminishing. Huggins was still looking to make a change at short in 1925. Some critics were of the opinion that the streak was taking on a life of its own, similar to comments heard years later about Cal Ripken when the Baltimore Orioles were losing. Others believed he was obsessed with the streak and shouldn't be playing every day. Still others believed Scott's age had prematurely caught up with him, and the blame was placed on his streak.

Pee Wee Wanninger was mentioned as a possible replacement for Scott. After all the talk, the Yankees opened the 1925 season with Scott at short and his streak intact at 1,291 games. The Yankees got off to a lousy start. Ruth was out of the lineup with "the bellyache heard round the world," a clever line by sportswriter W.O. McGeehan. Actually, the bellyache turned out to be an intestinal abscess that required surgery. Third baseman Joe Dugan had a bad knee. The rest of the team, with few exceptions, was not playing up to its potential. The slow start prompted Huggins to finally bench Scott on May 6 and end the streak at 1,307 games, the most remarkable endurance record ever established in baseball at the time. Ironically, Scott was 2-for-4 the day before the benching. A somewhat peeved Scott told reporters, "I was surprised when they benched me after I had hit well in Tuesday's game. If this had come while the team was losing I wouldn't have cared. It seems funny that it should happen the day after we win a game and I make two hits. Not that I care about the record. When I passed the 1,000 mark I lost interest in the matter. I didn't expect to go on forever. But I'll never sit on the bench."[5]

The Yankees made sure that Scott wouldn't be sitting on their bench. On June 17, 1925, he was sent to the Washington Senators for the $4,000 waiver price. He played well for manager Bucky Harris. In 33 games, he batted .272 as the Senators won another pennant but lost the World Series to the Pittsburgh Pirates in seven games. Scott did not play in the Series.

At age 33, Scott's durability streak and nagging injuries were finally taking their toll. The Senators placed him on waivers, and he was claimed by the Chicago White Sox and played in 40 games, batting .252. On July 6, Chicago sent Scott to the Cincinnati Reds on waivers. He played four games with the Reds before retiring from the major leagues but not from baseball. For the next three years, Scott played for three minor league teams: the Baltimore Orioles of the International League, the Toledo Mud Hens of the American Association and Reading in the International League.

In his retirement years, Scott successfully managed his bowling alleys and billiard parlors in Fort Wayne, Indiana. He was quite a bowler himself, participating in professional bowling tournaments and rolling numerous perfect games. He also authored a children's book for the Christy Mathewson series entitled *Third Base Thatcher*.

Everett Scott died on November 2, 1960, at Parkview Hospital in Fort Wayne, a little more than two weeks shy of his 68th birthday. Eight years later, he was inducted into the Indiana Baseball Hall of Fame. More recently, on November 7, 2008, Scott, along with first baseman Mo Vaughn, left fielder Mike Greenwell, pitchers Bill Lee, Frank Sullivan and Wes Ferrell, scout George Digby and former player development executive Ed Kenney Sr., were inducted into the Boston Red Sox Hall of Fame. The Red Sox Hall of Fame was established in 1995 to honor individuals for their outstanding contributions to the franchise.

The Yankees moved on to Philadelphia to play four games against Connie Mack's A's, who were now buried in seventh place. It's interesting to note how the fortunes of baseball teams can turn so rapidly. Early in the season, the A's were in second place, playing inspiring baseball and threatening New York for the league lead. But that challenge collapsed when the Yankees destroyed the A's by taking nine straight games during the season. Mack's mood dipped even lower when the Yankees swept the four-game series, making it 13 straight over Philadelphia.

There were two noteworthy events during the series: Sam Jones pitched a no-hitter, and Ruth slugged his 33rd home run off rookie Hank Hulvey. It turned out to be the first and only game Hulvey ever pitched, one of the short-est major league careers on record. If nothing else, Hank could tell his grand-children about the day Ruth hit a home run off him.

Jones pitched a marvelous game. It was the first no-hitter of the season. The last had been thrown on May 7, 1922, by Jess Barnes for the New York Giants against the Philadelphia Phillies, 6–0. It was Jones' first no-hitter of his career, and what a game he pitched. The right-hander was in rare form. He faced only 29 batters, two over the minimum. Surprisingly, Jones didn't strikeout a batter. Chick Galloway walked in the first inning. Frank Welch was safe on an error by, of all people, Scott, and that was all Jones gave up for the day. He recorded nine outfield outs and 18 in the infield, including two pop-ups to catcher Fred Hofmann. The play of the game came in the ninth inning with two out. The situation was intense. Jones recalls the exciting moment. "Along near the end of the game I started to get real tired, way more than usual. Chick Galloway, the A's shortstop, was the last man up in the bottom of the ninth. 'I'm gonna break it up if I can,' he yelled at me, and he bunted down the third base line. I fielded it and threw him out and there it was: a no-hitter."[6] Aside from the no-hitter, Jones' biggest thrill came the next day when he received telegrams of congratulations from people all over the country.

Three days later, while the Yankees were traveling to Washington for another single game, Howard Ehmke of the Boston Red Sox pitched a no-hitter against the A's. The score was 4–0 as the right-hander topped Jones' gem by facing only 28 men. Ehmke had two anxious moments during the game. In the sixth inning, Bryan Harris, the opposing pitcher, got a hit, but he was called out for not touching first base. In the eighth, Frank Welch hit a line drive to left which Mike Menosky fumbled. It was scored a hit but later changed to an error by the official scorer.

The Ehmke story is a fascinating one. He would enjoy a 15-year career in the major leagues with four different teams, including a year with Buffalo in the Federal League. After pitching in over 2,820 innings, Ehmke finished with a .500 record (166–166). Late in his career he was with the Philadelphia A's trying desperately to hold on to his job while coping with a sore arm. It looked like the end had come in August 1929. Manager Connie Mack approached Ehmke and told the pitcher he would have to release him. Ehmke objected and pleaded with Mack to keep him on the roster, explaining it was his last chance to be on a pennant winner and pitch in a World Series. The A's and the Cubs appeared on their way to pennants and, in fact, clinched in mid–September.

The shrewd Mack, who managed the A's for a half-century, asked Ehmke point blank if he believed he could win a World Series game. The answer was a resounding yes, Ehmke claiming he had one more good game in his sore arm that had limited him to only eight starts for Mack. An injury three years prior had forced Ehmke to reinvent his pitching mechanics which now featured sidearm and underhand deliveries. Whether it was out of the kindness of his heart (doubtful) or sound baseball judgment based on years of experience, Mack relented and told Ehmke he would pitch in the World Series against the powerful Cubs.

But first he wanted something from Ehmke. He instructed Ehmke to workout in Philadelphia and to attend the final series between the Phillies and Cubs and to study their hitters carefully. After one more start in September, which Ehmke won, Mack knew he had made the correct choice to start him in Game One, which he kept a secret. A wise judge of talent, personalities and baseball situations, Mack knew Ehmke's funky delivery was capable of fooling the Cubs' right-handed lineup, stars like Rogers Hornsby, Hack Wilson, Kiki Cuyler and Riggs Stephenson. He also knew that many of the fans in centerfield would be wearing white shirts, making it difficult for the Cubs' hitters to pick up Ehmke's delivery.

Ehmke made Mack look like a wizard. He beat the Cubs and Charlie Root, 3–1, striking out 13 and establishing a World Series record that would be broken in 1953 by Brooklyn's Carl Erskine when he whiffed 14 in a 3–2 victory against the Yankees. Ehmke's stunning pitching performance set the tone for the rest of the Series, which the A's captured in five games.

The immortal Cy Young, who had been retired as an active player for 18 years, had this to say about Ehmke's performance, "I never saw a pitcher with more stuff than Ehmke showed today. He was smart from start to finish, he never lost control of the game for a minute. It was one of the grandest displays of high pressure pitching that I have ever seen."[7]

True to his word, Howard Ehmke had just that one more good game in his right arm. The following year he pitched in only three games (10 innings), lost one of them and retired from baseball in June.

Now the story becomes real interesting. After retiring from baseball, Ehmke ran a successful canvas manufacturing company that produced some of the first tarpaulin used in the major leagues. Living near his company in Philadelphia, he would often watch young boys play baseball at the William Penn Charter School. So the story goes, he gave one of the boys, Dick Park, the glove he used during the 1929 World Series. Sixty years later, Park's son, Bill, donated the glove to the Hall of Fame where it is proudly displayed today. All this would never have happened if not for Connie Mack's faith in Howard Ehmke and the pitcher's belief in himself.

After the quick stop in Washington, where Paul Zahniser blanked the Yankees, 4–0, the club traveled back to Yankee Stadium to play Boston four games. The Yankees' first-place lead over Cleveland was stalled at 13 games. The last-place Red Sox were no match for the mighty Yankees. New York won the first three games and probably would have swept the series if not for the brilliant pitching of Howard Ehmke in the final game. Fresh off his no-hitter against the A's, the right-hander held the Yankees to one scratch single in the first inning by Whitey Witt. It's possible with a less lenient scorekeeper, Ehmke could have had back-to-back no-hitters. It was not to be, but Ehmke did set a new record of allowing only one hit over 18 innings. George Pipgras, the 23-year-old Yankees rookie, had the misfortune to make his debut against the veteran who pitched brilliantly for the second straight game. Pipgras pitched well and impressed Huggins enough to earn another start down the line. Pipgras was a quick study. Five years later he would lead the Yankees to a pennant and the American League in victories with 24 as New York won another World Series by sweeping the St. Louis Cardinals.

The day before Ehmke threw his one-hitter, Sam Jones fired a two-hitter, beating Boston, 8–1. The Red Sox couldn't touch Jones until George Burns singled with one out in the seventh. It gave Jones a record of 18–7 and 16 consecutive hitless innings. The string started on August 31 when he pitched against the Washington Senators for two-thirds of an inning. Then came the nine inning no-hitter and finally Burns' single in the seventh which all added up 16 hitless innings, quite an achievement.

During the series, Ruth banged out two more home runs, numbers 34 and 35, tying him with Cy Williams for the major league home run title. Both were inside-the-park gifts courtesy of the Boston outfielders and a generous scorer. One can imagine the Babe saying, "Hey, Keed, they all count." But Boston manager Frank Chance was not so understanding. No doubt frustrated over the long and arduous season, the outspoken Chance claimed the scorekeepers were wrong in awarding Ruth the two home runs. He believed the scorer should have given his center fielder, Dick Reichle, and left fielder Joe Harris errors. Chance did have some kind words for the Yankees, saying they were a splendid team and predicting they would beat the Giants in the World Series.

The Chicago White Sox followed Boston into Yankee Stadium for five games. It was another ugly series for the visiting team. The Yankees won four of five with Hoyt (15–8), Pennock (17–6), Bush (18–13) and Jones (19–7) pitching excellent baseball. Shawkey (16–10) was the only loser on the staff. Except for the first game that Hoyt won, 2–1, in a pitcher's duel, the Yankees bats were alive and well. During the five games, Dugan was 8-for-21 (.380), Ruth 7-for-20 (.350), Witt 7-for-22 (.318) and Pipp 6-for-19 (.315). Ruth also blasted his 36th home run.

The Yankees drew some decent crowds during the White Sox series,

30,000 for the doubleheader, not bad considering they enjoyed a commanding 16½-game lead over the Indians, an almost impossible mountain to climb. Fans were anticipating another World Series against the Giants and looking for revenge. It was not, however, the only sport on their minds. For months, boxing fans had been anxiously waiting for the match-up of the year. It finally arrived.

Across the Harlem River at the Polo Grounds, 90,000 people gathered to watch world heavyweight champion Jack Dempsey fight Luis Angel Firpo for the title. At about 4 P.M., some 25,000 fans outside the Polo Grounds, broke into a riot when the few remaining seats, priced at $3.30, were put on sale. It took close to 500 patrolmen and 25 mounted police to keep the unruly crowd under control. The line to buy tickets began forming the night before and by 10:00 A.M. the day of the fight 4,000 had assembled. By 4:30 P.M. the line had swelled to 20,000. The trouble started when the ticket van appeared containing the 3,500 tickets at $3.30 each. All hell broke loose when some latecomers spotted the van. According to the *New York Times*, "They made a dash for the wagon, sweeping patrolmen off their feet and overturning a Ford car which was parked close by, thousands of fight fans, who had waited long hours, ... swarmed forward to mob the intruders. Hats and clothes were torn, women in the crowd were crushed and hand to hand encounters followed."[8] Patrolmen had to resort to night sticks to maintain some semblance of order.

The melee taking place outside the Polo Grounds lasted longer than the fight inside. In a fierce battle, Dempsey knocked out Firpo fifty seven seconds into the second round. For their efforts, Dempsey received $486,750 and Firpo $156,250. The total gate was $1,250, 000.

Regardless of the length of the fight, it was jam-packed with excitement. Dempsey's speed, agility and powerful blows were evident right from the beginning of round one. He decked Firpo seven times, after five of which the Argentine fighter nearly took the full ten-count. The other two times Firpo went to his knees but recovered quickly without a count. It looked like Dempsey was going to put an end to the fight when suddenly Firpo landed one of his long smashing rights and caught Dempsey squarely on the jaw. It drove the Manassa Mauler through the ropes and clear out of the ring. A photograph shows Dempsey's legs straight up in the air. He landed on top of sportswriters and their typewriters in the first row. He was pushed back in the ring, and this is when Firpo missed the greatest opportunity in his boxing career. He had the heavyweight title in his grasp and let it slip away. Firpo could not deliver the finishing punch to a groggy and disoriented Dempsey. In his autobiography written with his wife Barbara, Dempsey recalled, "I don't remember climbing back into the ring, but I remember seeing about twenty

Firpos standing in front of me. I mumbled to Doc [Kearns, Dempsey's manager], 'what round was I knocked out in? What's all the fuss?'"[9]

Dempsey recovered and came out in round two and battered Firpo to the canvas twice before the final count. The first time Firpo rose on a two-count. The second time after a count of five. By this time, the Wild Bull of the Pampas was vulnerable to Dempsey's left-right combination which toppled Firpo and ended the fight. After the 10-count, Dempsey, in a magnanimous moment, helped the staggering Firpo to his feet.

A day later, a gracious Dempsey, slightly bruised, praised Firpo to the highest. "I've met a lot of tough fellows in my time, but Firpo's about the toughest of them all. He proved it last night and he'll prove it again if some of the other fellows who are yelling for a crack at the title will chance a bout with him."[10]

Firpo continued to fight but was never good enough to capture the heavyweight title. He gained fame in Latin America and throughout the world because of knocking Dempsey out of the ring, which might have been his greatest moment.

On September 16, Tris Speaker and the Cleveland Indians came into Yankee Stadium for four games confronted with the near-impossible task of overcoming a 16½-game lead with 23 games remaining, not a hopeful picture for the fiery competitor and his band of Indians. Making the job even tougher, the first two games were played as a doubleheader.

Yankees fans were keenly aware of the significance of the series. By 2 P.M., the starting time for the first game, there was standing room only in the grandstand. Later in the evening, Ed Barrow released the paid attendance at 60,331, the largest in the history of the sport. It was better than opening day when some 10,000 free tickets were handed out.

To the delight of throngs of Yankees fans, Ruth and company all but dashed any glimmer of hope the Indians were harboring by winning both ends of the doubleheader, 4–2 and 3–2. The young kid from Brooklyn, Waite Hoyt, showing no signs of jitters, kept the Indians in check, allowing seven hits and two runs for his 16th win of the season. In typical Ruthian style, with the Indians leading 2–1 in the sixth, he hoisted a home run into the right field bleachers to tie the score. It was the Babe's 37th of the season, and it came off ace George Uhle. The following inning Schang and Scott homered and the Yankees wrapped up game one.

The night cap saw a match-up of lefties, Herb Pennock against Jim Edwards. It had all the elements of an exciting game, which forced the 60,000-plus crowd to stay right to the end. First, an inside-the-park home run by Bob Meusel, which might have been caught if Speaker hadn't lost the ball in the sun. That run turned out to be the margin of victory. Second, Aaron Ward, who argued vehemently on two separate occasions with umpire Pants Rowland, finally got the heave-ho. Third, Pennock's gutsy clutch pitching in the ninth won the game and put the Yankees 18½ games in front and assured New York of at least a tie in the pennant race.

Realistically, the pennant race was over. The magic number for New York to clinch its third straight American League flag was one. One more victory for the Yankees or one more loss for the Indians and the pennant race would officially be history.

Give credit to Speaker and the Indians who were faced with the inevitable but showed great heart and pride. They would not give up. They whipped the Yankees the next two games, 6–2 and 8–3, postponing the victory celebration for New York and its fans. It was a valiant effort by the Indians, but all for nothing. The St. Louis Browns came to the Stadium a day later, and the Yankees defeated them, 4–3, clinching their third straight pennant riding the right arm of Sam Jones.

It was a big day for Jones. The victory was his 20th of the season, the magic number which pitchers strive to achieve. It didn't come easy. Coasting along with a 4–0 lead, Jones began to tire, giving up single runs in the seventh, eighth and another in the ninth before he was faced with a two-out, runner-on-third situation. Slugger Ken Williams, a lifetime .319 hitter, came to the plate. On the mound, Jones and Huggins conferred and elected to pitch to Williams. Jones ran the count to three-and-two before Williams popped to Schang behind the plate for the final out. The Yankees became only the second team in the history of the American League to win three straight pennants. It was first accomplished by the Detroit Tigers from 1907–09, managed by Hugh Jennings.

While the Yankees were idle for three days, mostly due to rain in the metropolitan area, American League president Ban Johnson announced that Babe Ruth was named Most Valuable Player for 1923. Ruth was the unanimous choice of the eight baseball writers, one from each city. Eddie Collins from the White Sox was second, and Detroit's Harry Heilmann was third. It was an extraordinary comeback for the Babe. The previous year he wasn't even among the top eight players.

The Browns left for Boston, having played the Yankees only one game due to inclement weather. It was, however, an important game—the pennant clincher. Ty Cobb brought his Tigers in for a meaningless (at least for the Yankees) three-game series. The Tigers and Indians were battling for second place. The Tigers took two of three. Jones and Bush lost. Hoyt was the only Yankees winner.

With the pennant clinched, Huggins called up Lou Gehrig from the

Eastern League to play in the Tiger series, mostly in late innings to give Pipp a well-deserved rest and have him ready for the World Series. In Lou's first game back, he pinch-hit for Pennock and struck out against left-hander Ray Francis. The following day, Gehrig doubled, driving in two runs to tie the score, but the Yankees lost in extra innings.

Baseball people now began to focus on the upcoming World Series. At a meeting at the Commodore Hotel attended by Commissioner Landis, his secretary Leslie O'Connor, Giants president Charles A. Stoneham, Yankee president Ruppert, James J. Tierney, secretary of the Giants and Yankees general manager Barrow, it was decided by a coin toss the World Series would begin October 10 at Yankee Stadium. The National League pennant winner had not been decided at the time, so alternate plans were made if the Giants or the Cincinnati Reds won. As it turned out, the Giants clinched their third straight pennant two days later, so the contingency plan was not necessary. The games between the Yankees and Giants would alternate between the Stadium and the Polo Grounds. Game time was set at 2 P.M. Box seats were priced at $6.60, reserved seats $5.50, unreserved grandstand $3.30 and bleacher seats $1.10.

In the meantime, the Yankees visited Fenway Park to play the last-place Red Sox in a meaningless four-game series. It was as exciting as watching grass grow. At least that is what most people anticipated. Not so. It turned out to be an interesting series. First, the good news. Ruth hit his 38th home run, tying him with Cy Williams of the Phillies for the major league lead. Young Gehrig had a monster series 9-for-19 (.474) including his first home run. In one game, he was 4-for-7 as the Yankees buried the Red Sox, 24–4! There were 30 hits in the game, a new American League record. Rookie George Pipgras picked up his first major league victory.

On the other side of the ledger, Huggins received some troubling news. Both Bob Meusel and Wally Pipp, two of his star players, sustained injuries. Meusel wrenched his knee sliding under a tag at home. He had to be carried off the field. Foolishly playing the next day, he re-injured the knee when he banged into the right field wall making a sensational catch. Pipp was injured even before the series began. In a freak accident, Pipp twisted his ankle getting off the train in Boston. Both players claimed they would be ready for the Series.

After the Boston series, the Yankees were idle for four days as no games were scheduled. It gave the club, especially Meusel and Pipp, a long-needed rest before facing the Giants. Conversely, there is always the concern a long layoff can dull the skills. The Yankees hobbled home to the Stadium to close out the season against their one-time pennant threat, the Philadelphia A's.

While the Yankees were resting and nursing their wounds, the Giants held two workouts at the Stadium. McGraw put his players through hours of batting practice and fielding drills getting them accustomed to the new field, a venue they saw for the first time. McGraw used all seven pitchers and ordered them to put plenty of "stuff" on the ball. McGraw, never one to ingratiate himself with opponents, opined that the infield was in excellent condition but that the outfield was "bumpy." Wally Pipp, who limped into the Stadium with a swollen and bandaged ankle, watched the Giants from the stands. He later defended the condition of the outfield, claiming it wasn't bumpy, but as a first baseman, he might not be the best judge or maybe Pipp didn't want McGraw, a master of intimidation, to go unchallenged.

Giants' coach Hugh Jennings, longtime friend of McGraw's, conducted one of the workouts. Jennings, nicknamed "Ee-Yah," played for 17 years in the major leagues, mostly at short, and finished with a .311 lifetime batting average. He also managed for 16 seasons and was named by the Veterans Committee in 1945 to the Hall of Fame. After the session, an upbeat Jennings commented, "I think we've got the feel of the park now. It was a bit strange at first, but the boys will be all right for the first game. The higher stand, of course, throws a shadow different from that at the Polo Grounds, especially at this time of the year. Did you notice, too, that the Polo Grounds diamond has a deeper depression between the pitching box and the second baseman's position? Little differences like that, however, will be overcome."[11]

Before the Yankees began their final four games of the season against the A's, an ailing Babe Ruth played in an exhibition game with the New York Giants. In today's baseball world, it is impossible to imagine a situation where a super-star of Ruth's caliber would play in an exhibition game days before the World Series. Yes, indeed, times have changed. Aaron Ward and Elmer Smith represented the Yankees along with Ruth. The game was played for the benefit of John B. Day and Jim Mutrie. Day was the former owner and Mutrie the manager of New York's first National League team. The Giants beat Baltimore, 9–3. Ruth, noticeably limping on an injured ankle, stole the spotlight and dazzled the small crowd with a monster home run that cleared the upper deck in right field and soared out of the park.

The Yankees and the A's split the final four games of the season at the Stadium before minuscule crowds who were anticipating the opening game of the World Series on Wednesday. Bush and Pennock each won their 19th, while Pipgras and Mays lost. It was Mays' last hurrah in a Yankee uniform. The controversial and troubled pitcher would be sold to Cincinnati in December.

In the first game against the A's, Ruth cracked out home run number 39 while Cy Williams belted his 41st to maintain his lead. The following day Ruth hit number 40 and in the last game of the season the Babe, in his first at-bat hit the first pitch from Slim Harriss to catch Williams for the major league home run title. Ruth had long ago locked up the title in the American League, besting Ken Williams of the St. Louis Browns, who finished the season with 29.

Ruth had an excellent opportunity to pass the 41 mark with four more turns at the plate. The best he could do was a single, two walks and a whiff, all the while being noisily supported by cheering fans who wanted to see the Babe win the title outright.

Even though the Yankees lost their last game to the A's, 9–7, and finished the season 98–54, they set a new American League record. The Yankees by virtue of being 16 full games ahead of the Tigers (who had slipped into second place the day before) boasted the greatest lead of any pennant-winning team in American League history. The previous record was held by the 1903 Red Sox and the 1910 A's at 14½ games. The major league record was set by the Pirates in 1902 over the Brooklyn Robins at 27½ games.

During the four games with the A's, Ruth played first base for the injured Pipp, and Meusel pinch-hit only once. Huggins was concerned about Pipp and did not think he would play in the Series. His ankle was swollen and painful. Huggins' plan was to play Ruth at first and Elmer Smith in right field. Not everyone agreed with Huggins' assessment of Pipp's ankle. In fact, Doc Woods, the Yankees trainer, believed Pipp's ankle was healing rapidly and would be ready by Wednesday's opener. Pipp's personal physician echoed Woods' sentiments. The ankle was improving and Pipp should be ready to play when the World Series opens at the Stadium. Based on the comments by two medical experts, could Huggins have been playing mind games with McGraw? Another question mark was left fielder Bob Meusel. There was a possibility he wouldn't be ready for Game One. If that was the case, Huggins would use the rookie Harvey Hendrick in left.

The Giants had their share of health problems too. Pitcher Hugh McQuillan (15–14, .341 ERA) had a sore arm, and Ralph Shinners, a reserve outfielder, came down with the flu. Ross Youngs, one of the brightest stars of the Giants, also had flu-like symptoms for several days, which left him weak and achy. Youngs batted .336 and led the league in runs scored with 121. His absence would be a serious blow to the Giants' offense.

While the Yankees and Giants were practicing at their respective fields waiting for the beginning of the World Series, ticket sales were booming. Personnel at both clubs were working overtime to fill the demand for reserved seats, which were quickly exhausted. Thousands of ticket requests poured into the American League headquarters at 226 West 42nd Street to be sorted, singling out true fans from the scalpers. Both teams made valiant efforts to keep tickets out of the hands of the scalpers, but they had limited success.

The wagering at the betting commission houses was ferocious. Although gambling was illegal, the city's gamblers conducted their business openly. They were protected by money in the right hands and strong political ties. The Yankees were favorites for more than a week, but by the eve of the Series, the odds dropped to even money. The betting was not confined to the New York metropolitan area. It was widespread. Chicago, Detroit, Cleveland, Pittsburgh, Boston and Philadelphia all wanted in on the action. The excitement was building, not just in New York, but throughout the country. This would be the third straight year the two clubs met in the Series and a genuine rivalry was formed. McGraw had no love for the Yankees and New York was on a mission of revenge. This was the perfect formula for record-breaking attendance, plus both parks boasted huge seating capacities to accommodate the anticipated crowds. Yankee Stadium held 62,000 and the Polo Grounds 52,000.

The local economy got a boost as well, as baseball fans arrived from every corner of the country by rail, traveling a few hours to four days. They came from as far south as Georgia, as far north as Canada and as far west as California and almost everywhere in-between. The hotels were jammed. The Commodore, Biltmore, Belmont, Murray Hill and Ansonia were only a handful of the hotels that were booked to capacity. Not a room was available. Some of the shrewder fans booked early in anticipation of the two teams meeting again.

The police force was beefed up to handle the huge crowd that was anticipated for the opening game at Yankee Stadium. Some 200 patrolmen and 20 mounted police were available to make sure the expected 60,000-plus fans got in and out of the Stadium safely and with a minimum of disorder.

Player injuries that were discussed and agonized over for days seemed to simply vanish into thin air on the eve of the opening game. Miraculously, everyone was ready to play, including Wally Pipp and Ross Youngs. Both McGraw and Huggins claimed their clubs were healthy and anxious to get the Series underway.

The New York press favored the Giants. To put it bluntly, they believed McGraw was the better manager. Dating back to 1904, McGraw's teams had won nine pennants and three world championships. This was more than any other manager in either league, including Connie Mack. McGraw's record was hard to argue against. Two years after he took over the Giants, he won the pennant. In 1905, led by the great Christy Mathewson, the Giants won their first World Series. They won pennants in 1911, 1912, 1913 and 1917 but lost the World Series each year. Four years later, McGraw and the Giants won consecutive pennants from 1921–1924. McGraw and the Giants rose to the occasion in the 1921 World Series in which the Yankees were favored. After the Giants lost the first two games, they came back to win the Series. They swept the Yankees in 1922, an embarrassment that still haunts New York from the front office to the dugout. A great deal of the credit goes to McGraw, a master psychologist and tactician. Some even claimed him to be an authoritative genius. There was no question the man had total authority vested in him right from the day he joined the Giants in 1902 as their manager. He made it abundantly clear to owner Andrew Freedman when he laid out the terms of his four-year contract which stipulated, "...I was to have absolute control of the team on the field; that I be empowered to purchase or trade for players and make releases as I saw fit; that my authority in that respect was to be absolute and that under no circumstances was I to be interfered with."[12]

McGraw played what's called today "small ball." He manufactured runs instead of waiting for the big home run. He often used the hit-and-run play and rarely had a player lay down a sacrifice bunt other than the pitcher. McGraw was more of a teacher than a manager. He loved to sign college players whom he believed were amenable to teaching and could learn quickly and, thus, overcome any weakness they might have. This suited McGraw's style perfectly. Burleigh Grimes, who pitched for McGraw, said he "taught me more about pitching in the first 15 minutes than I learned in 11 previous seasons."[13]

McGraw ran a tight ship, directing each move and counter-move on the field. He also liked to call the pitches thrown by his hurlers. Beside McGraw's field strategy, his dominant personality played a huge part in his style of managing. Dubbed "Little Napoleon" by the New York sportswriters, McGraw was fiercely combative, cocky, and brash, sparing no one. *In My Thirty Years in Baseball*, McGraw's autobiography, he claimed "...I never could see this idea of taking a defeat philosophically. I hate to lose and I never feel myself beaten until the last man is out.... I can appreciate the fine work of opposing players but, at the same time, I'm not much for that show of friendly feeling on the field."[14] Actually, pretty mild stuff for a manager who was not averse to fighting on and off the field. McGraw also fought with umpires, writers and harassed opposing players and even his own coach and long-time friend, Wilbert Robinson. After losing the 1913 World Series (third in a row) McGraw, with a few drinks in him, complained that Robinson had looked bad several times while coaching. Uncle Robbie, as he was affectionately called, shot back that McGraw had made more mistakes during the Series than the entire team. That was all he had to hear. The short-tempered McGraw fired Robinson. The feud between the two men lasted for many years.

No question McGraw possessed a Jekyll/Hyde personality. There were, however, many players, coaches, writers and baseball people who loved and respected him. Hall of Famer Frankie Frisch was counted among them. "McGraw in my opinion was the greatest manager I ever saw in action. He was tough, he was domineering, and he got the job done. He loved victory. He couldn't tolerate defeat or mediocrity. He had only one goal. He considered the Giants the greatest ball club in the world and at the same time I'm sure he considered himself the greatest manager."[15]

For the third straight year, Miller Huggins and the Yankees were up against the McGraw winning philosophy which was instilled in all his players. It was a daunting task for the Mighty Mite who was a fierce competitor in his own right. The petite Huggins was no pushover. When he took over the managerial job with the Yankees in 1918, he had to wrestle with a bunch of unruly characters. He did a lot of screaming at players and his temper tantrums were famous. Putting that character fault aside, Huggins, most experts believed was an exceptional judge of talent. He was also an intelligent man, having earned a law degree from the University of Cincinnati. While playing second base for Cincinnati, Huggins gained precious managerial experience observing three tough, hard-nosed field leaders: Joe Kelley, Ned Hanlon and John Ganzel (who played under McGraw). So it was not surprising Huggins was considered one of the smartest players in the game. After he joined the Yankees as manager, he recommended to owner Ruppert to try and get Ruth from Boston. When Ruth became available after the 1919 season, the Yankees quickly grabbed him. The two would battle each other for most of their time together until 1925. Ruth's over-indulgence, his carousing and poor play early in the season were getting to Huggins. When Ruth showed up an hour before game time in St. Louis, Huggins fined him $5,000 and suspended him for the season. Ruth was outraged. When Ruppert supported his manager, Ruth was humbled. It was a defining moment for Huggins and revealed much about the character of the man. Keep in mind, taking on Ruth, who was bigger than life at the time, was no small undertaking. It took a great deal of courage and inner strength.

Perhaps Miller Huggins didn't have the managerial track record of John McGraw, but he was no slouch. Three consecutive pennants proved he had the leadership qualities to match those of the great McGraw in a World Series.

Colonel Jacob Ruppert took a back seat to no one when it came to bargaining (ask Cap Huston) or giving his club an important edge whenever possible. Shortly before the Series began, he called the press into his office and announced he had signed Miller Huggins to a new one-year contract. It was a shrewd move by Ruppert who had learned from his mistake the previous year when he signed Huggins *after* losing the Series, which turned out to be more of a defensive move to show support for his manager. This time the

Famed sportswriter Fred Lieb chats with Yankees manager Miller Huggins. After Babe Ruth belted his three-run homer on opening day, 1923, at Yankee Stadium, Lieb penned the famous line, "The House That Ruth Built." The dean of baseball writers, Lieb was honored with the J.G. Taylor Spink Award in 1972 along with Dan Daniel and J. Roy Stockton. The award is the highest honor given by the Baseball Writers' Association of America. It is recognized in an exhibit at the Hall of Fame Library. (Courtesy National Baseball Hall of Fame Library, Cooperstown, New York.)

signing before the Series was a clear signal that Huggins was the boss, had control of his players and the full support of Yankee management. It was a brilliant move by Ruppert and a huge confidence builder for Huggins going into the World Series.

The game was still played on the field, however, not in the press or dugout. The Yankees had the edge in pitching; the Giants in hitting. Defensively, the Giants were better in the infield; the Yankees superior in the outfield. The bottom line? The teams were evenly matched. There would be no repeat of 1922 for the New York Giants.

The Yankees had a five-man rotation, all capable of pitching a brilliant game on any given day. Left-hander Herb Pennock (19–6, 3.13 ERA), Sam

Jones (21–8, 3.63 ERA), Waite Hoyt (17–9, 3.02 ERA), Bob Shawkey (16–11, 3.51 ERA), and Joe Bush (19–15, 3.43 ERA) were a manager's dream staff. Carl Mays was in the doghouse and didn't have a prayer of being used in a game.

The Yankees' hitting was far from feeble. Any club that can pencil Babe Ruth's name on the lineup card is one pitch away from a big inning. Ruth had a fabulous season. He batted .393, led the league with 41 home runs, 131 RBIs, 170 walks and 151 runs scored. Pipp and Meusel had solid years. Pipp hit .304 and drove in 108 runs batting clean-up. Meusel batted .313 with 91 RBIs and possessed a rifle for an arm. Whitey Witt, patrolling center field and leading off, was the plate-setter. He hit .314 and drove in 56 runs while scoring 113. Joe Dugan, the perfect number two batter, hit .283, drove in 67 and scored 111 runs. Schang, an outstanding defensive catcher who missed a number of games during the season due to an injury, batted .276. His prime value was in handling the pitching staff. Everett Scott anchored the infield and led all shortstops with a .961 fielding average. Catcher Fred Hofmann (.290) and outfielder Elmer Smith (.306) made major contributions during the season filling in for injured players.

Lou Gehrig, who finished the season with a vengeance, was ineligible to play in the World Series. It caused quite a stir. Huggins, not sure of Pipp's playing status, went to Ruppert and convinced him Gehrig was the man to play first in the Series. Technically, Gehrig was ineligible because he joined the club after the September 1 deadline. However, substitutions had been granted in the past for injured players and a precedent established. It happened in the 1920 World Series in an atmosphere of good sportsmanship. The Brooklyn Robins allowed shortstop Joe Sewell, fresh out of college, to play even though he arrived after the September 1 deadline. The Cleveland Indians reciprocated by allowing ineligible Jack Sheehan to play third. Ruppert believed Landis would be amenable to the idea. The commissioner was and when he approached McGraw with the idea, the manager was adamant. Absolutely not. "If the Yankees have had an injury, it's their hard luck," he snapped.[16] It was well known McGraw hated the Yankees. It started when Ruth came aboard and the Yankees began drawing tremendous crowds at the Polo Grounds. McGraw and the Giants were always THE team in New York and when the Yankees, led by Ruth, began making inroads into McGraw's popularity, it enraged him. Frankie Frisch, McGraw's star second baseman, revealed in his autobiography the extent of McGraw's hatred of the Yankees before the World Series. "He was so annoyed with the enemy [Yankees] that he wouldn't let us dress at the Stadium in the visitors' clubhouse. He insisted that we suit up at the Polo Grounds and make the trip to and from the Stadium in taxicabs."[17]

In spite of Ruth, the Giants still had the edge in hitting. They boasted five .300 hitters. Second baseman and future Hall of Famer Frankie Frisch led the team with a .348 average. He also hit 12 home runs and drove in 111 runs. His 223 hits led the National League as did his .973 fielding average for second basemen. Right fielder Ross Youngs (.336, 87 RBIs) led the league with 121 runs scored. Casey Stengel, another future Hall of Fame player, batted .339 in limited playing time, followed by George Kelly (.307, 16 home runs and 103 RBIs) at first base. Shortstop Dave Bancroft batted .304. Left fielder Irish Meusel, Bob's brother, along with Kelly, were the power in the lineup. Meusel batted .297 and led the team with 19 home runs and 125 RBIs, the most in the league. Heinie Groh hit a respectable .290 but also led the National League third baseman with a .975 fielding average. Center fielder Jimmy O'Connell (.250) and catcher Frank Snyder (.256) completed the Giants' starting team. The latter led all catchers with a .990 fielding average. Twenty-two year old infielder Travis Jackson (.275) and outfielder Bill Cunningham (.271) were McGraw's substitutes when needed.

The Giants' pitching staff was good but couldn't compare to the Yankees. Their five-man rotation of Hugh McQuillan (15–14, 3.41 ERA), Jack Scott (16–7, 3.89 ERA), Art Nehf (13–10, 4.50 ERA), Jack Bentley (13–8, 4.48 ERA) and Rosy Ryan (16–5, 3.49 ERA) were mediocre. McGraw's genius would be put to the test.

As the first game of the World Series neared and excitement mounted, it seemed everyone in the sporting world had an opinion as to the winner. Both the American and National League presidents were politically correct and partisan as expected. There were plenty of other opinions from men and women in baseball, boxing, billiards, horse racing and even in theatrical circles. The consensus was that the Giants would win. The chief reason was the superior managerial ability of McGraw, which probably stiffened the resolve of Huggins and the Yankees.

Both managers voiced their opinions, careful not to offend the other club, yet optimistic and positive in order to rally the troops. McGraw said, "I think the Giants ought to win, and I will be sorely disappointed if they don't win. The players, I am glad to report, are in a healthy frame of mind. Although not over-confident, they believe that they are as good as any other team in baseball...."[18] A less confident Huggins countered, "In all the time I've been manager of the Yankees I've never seen the players in better spirits. They are free from worry, happy and confident, and I am certain that you will not see any such failure as last year. It will be a close, hard-fought series, in my opinion."[19]

Let the games begin.

8

First World Series Championship

Game One—At Yankee Stadium

It was a mild, slightly overcast day as over 58,000 people crowded into Yankee Stadium to be part of the historic first World Series ever played at the Taj Mahal of the Bronx. The paid attendance was 55,307, a new record, beating the 42,620 crowd at the 1916 Series between Boston and Brooklyn. Spectators came from all parts of the country to be part of this wonderful event and to witness great baseball between two championship teams. Baseball fans came from near and far. Farmers, bankers, news boys, college students, society women, shop girls, actors, athletes, politicians, rich and poor, young and old came together as one mass of humanity to watch two baseball teams battle for the hearts and minds of New York City.

If you were a celebrity watcher, the Stadium was the place to be. It wasn't difficult to spot a famous or near-famous face in the crowd. It started with white-haired baseball Commissioner Kenesaw Mountain Landis prominently seated in a special box. He was flanked by President Ban Johnson of the American League and President John Heydler of the National League. The rest of the celebrity cast made up a who's who of widely known and esteemed notables. Seated elbow to elbow were some of the most prominent names of the era—famed boxing promoter Tex Rickard, police commissioner Richard E. Enright, U.S. Senator Royal S. Copeland, world famous Irish tenor and operatic star John McCormick and Princeton's ex–football great Bill Edwards. As expected, the world of baseball was well represented, beginning with the most famous Giant of them all, Christy Mathewson. Other notables included Connie Mack, Branch Rickey, George Stallings, Roger Bresnahan and Johnny Evers of the famous double play combination.

Early arrivals were in for a real treat. Baseball's two greatest clowns, Nick Altrock and Al Schacht, performed for the crowd. Both pitchers were out of baseball in 1923, but Altrock would return the following year at age 48 and appear in one game for the Senators. In his only at-bat, he hit a triple, slightly tainted since the opposing players didn't hustle after the ball. It was all in good fun. In 1929 at age 53, Altrock singled in a game and in 1933 he made his final big league appearance as a pinch-hitter for the Senators at age 57. These two pantomime clowns put the fans in a festive mood by performing several of their most hilarious stunts.

Entertainment wasn't exclusively confined to on-field activities. At 1:30 P.M., radio station WEAF, located at 195 Broadway in Manhattan, would begin the broadcast of the 1923 World Series. The announcer was Graham McNamee, who made his professional debut as a baritone at Aeolian Hall in 1921. Looking for something more rewarding, McNamee was hired by WEAF in the spring of 1923 at $30 a week. By September, he was broadcasting the 1923 World Series. As author Joseph Durso explains, "Now he was being handed a saucer-shaped microphone, an engineer, a seat in the open, no precedents and the job of describing one of the great spectacles of the day."[1]

Listeners along the Eastern seaboard also heard the broadcast on stations WJZ in New York, WMAF in South Dartmouth, Massachusetts, and WCAP in Washington D.C. It was transmitted simultaneously with WEAF via telephone lines connected to microphones controlled by the stations. McNamee was a huge hit, receiving over 1,700 letters after the Series and eventually becoming a celebrity at other historic events.

McNamee summed up his approach to broadcasting the World Series in these words, "You must make each of your listeners, though miles away from the spot, feel that he or she too is there with you in that press stand, watching the pop bottles thrown in the air; Gloria Swanson arriving in her new ermine coat; McGraw in his dugout, apparently motionless, but giving signals all the time."[2]

When the game finally began, some of the baseball experts were surprised McGraw's pitching choice was John Watson, a right-hander whom the Giants picked up during the summer in a trade with the Boston Braves. He finished the regular season 8–5 with a 3.41 ERA. He also finished the season early when McGraw suspended him and slapped him with a $500 fine for violating team discipline. Some speculated that McGraw selected Watson over Nehf (whom he had warming up before the game) because of his cool, impassive and unconcerned manner. Huggins selected young Waite Hoyt, also an odd choice, considering 21-game winner Sam Jones was well rested.

The Yankees jumped on Watson in the first inning. After Witt lined out,

Dugan walked and was forced at second by Ruth. It appeared Watson would have a relatively easy inning until Meusel doubled, sending Ruth scampering all the way from first to score. The next inning the Yankees scored a pair of runs. Ward led off with a single to left. Schang followed with a single to center. Scott bunted along the first base line with Kelly making the unassisted out. Ward moved to third, Schang to second. Hoyt fanned for the second out, but Witt came through in the clutch when he singled to center scoring both base runners and giving the Yankees an early 3–0 lead.

In the top of the third, the roof caved in on Hoyt as the Giants scored four times to take a 4–3 lead. George Kelly opened with a single. Hank Gowdy walked. McGraw saw an opportunity to get more speed on the bases and sent in young 24-year-old Freddie Maguire to run for Gowdy. Watson was up next, but McGraw didn't like what he saw so far from his pitcher. He sent Jack Bentley, a good-hitting pitcher, to bat for Watson. Bentley singled, loading the bases with no out. McGraw, the master strategist, wasn't quite finished. He pulled Bentley, a slow runner, and replaced him with Dennis Gearin, recently called up from the minors. The next batter, Dave Bancroft, grounded to short, forcing Gearin at second for the first out while Kelly scored. With runners on first and third, Hoyt momentarily lost concentration and went into a full wind-up. Bancroft took off, putting runners on second and third. Heinie Groh lined the next Hoyt pitch inside the first base line into right field where Ruth let the ball get by him. Maguire and Bancroft scored, tying the game at 3–3 while Groh wound up at third with a triple. That brought Huggins to the mound. He replaced Hoyt with Joe Bush. The first man he faced was Frankie Frisch, who grounded sharply to Pipp, but with his weak ankle he let the ball get by and go into right for a single scoring Groh and handing the Giants the lead.

Rosy Ryan was now on the mound for the Giants. Both Bush and Ryan threw goose eggs until the Yankees broke through in the seventh. Bush led off with a single to center. Witt flied out. Dugan promptly drove a Ryan pitch to right center for a triple, scoring Bush and tying the game at 4–4. Ruth came to the plate and smacked a vicious grounder down the first base line on which Kelly made a clutch play knocking the ball down and then throwing to Frank Snyder to nail Dugan at home. Meusel made the final out to end the inning.

The game remained tied entering the top of the ninth. Bush's fast ball had the Giants baffled since Frisch greeted him in the third with a single. The ninth looked like another routine inning for Bullet Joe. Ross Youngs lined to Witt in center. Dugan tossed out Irish Meusel and there were two quick outs. Casey Stengel strolled to the plate, worked the count full, then hit the next pitch on a line to left center with Witt and Meusel in hot pursuit. Witt was playing Stengel to pull and Meusel was hugging the left field line, so there was a huge gap in left center. Stengel, not as spry as he once was and also favoring a heel he injured in a game in Chicago banging against a fence and landing on a concrete base, ran the bases as if his life depended on it. Witt retrieved the ball and threw it to Meusel, who had a great arm and fired a perfect strike to Scott at short. Yankee third baseman Joe Dugan could hear Casey rounding third yelling to himself, "Go, Casey, go, go, Casey go." Here's how the *New York Times* described the final 90 feet, "By now Stengel was rounding third, badly winded but still going strong. It was a race between man and ball, but the man won easily, for Casey slid into the plate and up onto one knee in a single motion. Then he waved a hand in a comical gesture that seemed to say, 'Well, there you are,' and the game was as good as over."[3]

Casey's flippant wave of the hand was right on target. The game was as good as over as Ryan retired the Yankees in the ninth in order, three up, three down. It was a bitter and frustrating loss for the Yankees. Dating back to the 1921 Series, the Giants had now beaten the Yankees eight straight World Series games, not counting the tie in 1922. Adding to the Yankees' anxiety was the fact they outhit the Giants, but it was the Giants defense that won the game. McGraw's club made some magnificent plays throughout the game, nipping potential big innings for the Yankees, keeping the game close.

Key plays by the Giants cropped up in almost every inning. A smart double play in the fourth involving Ryan, Groh and Frisch; a great catch by Frisch and even a greater throw home to nail Ruth in the fifth; Frisch's play on Scott to choke off a rally in the sixth; in the seventh Kelly made a marvelous stop of a Ruth smash and then his throw cut down Dugan at the plate; Snyder picked off Pipp at second base in the eighth and Groh's amazing backhand stop in the ninth.

The Yankees clubhouse was a dreary, gloomy site. Players were milling about in a state of shock. The end came so quickly. How could it happen? Two out, bases empty and a tie game suddenly turned into a heartbreaking defeat. Ruth dressed hurriedly, saying nothing as he left the clubhouse to cheers from his loyal fans outside. Bush, totally dejected, sat mulling over and over in his mind the pitch Casey hit for the inside-the-park home run. Witt, Meusel, Dugan and Pipp followed Ruth out of the clubhouse wanting to flee the scene of defeat and hopefully erase the memory. Were the Yankees capable of beating the Giants? After eight straight losses, were they spooked? These and other questions had to be foremost on the minds of Huggins and his players. Huggins, true to his character, made no excuses. He complimented the Giants on their victory, singling out Frisch and Kelly for their defensive gems. Outwardly, he remained positive and upbeat throughout his press conference. Who knew what was truly going through his mind? He calmly told the newspaper men he was looking forward to the next game and believed the breaks would go the Yankees way. He named 19-game winner Herb Pennock as his starting pitcher.

Game Two—At Polo Grounds

Although the Giants won the first game of the Series and Stengel provided fans with an exciting ninth inning, attention was still focused on Babe Ruth and his dangerous bat. The crowds were anxiously waiting for the big guy to explode. The anticipation was mounting and his every at-bat chronicled. Each day, the *New York Times* ran a prominent box on the sports page titled, "What Babe Ruth Did at Bat" in the first World Series game, second World Series game and so on, for six days. Even announcer McNamee confessed he had trouble speaking when Ruth came to bat. The adulation for Ruth was way too much for McGraw and his titanic ego to remain silent. In spite of the Giants remarkable record of holding Ruth in check, the inflamed McGraw still had to let the baseball world know he had Ruth's number. As it turned out, not a smart thing to do. "Why shouldn't we pitch to Ruth? I've said it before, and I'll say it again, we pitched to better hitters than Ruth in the National League."[4]

Another record crowd of 40,402 paid customers turned up at the Polo Grounds for Game Two of the World Series. Although attendance was considerably below that of the game at Yankee Stadium, it was still the largest crowd that ever watched a baseball game at the Polo Grounds. There were a few empty seats in the grandstand, but in the choice viewing area hundreds stood two and three deep. With gate receipts for the two games already at $340,410, it appeared baseball was on its way to a long-held dream of a $1 million World Series.

Huggins, true to his word, started Herb Pennock while McGraw went with Hugh McQuillan, who won 15 games for him during the season. Once again, the Yankees jumped off to an early lead. In the top of the second after Pipp grounded out on a fine play by third baseman Groh, Aaron Ward followed with a long home run into the upper deck in left field to give the Yankees a 1–0 lead. In the Giants' half of the second, Irish Meusel, who hit 19 home runs during the season, answered Ward's blow with one of his own. The ball landed in the upper deck, traveling a little further than Ward's.

Both teams were scoreless in the third. Then in the top of the fourth, Ruth led off the inning, ran the count to two balls and one strike. Snyder, the Giants' catcher, "...sneaked a look at the little logician in the dugout. McGraw blinked twice, pulled up his trousers, and thrust the forefinger of his right hand into his left eye. Snyder knew that he meant: 'Try the Big Bozo on a slow curve around the knees, and don't forget to throw to first if you happen to drop the third strike.'"⁵ Snyder didn't have to worry about dropping the third strike. It never happened. Ruth promptly blasted the slow curve for his first home run of the Series. It was a gigantic shot that cleared the roof and landed in Manhattan Field, which adjoined the Polo Grounds. A policeman picked up the errant ball and stuck it in his pocket. No doubt, it was the main topic at the family dinner table that evening. Ruth circled the bases like a young boy who was just let out of school. He had a wide grin on his face and when he touched home plate, he removed his cap and waved at the thousands of jubilant fans. In right field, torn bits of paper rained down like confetti at a parade.

Meusel followed Ruth and struck out, but Pipp blooped a single into right field. Ward popped to Kelly for the second out, and it looked like McQuillan was going to get out of the inning with only minimal damage. Schang kept the inning alive by singling to right and when Youngs bobbled the ball, Pipp alertly scampered to third. Scott, who was hitless in the first game, followed with a clutch single scoring Pipp and giving the Yankees a 3–1 lead. McGraw had enough of McQuillan and called for Jack Bentley, who hit Pennock in the back with his first pitch. Pennock fell to the ground as both benches cleared. After a short delay, the left-hander struggled to his feet and walked to first holding his hand over his left side. An angry Huggins shouted at Bentley, believing the wild pitch was intentional. Nothing more was said. The bases were now full. Bentley recovered and induced Witt to fly out to center, avoiding a big inning.

Pennock recovered nicely and set the Giants down in order in the fourth. With one out in the fifth inning, Ruth connected again, lining the ball into the lower tier of the right field stands to increase the Yankees' lead to 4–1. McGraw's comments apparently aroused the sleeping giant. It was the first time in World Series history that a player hit two consecutive home runs in one game. Another Yankee, Reggie Jackson, would shatter that record in the 1977 World Series against the Los Angeles Dodgers. In the fourth inning of Game Six, Jackson hit Burt Hooton's first pitch over the right field wall. In the fifth, he hit Elias Sosa's first pitch for another home run. In the eighth, he faced knuckleballer Charlie Hough. The Yankees were leading, 7–4, and Jackson pickled Hough's first pitch into dead centerfield. Three consecutive pitches, three home runs.

Entering the bottom of the sixth with the Yankees leading, 4–1, Pennock had retired the last seven batters and looked like he was in complete control of the Giants. Then Groh opened with a single followed by a Frisch single, and suddenly the Giants were threatening with runners on first and third with no out. Ross Youngs singled, scoring Groh and putting runners on first and second, still no out, and the score now uncomfortably close at 4–2. The Yankees fans at the Polo Grounds were squirming in their seats. Huggins was pacing nervously in the dugout. Pennock was in trouble as the dangerous Meusel stepped to the plate. Pennock was looking for a ground ball and he got it. Irish grounded to Scott who threw to Ward to start the double play, but Youngs crashed into Ward and both players were upended. The Yankees immediately began arguing with second base umpire Robert Hart, claiming interference and that Meusel should be ruled out too. The Yankees lost the argument and when play resumed, the Giants had runners on first and third with one out. The next Giant batter, Bill Cunningham, gave the Yankees another chance at the double play when he grounded to Scott at short who tossed to Ward and on to Pipp. Pennock wiggled out of that jam and went on to blank the Giants for the next three innings, gaining the 4–2 victory and knotting the Series at one apiece.

Beside the Yankees victory, it was a huge boost to Ruth's confidence and a satisfying moment for his loyal fans. Memories of the 1922 Series, when Ruth was simply awful, still lingered in the minds of many. The two home runs helped erase those memories and were the Babe's answer to McGraw's slow pitch theory, effective but not invincible. You can go to the well once too often. McGraw was also second-guessed on his choice of McQuillan as his starting pitcher. Some thought Art Nehf or Jack Scott would have been better selections.

Huggins' choice of Pennock made him look like a genius. He knew how important, if not critical, a victory meant to his club and its chances of winning the World Series. A loss would have further demoralized the team and put them mentally in a deep hole which would have been almost impossible to dig out of. His demeanor during the entire game demonstrated its importance. Huggins, coaching at first base, was in constant motion, pacing back and forth, shouting and cajoling his players with words of encouragement. The Mighty Mite, in frenzied determination, was sending a message to his team and that message was: we can beat the Giants, don't give up. In the Giants' dugout, McGraw was almost invisible. It was totally out of character for a man who thrived on a hard fought battle.

Pennock might have had something to do with McGraw's mood. He pitched a marvelous game. He kept the ball low and used his change-up and curve effectively all day. There was one exception, Meusel's home run in the second inning. It came off a low fast ball, Meusel's favorite zone, and he didn't miss it. Pennock walked only one batter and was especially tough with men on base, wiggling out of several jams.

After the game, it was a joyous bunch of Yankees, a marked difference from the day before. Players were laughing, yelling and shouting, congratulating each other on a splendid victory. Ruth stood in the center of the melee with a broad grin that stretched from ear to ear. Dugan, Meusel and Ward led the cheering with unconcealed delight. Even the quiet and reserved Deacon Scott joined in the excitement of the moment.

Most of the praise went to Pennock and deservedly so for his splendid effort. His reaction was one of modesty and class. "Yes, my curve was breaking better than usual, but Babe's great hitting and Joe Dugan's fast fielding did more to win for us than anything I contributed. That was a nice little crack I got on the back. I thought for a minute that I was through, but the pain eased up after a while and it didn't bother me much in the last few innings. I'll be ready to go back in there any time Huggins wants me."[6]

Huggins was in an upbeat mood, praising the team for playing sound, fundamental baseball with determination and spirit. He was pleased with Pennock's performance, especially after getting plunked by Bentley. He also singled out Dugan for his fine defensive work and Ruth for his two homers. Huggins made it clear he believed the Babe had regained his confidence, and he was expecting more production from him during the rest of the Series.

McGraw was gracious in defeat. Like Huggins, he praised Ruth, Pennock, Dugan and even mentioned Ward. It was somewhat out of character for the hard-nosed Giant manager. Once he finished talking to the press, he gathered the team together in the clubhouse beneath the Polo Grounds and laid out the strategy for Game Three. In his short, jerky sentences, in no uncertain terms and language, he made it clear what he wanted and expected of them. Diplomacy was not McGraw's strength, so the message was forthright and to the point. The Giants must win the next game and regain the advantage.

Game Three—At Yankee Stadium

Another attendance record was shattered as 62,430 baseball fans paid their way into Yankee Stadium for Game Three. The previous record was 60,331 for a doubleheader on September 16 between the Yankees and the Cleveland Indians at Yankee Stadium. The next largest crowd was opening game of this World Series. The exact sum taken at the gate of Game Three was $201,072. Every seat in the cavernous Stadium was taken, and hundreds were standing. It was also estimated that 25,000 frenzied and disappointed fans were turned away. At game time, the line of ticket holders trying to get through the turnstiles was two blocks long. Numerous taxi cabs and private automobiles created massive gridlock until the police arrived and untangled the mess. Many simply abandoned their cars and walked to the Stadium. The excitement and enthusiasm of this World Series was unparalleled at the time.

The fans certainly got their money's worth. It was a classic pitcher's duel between 21-game winner Sam Jones, the ace of the staff, and Art Nehf, the Giants' veteran left-hander who had a mediocre season at 13–10. For the first six innings, both pitchers were in total control, matching each other pitch for pitch. Then in the top of the seventh, after Irish Meusel lined out to his brother Bob in left field, the hero of Game One, Casey Stengel, came to the plate. This wasn't the Casey of the mythical Mudville in the poem by Ernest L. Thayer. This was the Casey of Game One. The outfielder with the floppy ears whose career McGraw revived came through once more with a home run that barely cleared the right field fence as Ruth watched in frustration and the Giant fans went nuts. Casey throughout his career as player and manager always caused excitement and often controversy. This home run was a perfect example. There are two versions of what happened when Stengel circled the bases. One account claims the frolicsome Stengel thumbed his nose at the Yankee bench as he trotted home. The other account relates that when Stengel reached third base, he thumbed his nose at Sam Jones. If either scenario happened today, there would be a riot on the field involving every player on both teams. In most instances, today's players do not participate in bench jockeying and refrain from showing up the opposition. They have greater respect for each other as professionals. Apparently, Ruppert was ahead of his time. He took offense at Stengel's conduct, saying it "lacked dignity" and was insulting to patrons. He was so infuriated, he filed an official complaint with Landis, who laughed it off, slapped Stengel with a $50 fine and said, "I guess Stengel just can't help being Stengel." Sound familiar? That's just Manny being Manny, an old refrain that wore thin with the Red Sox after years of Ramirez's juvenile antics. The home run gave the Giants a 1–0 lead, which was all Nehf needed as he continued to blank the Yankees over the final three innings.

The Giants were back on top in this best-of-seven World Series, two games to one. McGraw was elated and had visions of his dream of three consecutive World Series championships coming true. He had nothing but admiration for Stengel. "To Stengel goes the credit for winning. His homer was the one big drive in the Giant attack. Casey is one of those players who can drive the ball when he meets it squarely. He met it squarely in the first game and he did the same thing yesterday. The only difference was that he did not have to run himself out for the home run. It was a whale of a wallop. Stengel is going great guns in this series."[7] Most of the praise, however, was reserved for Nehf, who pitched a marvelous game. Some say it was the best game of his career with the Giants while many old timers said it was the finest pitched

World Series game they had ever seen. He scattered six hits, limited Ruth to a single and stymied Meusel and Pipp, the fourth and fifth hitters, who went a combined 0-for-6. He also demonstrated a coolness under pressure. He was never rattled. He was aided in several innings by the pitcher's best friend, the double play, and some fine fielding by Heinie Groh at third.

Jones, the hard-luck loser, pitched an outstanding game, scattering four hits and walking only two batters. He made one mistake and paid for it dearly. Many years later, Jones recalled that World Series with dignity. "Art Nehf and I both pitched shutouts through six innings, but then in the seventh Casey Stengel hit one of my fast balls into the right field stands. That was the only run of the game, and Nehf beat me, 1–0. Oh, that really hurt! But you know, that Art Nehf, he was an awfully nice fellow—awfully nice. And a wonderful pitcher, too."[8]

Not to take anything away from Nehf's pitching gem, but the Yankees did have an opportunity in the fourth for a potentially big inning, but because of Bob Meusel's blunder, they failed to capitalize. Dugan led off the inning by doubling to left center. Ruth walked on four straight pitches as the crowd voiced its displeasure. This set the stage for clean-up hitter Meusel. In today's game, managers would have let Meusel swing away, looking for a big inning, especially early in the game. In 1923, baseball was played differently. Huggins called for a bunt. Meusel ignored the order and swung at Nehf's first pitch, which by all accounts was not a hitter's pitch. What happened next is what Huggins wanted to avoid so dearly. Meusel grounded to Bancroft at short for the dreaded double play. Dugan took third. Pipp, the next batter, grounded to Frisch and just like that, the inning was over. The obvious question arises: could Meusel have missed the sign? Not possible. After the game, Huggins met Ruppert and told the owner, "I told Meusel to bunt and he didn't follow orders. What can I do with a player like that."[9]

Inside of twenty-four hours, the Meusel story changed dramatically. Huggins explained to the press that Ruppert misunderstood his remarks. What Huggins really said to Meusel was to swing at the first pitch if it's good. If you don't connect, then bunt the second pitch. Huggins' explanation was flimsy at best. It appeared someone was covering up the truth. It's the author's opinion that Meusel didn't want to bunt in that situation and disobeyed Huggins' order. Huggins told Ruppert the unvarnished truth. Over night, Huggins had an epiphany, realizing his words made the team look like it was not playing together and he was losing control of the club and his authority was being challenged. Hence, the backtracking.

That wasn't the only setback Huggins endured during the game. After Stengel's home run gave the Giants a 1–0 lead, the Yankees came to bat in their half of the seventh. Meusel, who was now looming as the "goat" of the game, started the inning with a line drive out to Youngs in right field. Pipp walked. Aaron Ward grounded back to the box; the ball was deflected by Nehf to shortstop Bancroft, who threw to Frisch for the attempted force out at second. Pipp, running hard to beat the throw, slid into second, twisting his already weak ankle and landing flat on his back. Frisch ran over and held his ankle in the air. Moments later, all the players along with trainer Doc Woods surrounded the injured first baseman. Woods taped the ankle on the spot, and Pipp, leaning on the trainer, hobbled off the field to a loud ovation. The next inning Ruth replaced Pipp at first and Hinkey Haines went to right field. At first, it appeared Pipp was finished for the Series. Fortunately, his ankle did not swell bad enough overnight and he played the rest of the Series. No question, the injured ankle affected Pipp's hitting. He played in all six games, batted a modest .250, and his five hits were all singles. Even injured, Pipp's presence in the lineup strengthened the Yankees and provided encouragement to the rest of the club.

Although the Yankees were behind in the Series, the mood in the club house was entirely different than after Game One. No one was despondent or dejected. On the contrary, the players were upset over the narrow loss, knowing they could have easily won the game with a few breaks. Ruth was miffed that Nehf wouldn't pitch to him in the eighth, giving him an unintentional intentional walk that put Dugan on second with the tying run. Ward was the most upset, claiming catcher Frank Snyder interfered with his swing in the ninth inning and he should have been awarded first base. Ruth and Huggins were all over umpire Dick Nallin, arguing Ward's case. Nallin didn't see it their way and Ward was called out on strikes. In spite of the tough loss, the Yankees displayed confidence and were eager for Game Four to begin.

Game Four—At Polo Grounds

Another World Series game, another attendance record. This time 46,302 persons paid to watch the Yankees and Giants play Game Four at the Polo Grounds. The total receipts were $181,022, almost a guarantee the total would be well over a million dollars, another first in World Series history.

Unfortunately for Giants fans who paid their hard-earned money, this game did not live up to the excitement of the first three games. There was one exception and that came in the Giants' half of the eighth inning when they put a scare into Huggins and the Yankees rooters. Realistically, the game was over after the second inning when the Yankees scored six runs on five hits! Jack Scott, 16–7, 3.89 ERA, started for the Giants and had an easy first inning. Then came the devastating second and the Yankee bats exploded. The gimpy Pipp started the debacle with a single to center followed by another off the bat of Ward. Schang bunted back to the mound. Scott fielded it and turned to throw to third but realized he couldn't get Pipp, then threw to first but too late to get Schang. The bases were loaded, no outs. Everett Scott, who had a long history of not hitting in World Series play, came through with another single, scoring Pipp and Ward with Schang reaching third.

McGraw, not waiting any longer for the game to get out of hand, called on Rosy Ryan, hoping his right-hander could stop the Yankees as he did in Game One. It was not to be as McGraw's luck ran out. It would turn out to be a long day for "Little Napoleon." The first batter Ryan faced was Yankee pitcher Bob Shawkey, who flied to Stengel in center, scoring Schang with the third run of the inning. Witt, who had been quiet so far during the Series, doubled to left center scoring Scott all the way from first with run number four. Dugan grounded to Groh at third who tagged Witt trying to advance, a baserunning blunder, for the second out. At this point, it looked like Ryan was out of the inning. Pitching too carefully to Ruth, he wound up walking him. Bob Meusel, who was 0-for-4 in Game Three and hit into the double play that killed a Yankees rally, stepped to the plate. With one swing Yankees fans forgave Meusel as he lined a triple to left field, scoring Dugan and Ruth with runs five and six. McGraw, desperately trying to end the madness, brought in veteran Hugh McQuillan, the third pitcher of the inning. Mercifully, McQuillan induced Pipp, batting for the second time, to fly out and end the farce.

McGraw's misery wasn't over as the Yankees padded their lead by scoring two more runs. In the third, Witt doubled in a run with his third hit of the day. In the fourth, Ward drove in Ruth, and the Yankees' lead increased to 8–0. In the meantime, Yankees starter Bob Shawkey was pitching a magnificent game. Over the first seven innings, he scattered eight hits and kept the Giants from scoring. Then came the eventful eighth. The crowd began clapping in unison, calling for a rally in spite of the 8–0 deficit. Shockingly, the Giants responded. Youngs singled, and Meusel rapped a grounder to Scott at short that looked like a tailor-made double play, but the ball hit a pebble and bounced over Scott's head. Youngs took third. The hot hitting Stengel came to the plate and singled to right, driving in the Giants first run. Ruth's throw to third was way off the mark, allowing Meusel to go to third and Stengel to second. The Babe was charged with an error. Shawkey settled down and got Kelly to ground out, Meusel scoring and Stengel taking third. Snyder also grounded out, Stengel scoring the third run of the inning. With the bases empty and two outs, it appeared the Giants' rally was over after three runs. Jimmy O'Connell, making his first appearance of the Series, hit for Claude Jonnard, who had replaced McQuillan in the top of the inning. Shawkey, who was getting tired, tried to pitch O'Connell tight and wound up hitting him. Bancroft singled to right, and when Groh walked on four consecutive pitches, it was clear Shawkey was out of gas. The bases were loaded, and the partisan crowd was screaming with joy. The Yankees bullpen was heating up in earnest. Huggins, without any hesitation, went to Pennock, the Game Two winner, to replace Shawkey. The ever-dangerous switch-hitting Frisch stepped to the plate to face Pennock. Up to this point in the Series, Frisch was 7-for-16, a .437 average, including two hits in this game. Pennock ran the count to three and two. Avoiding a walk at all cost, the left-hander threw a strike, Frisch swung and hit a weak pop up that Scott corralled in foul territory down the left field line. The raucous partisan crowd let out a collective sigh of disappointment. Virgil Barnes, the Giants' fifth pitcher of the day, retired the Yankees in order in the ninth. Youngs led off the Giants' ninth with a home run, making the score 8–4, but Pennock retired the next three batters, securing the victory for Shawkey as the Series was now tied at 2–2.

There was no joy in the Giants clubhouse. McGraw was furious. He complained about the lacking of pitching, pointing out that this was a problem during the regular season when he had to use two, three and in some cases, four pitchers during a game. He singled out Scott, Ryan and McQuillan as having nothing on the ball. In his opinion, there was no one on his staff that was dependable. Game Five would only add to McGraw's frustration.

It was a different Yankees team after the Game Four victory. Unlike the loud and boisterous celebration after Game Two, this time the Yankees were subdued. The players were happy, smiling and yelling, but there was also, for the first time, an air of confidence. Huggins was forthright in praising his pitchers, especially Shawkey, even though he collapsed in the eighth and didn't finish the game. He also pointed out Pennock's clutch pitching against Frisch. In spite of two walks, Ruth was satisfied that the Giants were pitching to him and boasted he would hit more home runs in the remaining games. Pipp said he was feeling fine and that the intense rubdown he received the night before really helped. He was confident he would play the rest of the Series so long as he didn't wrench the ankle.

Yankees second baseman Aaron Ward, having an outstanding Series, batting .437 (7-for-16), was the most positive in expressing the new found confidence. "There isn't much doubt now about who's going to win. We've got them on the run and we are going to keep them moving. They can't stop us from now on."[10]

Game Five—At Yankees Stadium

After the Yankees trounced the Giants in Game Four of the World Series, baseball fans began to sense a shift in momentum and were eager to witness the club continue its march towards their first championship. Dozens of loyal and enthusiastic fans camped out all night at Yankee Stadium so they could be first in line to purchase the $1.10 bleacher seats. They came well equipped with food and blankets. The latter they didn't need since it was a warm evening for October.

More fans arrived at the Stadium by subway and the El as dawn broke, and by 7:30 A.M. nearly 2,000 people were in line at the various ticket entrances. One load of passengers was quite annoyed when their train failed to stop at 161st Street and continued on to 167th. The explanation given was that the platform at 161st was too congested and to stop would have endangered a lot of people. At 8:45 A.M., fifteen minutes earlier than planned, the 20,000 bleacher seats went on sale. By 11:30 A.M., they were sold out. At 9:00 A.M., the grandstand seats, priced at $3.30, went on sale. At one point, fans broke through the orderly lines and had to be restrained by the police. The grandstand seats were sold out by noon.

Shortly after, the holders of reserved seats began to show up via automobiles and taxi cabs. There was a steady stream of cars, three abreast, that crossed over the 161st Street bridge headed for the Doughty Street entrance to discharge passengers. This mass of cars continued to advance well after the game started. In spite of the police's vigilant efforts to stop ticket scalpers, some still succeeded in exacting an inflated price from desperate fans wanting to see the game at almost any price. A $3.30 ticket went for as high as $15.

The paid attendance was 62,817, which resulted in cash receipts of $201,459. The total attendance was somewhere in the neighborhood of 67,000. Once again, huge crowds of people were turned away. Estimates ran as high as 50,000, which seems a tad high. Regardless of the accuracy of the number, it is safe to say thousands were sent home disappointed. But the fans that made it into the Stadium were a joyous bunch. If you enjoy lopsided games with plenty of hitting and runs by your favorite club, this was the game for you.

The Yankees won the game, 8–1, behind the three-hit pitching of Bullet Joe Bush. The press was quick to conclude that the Yankees were "probably" going to win the World Series, hedging their bet slightly. McGraw chose Jack Bentley and his curve ball to start the game, but the left-hander walked right smack into a buzz saw in the first inning. With one out, Dugan singled to right, the first of his four hits. Ruth walked. Meusel wasted no time driving a Bentley pitch he liked to left center for a stand-up triple. The Yankees had two quick runs. Pipp, still limping, whacked the first pitch to right field where Youngs made a sparkling catch robbing Wally of an extra-base hit. Meusel scored, and the Yankees were off to a fast 3–0 lead.

The Giants scored in the top of the second when Irish Meusel, not to be outdone by his brother, tripled and later scored on Stengel's ground out to Pipp at first.

The bottom of the second started harmlessly as Bentley retired Scott on a fly to center. Bush, not satisfied with a three-run lead and wanting to help his cause, singled to center to start another rally. Bentley didn't help his situation when he walked the weak-hitting Scott. That set the stage for Joe Dugan to become the hero of the day. The Yankees third baseman drove the ball to right center. Both Stengel and Youngs came running in fast as the ball began to sink. Stengel, closest to it, made a valiant effort for a shoe-string catch but came up short as the ball bounced over his glove, and with no one backing up, the ball rolled forever with Casey and Youngs in hot pursuit. It was all in vain as Dugan flew around the bases with the second inside-the-park home run of the Series. The homer gave Bush and the Yankees a 6–1 lead. The *New York Times* described the reaction of the Yankees fans in these words: "The crowd gave way to a riot of enthusiasm. Yankee rooters stood up and yelled themselves purple in the face. Programs and newspapers flew from stands and bleachers. On the field Huggins danced and waved his arms. The whole Yankee team rushed out to shake the hero's hand, and somebody on the bench picked up the bats two at a time and threw them high into the air."[11]

Once the crowd settled down, Bentley had to face Ruth, who grounded sharply to Kelly, who booted the ball for an error. The vaunted Giants defense began to show signs of cracking. McGraw had seen enough and motioned for Jack Scott, who was hit hard the day before and lasted only one inning. Apparently, McGraw was running out of options. On Scott's first pitch, Meusel singled to right, sending Ruth to third. Pipp, up next, smacked a sharp grounder to Frisch, who made a great play getting to the ball but then threw wide to home as Ruth slid in safely with the fourth and final run of the inning.

Bush now had a 7–1 lead, and the Giants were demoralized. The Yankees tacked on another run in the fourth on Meusel's RBI single that scored Dugan. The run was superfluous as Bush pitched a masterful game. He was almost unhittable. From the third inning on, he blanked the Giants, allowing only three hits, all by Irish Meusel. He was stingy with the free passes, too, walking only two batters. Six of the nine innings Bush retired the Giants in order, one-two-three. Only two runners, Meusel and Youngs, reached as far as third. It was a memorable day for Bullet Joe. In addition to his marvelous pitching performance, it was his ninth wedding anniversary. In fact, prior to the game Bush had asked his teammates to get him 10 runs as an anniversary gift. They didn't quite reach the mark, but Bush was more than satisfied with eight. Three unexpected guests added to his unforgettable day. Bush's parents and uncle arrived at the Stadium from their home in New Haven, Connecticut, without tickets. A gracious Ed Barrow found tickets for the three and escorted them to seats in the mezzanine section near the press. All in all, it was a wonderful day for the Bush family.

The Yankees continued their ferocious attack, pounding out 14 hits as McGraw used four pitchers to try and stop the onslaught. Over the last two games, the Yankees scored 16 runs on 27 hits, manhandling nine Giant pitchers. Some in the press were quick to remind everyone that what McGraw feared for the last three years, that his pitching rotation was suspect, had finally come to pass. Except for the brilliant game Nehf pitched, the 1–0 victory, the Giants hurlers were simply no match for the powerful Yankee batters. McGraw's club was now on the brink of elimination, and he had little choice but to go with his veteran southpaw, Art Nehf, in Game Six on only two days' rest.

Huggins, the ex-lawyer from Cincinnati, knew he was close to an historic moment and smart enough to know that now was not the time for his club to get overconfident. He knew McGraw as well as anyone and knew the Giants manager would not let his players go down to defeat without a real battle. He was correct. Before Game Six, McGraw delivered one of his legendary speeches, a final attempt to ignite the team and extend the Series to seven games. Huggins, as the saying goes, was cautiously optimistic. He was secure in his belief the team would continue to hit and he had the better pitching. It was a fine line he was walking, praising the team for their efforts but not to the extent they would become cocky and self-assured and let their hard fought gains slip away. Ruth realized the dilemma, too. He cautioned everyone to be alert for Game Six. Scott, the team captain, echoed Ruth's sentiments and told the players to get a good night's sleep and save the celebration until the Series was won.

Game Six—At Polo Grounds

The massive crowds that stormed Yankee Stadium and set new World Series attendance records were nowhere to be found at the Polo Grounds for Game Six. For some unexplained reason, a mere 34,172 fans paid to see the game, a drastic decrease compared to the other two games at the Polo

Three of the most valuable tickets in the baseball memorabilia world. They are all from the 1923 World Series between the Yankees and Giants. Game One: the first ever World Series game played at Yankee Stadium. Game Five: the only game the Yankees won at the Stadium. Game Six: played at the Polo Grounds, the game that clinched the World Series for the Yankees, their first championship. (Courtesy Howard Haimann from his personal collection.)

Grounds. Game Two attendance was 40,402, and Game Four 46,302. One can only guess the last two drubbings the Yankees gave the Giants discouraged many fans. Perhaps they believed like many in the press that this year the Giants were overmatched and McGraw's dream of winning three consecutive World Series was just that, a dream. Maybe it was the misty rain that kept less venturesome fans from attending. Regardless of the disappointing attendance, the receipts of $139,252 set an all-time World Series record and broke the one million dollar goal. The exact amount was $1,063,865.

The fans that stayed home and listened to Graham McNamee on radio station WJZ missed a whale of a game. The pitching match-up was no surprise. McGraw went with Art Nehf, who shut out the Yankees in Game Three. Huggins selected Herb Pennock, the southpaw who won Game Two and saved Game Four when he got Frisch out with the bases loaded and the Giants threatening a comeback victory.

In the first inning, Nehf retired Witt and Dugan without any trouble. Then came Ruth and with Nehf pitching cautiously to the Babe, he ran the count to three and two. On the next pitch, Nehf threw Ruth a slow curve that the big guy hammered into the upper deck in right field, giving the Yankees a

1–0 lead. The Giants, however, tied the game in their half when Groh, Frisch and Youngs hit consecutive singles off Pennock.

Both pitchers settled down over the next two innings. Then the Giants began pecking away at Pennock, scoring single runs in the fourth, fifth and sixth innings, building a 4–1 lead for Nehf. In the fourth, Frisch playing the game of his life, beat out a bunt down the first base line. Youngs grounded to Ward while Frisch took second. When Meusel flied to center, it looked like Pennock would get out of the inning. Bill Cunningham, playing center field in place of Stengel, was up next, and he came through with a timely single to right, scoring Frisch. It was Cunningham's only hit of the Series.

The following inning, the Giants tacked on another run. Frank Snyder hit Pennock's first pitch into the upper deck in left field, giving the Giants a 3–1 lead. In the sixth Frisch, who was wielding a hot bat all Series, led off with a triple between Meusel and Witt in left center. It was the "Fordham Flash's" third hit of the game. Down, 3–1, Huggins brought the infield in for a play at the plate. The strategy worked. Youngs grounded to Ward at second. Frisch held third. With the infield still in, Meusel slapped a single past Ward, and the Giants now led, 4–1.

In the meantime, Nehf was pitching another strong game and doing it on two days' rest. Entering the top of the eighth, the lefty from Terre Haute with impeccable control hadn't allowed a hit since Ward's single in the second inning. Granted, he had some nifty defensive plays behind him. Frisch made three outstanding plays, one in the fourth catching Dugan's pop fly in right field; two more in the fifth, a sharp grounder by Schang and a slow roller by Scott. It seemed Frisch was all over the field. He was a man inspired.

Nehf had all his pitches working for him. To quote an old and worn-out cliché, "he had the Yankees eating out of his hand." A perfect example came in the top of the seventh. With two out, Ruth came to the plate and Nehf toyed with the Babe. It was a thing of beauty. Nehf picked up two quick strikes on Ruth. The next two were purpose pitches. He threw the first inside, driving Ruth off the plate; the second was high and tight. Now he had Ruth all set for the curve over the outside corner. Ruth took a feeble swing but missed by a foot. It was an outstanding pitching sequence to a formidable hitter.

Pennock worked the bottom of the seventh, shut the door on the Giants and was finished for the day. Then came the top of the eighth. After fanning Ruth with such ease the previous inning, Nehf was beaming with confidence and eager to finish off the Yankees. The left-hander started the inning by getting Ward on a feeble pop-up to Kelly at first. It appeared Nehf was on his way to another victory when the inning suddenly turned ugly, real ugly. Wally Schang, the next batter, trying to avoid a beaning, pulled away from the pitch, but his bat accidentally hit the ball and drove it over third base for a single.

It was an omen of things to come. Scott followed with a clean single to right, Schang moving to third. Author Joe Durso in his book *Casey & Mr. McGraw*, described the reactions of the two managers," ... McGraw stood in his dugout and began to watch his dream [three consecutive World Series titles] come a little undone. Huggins standing in his dugout, now went to his bench and a war of grand strategy broke out between the two old rivals who had ferried their troops across the river for six days like field marshals."[12]

Huggins pulled Pennock and sent back-up catcher Fred Hofmann to hit. Nehf, noted for his superb control, who walked only 640 batters in 2,707 innings in his career, couldn't find home plate with a radar gun. He proceeded to walk Hofmann on four pitches, loading the bases. Huggins, sensing the game was on the line, made another move, sending yesterday's pitching hero, Joe Bush, to hit for Witt and Hinkey Haines to run for Hofmann. Nehf walked Bush on four pitches, forcing in a run and making the score 4–2. Huggins, looking for more speed on the bases, sent in Ernie Johnson to run for Bush.

Eight straight balls was enough for McGraw. He called for Rosy Ryan, who, believe it or not, threw four consecutive pitches off the plate to Dugan, forcing in yet another run without the benefit of a hit. Heck, without the benefit of a single strike. Twelve straight balls. Unbelievable! The score was now 4–3 with McGraw's worst nightmare coming to bat, Babe Ruth. At this point, McGraw rolled the dice and ordered Ryan to pitch to the Babe. "Ruth was so anxious to hit," McGraw said, "that I knew he didn't have a chance. So I ordered Ryan to throw him three pitches right in the dirt."[13] On the first pitch Ryan threw a strike and the crowd went wild. It was the first strike after 12 straight balls. Ruth fouled off the second pitch, took the next for a ball, then swung and missed for out number two. Ryan was almost out of the inning. His first pitch to Meusel was a called strike as the Giant fans continued to cheer. But Meusel slapped the next pitch up the middle, scoring Haines and Johnson. Cunningham retrieved the ball in center and uncorked a throw trying to cut down Dugan going to third, but the ball took a bad hop, skipped by Groh, allowing Dugan to score all the way from first with the fifth and final run. It was one of the weirdest innings in World Series play.

Sam Jones, the Yankees 21-game winner, pitched the eighth and ninth, allowing one hit, an Irish Meusel single, while preserving the victory for Pennock. The game and the Series ended when Jack Bentley, hitting for Ryan, grounded to Ward. The New York Yankees had won their first World Series championship!

The Yankees clubhouse was a cacophony of shouting and cheering almost matching the deafening sound level of the thousands of fans outside. Commissioner Landis, batting champ Harry Heilmann and Colonel Ruppert were among the elite who congratulated the new world champions. Cham-

1923 New York Yankees World Champions. (Courtesy Howard Haimann from his personal collection.)

pagne flowed freely. Ruth led the celebration, hugging the hero of the moment, Bob Meusel. Huggins, who took a considerable amount of abuse for the 1921 and 1922 World Series defeats, was next to receive the congratulations of the players. Finally, Bush and Ruth, sensing the euphoria of the moment, jumped on the rubbing table and called the players to gather around. Ruth, looking surprisingly bashful, presented Huggins with a diamond ring as an expression of their admiration for the little guy. While Huggins was admiring the ring, all the players hoisted their manager onto the table demanding a speech. Choked up and on the verge of tears, Huggins remained silent for awhile until he regained his composure.

"Fellows," he began, "It is a fine thing to win the American League pennant; it is still finer to go on and win the world's championship, but this ring which you have given me has brought to me more real happiness than either of the victories we have won on the diamond. It is the association with such players as you, players who go on fighting in the face of odds and never give up that brings the most happiness.

"We had our little arguments during the season, but they were not real hard feelings; they only appeared so at the time. Underneath it all and when it is all over there can't help but be a great friendship between all of us who have fought the greatest battle of all and come out on top. This token of your friendship is one that I shall always treasure and I want to thank you all for the loyal spirit in which it is given."[14]

Huggins went on to praise the Giants in general and specifically Nehf and Frisch. He applauded Frisch's five outstanding defensive plays and his always dangerous bat.

The scene in the Giant clubhouse, as expected, was quiet and solemn. McGraw was the center of attention surrounded by baseball people, friends, officials and newspapermen. For a few moments while talking to the press, McGraw seemed to wallow in self-pity bemoaning the fact he had failed to win three straight World Series. Some claimed he appeared to be talking to himself. He quickly snapped out of his reverie and graciously lauded the victorious Yankees. "The best team won; there's no disputing that," he said. "The Yankees sure put a great ball club on the field this year. You can't take a thing away from them. Nobody should have any desire to detract from their victory, anyhow. I know I haven't. They're a good bunch of ball players. They showed that to everybody's satisfaction in this series."[15]

He went on to praise the Yankees pitching staff, Bob Meusel for his clutch hit, Aaron Ward and Joe Dugan for their outstanding defense and fine hitting. McGraw was in such an affable mood that he said he would shake hands with everyone in the Yankees organization from Colonel Ruppert on down to the bat boy.

McGraw even went into the enemy's clubhouse and spoke to Huggins and the players. "You fellows beat us fairly," said the Little Napoleon, "and I wish you all the best of luck this winter and next year. Huggins, you have a great team. I hope you will win another pennant and that the Giants will have the good fortune to meet you again for the world's championship."[16]

Looking back on the Series, it is evident the Yankees had the stronger pitching staff. Pennock won two games and helped Shawkey get out of a jam in the fourth game. Bush dominated the Giants in Game Five, and Jones pitched brilliantly in the third game only to lose when Nehf shut out the Yankees. Sadly for the Giants, Nehf was the only pitcher McGraw could rely on and had to use him on two days' rest which finally caught up with the veteran in the deciding game.

As a team, the Yankees batted .293 (90 points over there average the year before) compared to the Giants' weak .234. Ruth hit .368, scored eight runs and belted three home runs, which vindicated his miserable showing the year before. Meusel batted .269 but had two triples and the key hit in Game Six. Ward, who hit .284 during the regular season, batted .417 and played a brilliant second base. Dugan batted a respectable .280, but as McGraw said, "was a tower of strength on defense." Pipp, nursing a heavily taped ankle, hit only .250 but played flawlessly at first. His presence in the lineup was an inspiration to his teammates.

Frisch, Stengel, Youngs and Meusel, in a losing cause, all had an outstanding Series. Frisch batted .400, Stengel .417 with two home runs, Youngs chipped in with a .348 average and Meusel .280 with a double, triple and home run. But the Giants' pitching, as it had done all year, failed McGraw in the end and left his dream of three straight World Series championships unfulfilled.

The day after the World Series ended, both Yankee Stadium and the Polo Grounds were silent caverns save for a groundskeeper and night watchman. But the Yankees celebration continued at an undisclosed location away from the maddening crowds. Colonel Ruppert hosted the event for Huggins, club officials and all the players, who were now looking forward to receiving their World Series checks. Each Yankees player was voted a full share which amounted to $6,160.46, a tidy sum in 1923; each Giants player received $4,112.88. Both amounts were World Series records.

At the celebration, Ruppert, the proud owner of the New York Yankees and their first World Series championship, paid tribute to his little manager. "Give the credit to Miller Huggins," he said. "He made the team what it is, and he can have a job with me as long as he wants it. The Yankees played the kind of ball I knew they could play. It took lots of faith to keep a brave front in the last two years, but I always felt that Huggins and the players would justify my confidence in them. When the Yankees did win a world's series, it was the greatest one that was ever played."[17]

Whether it was the greatest World Series ever played is debatable. In the excitement of the moment, an emotional Ruppert can be forgiven for his exaggeration. What the Colonel and baseball experts didn't know at the time and could never imagine in their wildest dreams was that the 1923 world championship was only the beginning of a long, enduring and exciting journey into baseball domination.

From Ruppert to Steinbrenner, from general managers Barrow to Cashman, from field managers Huggins to Girardi, the New York Yankees have become synonymous with a tradition of excellence. Joe McCarthy, the so-called push button manager, captured four straight World Series championships from 1936 through 1939. Casey Stengel, the colorful and brilliant manager, established a record that will stand for many years, if not forever. All Casey did was win five consecutive world championships from 1949–1953. Joe Torre, the unflappable leader, added to the dynasty by winning three Fall Classics in a row from 1998–2000. Perhaps Joe Girardi, the young, bright manager, who led the Yankees to their 27th World Series Championship in 2009, might be the next leader to run off another string of

World Series championships and join this small, elite group. Only time will tell.

Front office personnel and managers are critical elements to any dynasty, but the players on the field make it a reality. The Yankees' list of stars is endless. The following Hall of Famers (two destined to be) represent only a smattering of the greats that have contributed to the Yankees' dominance: Ruth, the greatest ballplayer of all time; Gehrig, a superstar who teamed up with the Babe to form the most feared tandem in baseball history; DiMaggio, the personification of grace and excellence on a diamond; Mantle, a rare combination of power and speed; Berra, an American treasure who played in 75 World Series games; Ford, a street-wise kid who became the premier pitcher for the Yankees through 18 seasons; Jackson, a talented and complex man considered by some the greatest clutch player of his generation; Jeter, a gifted athlete, captain of the Yankees and the epitome of a team player; and Rivera, a first-ball Hall of Famer who will be remembered as one of the most brilliant closers in baseball. These giants and hundreds more have transformed excellence into legendary status.

Through wealth, talent and an unquenchable thirst to win, the New York Yankees over the many decades have captured an unprecedented 40 American League pennants and 27 world championships. This brilliance has been played out on a stage so majestic that the Stadium has taken on a life of its own. Spacious and breathtaking, Yankee Stadium has been the scene of many iconic moments in baseball and non-baseball history. Some have even compared it to the Colosseum of ancient Rome. Based on 2009's success, it appears the new stadium (at a cost of $1.5 billion) will continue to be the world class venue for Yankees baseball and other major events.

And, to think, it all began in 1923 when the first Stadium was built and the Yankees won their first World Series championship ... and the counting continues.

Appendix A:
American League
Final Standings

Team	G	W	L	PCT	GB
New York	152	98	54	.645	
Detroit	155	83	71	.539	16
Cleveland	153	82	71	.536	16½
Washington	155	75	78	.490	23½
St. Louis	154	74	78	.487	24
Philadelphia	153	69	83	.454	29
Chicago	156	69	85	.448	30
Boston	154	61	91	.401	37

SOURCE: *Total Baseball*, sixth edition

Appendix B:
New York Yankees
Game-by-Game
Won/Lost Record

| | | | Yankee Pitcher | |
Date	Winner	Loser	Winner	Loser
April 18	New York Yankees 4	Boston Red Sox 1	Shawkey	
April 19	New York Yankees 8	Boston Red Sox 2	Bush	
April 20	New York Yankees 4	Boston Red Sox 3	Jones	
April 21	New York Yankees 7	Boston Red Sox 6	Mays	
April 22	Washington Senators 4	New York Yankees 3		Shawkey
April 23	Washington Senators 2	New York Yankees 1		Bush
April 24	New York Yankees 4	Washington Senators 0	Jones	
April 25	New York Yankees 7	Washington Senators 1	Pennock	
April 26	Boston Red Sox 5	New York Yankees 4		Bush
April 27	New York Yankees 4	Boston Red Sox 2	Shawkey	
April 28	Boston Red Sox 5	New York Yankees 3		Bush
April 29	Exhibition Game with Dougherty Silk Sox			
April 30	New York Yankees 17	Washington Senators 7	Jones	
May 1	New York Yankees 8	Washington Senators 7	Bush	
May 2	Washington Senators 3	New York Yankees 0		Shawkey
May 3	New York Yankees 3	Washington Senators 2	Pennock	
May 4	Philadelphia Athletics 8	New York Yankees 6		Jones
May 5	New York Yankees 7	Philadelphia Athletics 2	Bush	
May 6	Philadelphia Athletics 5	New York Yankees 1		Jones
May 7	No Games Scheduled			
May 8	New York Yankees 3	Cleveland Indians 2	Shawkey	
May 9	No Game—Cold Weather			
May 10	New York Yankees 13	Cleveland Indians 4	Pennock	

			Yankee Pitcher	
Date	*Winner*	*Loser*	*Winner*	*Loser*
May 11	No Game—Rain			
May 12	New York Yankees 3	Detroit Tigers 2	Bush	
May 13	Detroit Tigers 4	New York Yankees 1		Jones
May 14	New York Yankees 16	Detroit Tigers 11	Bush	
May 15	New York Yankees 9	Detroit Tigers 5	Mays	
May 16	New York Yankees 4	St. Louis Browns 1	Hoyt	
May 17	New York Yankees 9	St. Louis Browns 2	Bush	
May 18	New York Yankees 9	St. Louis Browns 4	Shawkey	
May 19	New York Yankees 6	St. Louis Browns 5	Mays	
May 20	New York Yankees 3	Chicago White Sox 2	Jones	
May 21	New York Yankees 5	Chicago White Sox 0	Hoyt	
May 22	New York Yankees 3	Chicago White Sox 1	Pennock	
May 23	No Game Scheduled			
May 24	Philadelphia Athletics 1	New York Yankees 0		Bush
May 25	Philadelphia Athletics 4	New York Yankees 2		Shawkey
May 26	New York Yankees 10	Philadelphia Athletics 8	Pennock	
May 27	New York Yankees 8	Washington Senators 1	Jones	
May 28	No Game Scheduled			
May 29	New York Yankees 4	Washington Senators 2	Hoyt	
May 30	New York Yankees 6	Washington Senators 4	Pennock	
May 30	New York Yankees 9	Washington Senators 5	Bush	
May 31	New York Yankees 8	Boston Red Sox 1	Shawkey	
June 1	Boston Red Sox 5	New York Yankees 0		Jones
June 2	Boston Red Sox 7	New York Yankees 3		Hoyt
June 3	No Game—Rain			
June 4	Washington Senators 5	New York Yankees 2		Bush
June 5	New York Yankees 7	Chicago White Sox 6	Mays	
June 6	Chicago White Sox 4	New York Yankees 1		Pennock
June 7	No Game—Rain			
June 8	Chicago White Sox 7	New York Yankees 3		Jones
June 9	Cleveland Indians 13	New York Yankees 3		Bush
June 10	New York Yankees 8	Cleveland Indians 7	Jones	
June 11	Cleveland Indians 4	New York Yankees 3		Pennock
June 12	Cleveland Indians 8	New York Yankees 4		Shawkey
June 13	New York Yankees 5	St. Louis Browns 0	Bush	
June 14	St. Louis Browns 3	New York Yankees 1		Hoyt
June 15	New York Yankees 10	St. Louis Browns 0	Pennock	
June 16	New York Yankees 9	St. Louis Browns 4	Shawkey	
June 17	New York Yankees 9	Detroit Tigers 0	Bush	
June 18	Detroit Tigers 11	New York Yankees 3		Hoyt
June 19	New York Yankees 6	Detroit Tigers 5	Jones	
June 20	Detroit Tigers 9	New York Yankees 7		Bush
June 21	No Game Scheduled			
June 22	New York Yankees 4	Boston Red Sox 2	Shawkey	
June 23	New York Yankees 4	Boston Red Sox 0	Bush	

Date	Winner	Loser	Yankee Pitcher Winner	Loser
June 24	No Game Scheduled			
June 25	New York Yankees 14	Boston Red Sox 6	Jones	
June 26	Boston Red Sox 3	New York Yankees 1		Hoyt
June 27	No Game Scheduled			
June 28	New York Yankees 4	Philadelphia Athletics 2	Shawkey	
June 29	New York Yankees 10	Philadelphia Athletics 9	Hoyt	
June 30	New York Yankees 6	Philadelphia Athletics 1	Pennock	
July 1	New York Yankees 4	Philadelphia Athletics 0	Jones	
July 2	New York Yankees 13	Washington Senators 1	Shawkey	
July 3	New York Yankees 2	Washington Senators 1	Bush	
July 4	New York Yankees 12	Washington Senators 6	Pennock	
July 4	New York Yankees 12	Washington Senators 2	Jones	
July 5	Exhibition Game with Pittsburgh Pirates			
July 6	New York Yankees 5	St. Louis Browns 2	Hoyt	
July 7	St. Louis Browns 13	New York Yankees 3		Shawkey
July 8	New York Yankees 6	St. Louis Browns 4	Bush	
July 9	New York Yankees 9	St. Louis Browns 3	Pennock	
July 10	New York Yankees 3	Chicago White Sox 2	Jones	
July 11	New York Yankees 3	Chicago White Sox 1	Hoyt	
July 12	New York Yankees 10	Chicago White Sox 6	Shawkey	
July 13	Chicago White Sox 4	New York Yankees 3		Bush
July 14	Cleveland Indians 4	New York Yankees 2		Pennock
July 14	New York Yankees 10	Cleveland Indians 7	Jones	
July 15	New York Yankees 4	Cleveland Indians 2	Hoyt	
July 16	Cleveland Indians 6	New York Yankees 0		Shawkey
July 16	New York Yankees 11	Cleveland Indians 7	Bush	
July 17	Cleveland Indians 13	New York Yankees 0		Mays
July 18	New York Yankees 4	Detroit Tigers 1	Hoyt	
July 19	Detroit Tigers 9	New York Yankees 2		Jones
July 20	No Game Scheduled			
July 21	New York Yankees 3	Detroit Tigers 2	Shawkey	
July 22	New York Yankees 7	Detroit Tigers 4	Hoyt	
July 23	No Game Scheduled			
July 24	New York Yankees 9	Philadelphia Athletics 2	Mays	
July 25	New York Yankees 5	Philadelphia Athletics 4	Shawkey	
July 26	New York Yankees 4	Philadelphia Athletics 3	Jones	
July 27	New York Yankees 7	Philadelphia Athletics 3	Pennock	
July 28	Chicago White Sox 3	New York Yankees 1		Hoyt
July 29	Chicago White Sox 3	New York Yankees 2		Bush
July 29	New York Yankees 8	Chicago White Sox 2	Shawkey	
July 30	New York Yankees 5	Chicago White Sox 3	Jones	
July 31	No Game—Rain			
Aug. 1	Cleveland Indians 5	New York Yankees 3		Pennock
Aug. 2	New York Yankees 4	Cleveland Indians	Hoyt	
Aug. 3	No Game—Death of President Harding			

			Yankee Pitcher	
Date	*Winner*	*Loser*	*Winner*	*Loser*
Aug. 4	Cleveland Indians 15	New York Yankees 7		Shawkey
Aug. 5	New York Yankees 9	St. Louis Browns 8	Hoyt	
Aug. 6	New York Yankees 5	St. Louis Browns 3	Bush	
Aug. 7	St. Louis Browns 12	New York Yankees 10		Shawkey
Aug. 8	St. Louis Browns 4	New York Yankees 3		Pennock
Aug. 9	Detroit Tigers 11	New York Yankees 3		Hoyt
Aug. 10	No Game—Funeral of President Harding			
Aug. 11	New York Yankees 10	Detroit Tigers 4	Bush	
Aug. 11	New York Yankees 9	Detroit Tigers 8	Hoyt	
Aug. 12	Detroit Tigers 5	New York Yankees 2		Bush
Aug. 13	No Game Scheduled			
Aug. 14	Exhibition Game against Indianapolis			
Aug. 15	St. Louis Browns 5	New York Yankees 3		Hoyt
Aug. 16	New York Yankees 3	St. Louis Browns 1	Pennock	
Aug. 17	New York Yankees 5	St. Louis Browns 4	Bush	
Aug. 18	New York Yankees 6	Chicago White Sox 5	Jones	
Aug. 19	Chicago White Sox 4	New York Yankees 3		Hoyt
Aug. 20	New York Yankees 16	Chicago White Sox 5	Pennock	
Aug. 21	No Game—Rain			
Aug. 22	Detroit Tigers 6	New York Yankees 3		Bush
Aug. 23	Detroit Tigers 2	New York Yankees 1		Shawkey
Aug. 24	New York Yankees 7	Detroit Tigers 1	Pennock	
Aug. 25	Cleveland Indians 5	New York Yankees 2		Jones
Aug. 26	Cleveland Indians 4	New York Yankees 3		Bush
Aug. 27	New York Yankees 10	Cleveland Indians 3	Shawkey	
Aug. 28	Exhibition Game with Toronto Leafs			
Aug. 29	No Game Scheduled			
Aug. 30	New York Yankees 4	Washington Senators 3	Pennock	
Aug. 31	New York Yankees 4	Washington Senators 2	Jones	
Sept. 1	New York Yankees 6	Washington Senators 1	Hoyt	
Sept. 2	Washington Senators 7	New York Yankees 2		Bush
Sept. 3	New York Yankees 2	Philadelphia Athletics 1	Shawkey	
Sept. 3	New York Yankees 7	Philadelphia Athletics 4	Pennock	
Sept. 4	New York Yankees 2	Philadelphia Athletics 0	Jones	
Sept. 5	New York Yankees 6	Philadelphia Athletics 3	Hoyt	
Sept. 6	No Game Scheduled			
Sept. 7	No Game Scheduled			
Sept. 8	Washington Senators 4	New York Yankees 0		Pennock
Sept. 9	New York Yankees 6	Boston Red Sox 2	Bush	
Sept. 9	New York Yankees 4	Boston Red Sox 0	Shawkey	
Sept. 10	New York Yankees 8	Boston Red Sox 1	Jones	
Sept. 11	Boston Red Sox 3	New York Yankees 0		Pipgras
Sept. 12	New York Yankees 2	Chicago White Sox 1	Hoyt	
Sept. 12	New York Yankees 5	Chicago White Sox 3	Pennock	
Sept. 13	New York Yankees 9	Chicago White Sox 5	Bush	

Date	Winner	Loser	Yankee Pitcher Winner	Loser
Sept. 14	Chicago White Sox 7	New York Yankees 4		Shawkey
Sept. 15	New York Yankees 10	Chicago White Sox 4	Jones	
Sept. 16	New York Yankees 4	Cleveland Indians 2	Hoyt	
Sept. 16	New York Yankees 3	Cleveland Indians 2	Pennock	
Sept. 17	Cleveland Indians 6	New York Yankees 2		Bush
Sept. 18	Cleveland Indians 8	New York Yankees 3		Shawkey
Sept. 19	No Game Scheduled			
Sept. 20	New York Yankees 4	St. Louis Browns 3	Jones	
Sept. 21	No Game Scheduled			
Sept. 22	No Game—Rain			
Sept. 23	No Game—Rain			
Sept. 24	New York Yankees 12	Detroit Tigers 4	Hoyt	
Sept. 25	Detroit Tigers 5	New York Yankees 4		Jones
Sept. 26	Detroit Tigers 8	New York Yankees 3		Bush
Sept. 27	New York Yankees 8	Boston Red Sox 3	Pipgras	
Sept. 28	New York Yankees 24	Boston Red Sox 4	Jones	
Sept. 29	Boston Red Sox 5	New York Yankees 4		Hoyt
Sept. 29	Boston Red Sox 3	New York Yankees 2		Pipgras
Sept. 30	No Game Scheduled			
Oct. 1	No Game Scheduled			
Oct. 2	No Game Scheduled			
Oct. 3	No Game Scheduled			
Oct. 4	Philadelphia Athletics 7	New York Yankees 6		Mays
Oct. 5	New York Yankees 8	Philadelphia Athletics 4	Bush	
Oct. 6	New York Yankees 3	Philadelphia Athletics 1	Pennock	
Oct. 7	Philadelphia Athletics 9	New York Yankees 7		Pipgras

Appendix C:
New York Yankees Final
Individual Statistics/Roster

Starting Line-Up

Pos	Player	AB	R	H	2B	3B	HR	RBI	BB	SO	AVG
CF	Whitey Witt	596	113	187	18	10	6	56	67	42	.314
3B	Joe Dugan	644	111	182	30	7	7	67	25	41	.283
RF	Babe Ruth	522	151	205	45	13	41	131	170	93	.393
1B	Wally Pipp	569	79	173	19	8	6	108	36	28	.304
LF	Bob Meusel	460	59	144	29	10	9	91	31	52	.313
C	Wally Schang	272	39	75	8	2	2	29	27	17	.276
2B	Aaron Ward	567	79	161	26	11	10	82	56	65	.284
SS	Everett Scott	533	48	131	16	4	6	60	13	19	.246

Reserves

C	Fred Hofmann	238	24	69	10	4	3	26	18	27	.290
OF	Elmer Smith	183	30	56	6	2	7	35	21	21	.306

First Year

1B	Lou Gehrig	26	6	11	4	1	1	9	2	5	.423

Pitching Staff

Player	T	W	L	PCT	G	GS	CG	SH	IP	ERA
Bob Shawkey	R	16	11	.593	36	31	17	1	258.2	3.51
Joe Bush	R	19	15	.559	37	30	22	3	275.2	3.43
Sam Jones	R	21	8	.724	39	27	18	3	243	3.63
Herb Pennock	L	19	6	.760	35	27	21	1	238.1	3.13
Waite Hoyt	R	17	9	.654	37	28	19	1	238.2	3.02
Carl Mays	R	5	2	.714	23	7	2	0	81.1	6.20
George Pipgras	R	1	3	.250	8	2	2	0	33.1	5.94

As part of the 1923 team, the following players made minor contributions to the season: Mike Gazella, Ernie Johnson, Mike McNalley, Harvey Hendrick, Benny Bengough, Hinkey Haines and Oscar Roettger.

SOURCE: *Total Baseball*, sixth edition

Appendix D:
Babe Ruth's 1923
Home Runs vs. Opposition

Date	Team	Pitcher	Number	Location
April 18	Boston	Howard Ehmke	1	Home
April 24	Washington	Allan Russell	2	Home
May 12	Detroit	Herman Pillette	3	Away
May 15	Detroit	Rip Collins	4	Away
May 17	St. Louis	Bill Bayne	5	Away
May 18	St. Louis	Wayne Wright	6	Away
May 19	St. Louis	Hubert Pruett	7	Away
May 22	Chicago	Mike Cvengros	8	Away
May 26	Philadelphia	Bob Hasty	9	Away
May 30	Washington	Walter Johnson	10	Away
May 30	Washington	George Mogridge	11	Away
June 8	Chicago	Mike Cvengros	12	Home
June 13	Cleveland	George Uhle	13	Home
June 17	Detroit	George Dauss	14	Home
July 2	Washington	Tom Zachary	15	Home
July 3	Washington	George Mogridge	16	Home
July 7	St. Louis	Elam VanGilder	17	Away
July 7	St. Louis	Elam VanGilder	18	Away
July 9	St. Louis	Dixie Davis	19	Away
July 12	Chicago	Ted Lyons	20	Away
July 14	Cleveland	Dewey Metivier	21	Away
July 18	Detroit	Ken Holloway	22	Away
July 25	Philadelphia	Rube Walberg	23	Away
July 27	Philadelphia	Rollie Naylor	24	Away
August 1	Cleveland	Sherry Smith	25	Home
August 5	St. Louis	Ray Kolp	26	Home

Date	Team	Pitcher	Number	Location
August 5	St. Louis	Ray Kolp	27	Home
August 11	Detroit	George Dauss	28	Home
August 12	Detroit	Sylvester Johnson	29	Home
August 15	St. Louis	Urban Shocker	30	Away
August 17	St. Louis	Elam VanGilder	31	Away
August 18	Chicago	Mike Cvengros	32	Away
September 5	Philadelphia	Hank Hulvey	33	Away
September 9	Boston	George Murray	34	Home
September 10	Boston	Jack Quinn	35	Home
September 13	Chicago	Ted Blankenship	36	Home
September 16	Cleveland	George Uhle	37	Home
September 28	Boston	Howard Ehmke	38	Away
October 4	Philadelphia	Bob Hasty	39	Home
October 5	Philadelphia	Rube Walberg	40	Home
October 7	Philadelphia	Slim Harriss	41	Home

Appendix E: Wally Pipp's 21-Game Hitting Streak

Date	AB	H	AVG	Team/Score	
May 8	3	1	.333	New York 3	Cleveland 2
May 9	Game Postponed—Cold Weather				
May 10	6	1	.222	New York 13	Cleveland 4
May 11	Game Postponed—Rain				
May 12	4	3	.385	New York 3	Detroit 2
May 13	4	1	.353	Detroit 4	New York 1
May 14	6	4	.435	New York 16	Detroit 11
May 15	5	2	.429	New York 9	Detroit 5
May 16	4	1	.406	New York 4	St. Louis 1
May 17	4	1	.389	New York 9	St. Louis 2
May 18	5	3	.415	New York 9	St. Louis 4
May 19	3	1	.409	New York 6	St. Louis 5
May 20	4	1	.396	New York 3	Chicago 2
May 21	5	1	.377	New York 5	Chicago 0
May 22	8	3	.377	New York 3	Chicago 1
May 23	No Game Scheduled				
May 24	4	1	.369	Philadelphia 1	New York 0
May 25	3	1	.368	Philadelphia 4	New York 2
May 26	6	2	.365	New York 10	Philadelphia 8
May 27	3	1	.364	New York 8	Washington 1
May 28	No Game Scheduled				
May 29	5	1	.354	New York 4	Washington 2
May 30	4	1	.349	New York 6	Washington 4
May 30	5	2	.352	New York 9	Washington 5
May 31	3	1	.351	New York 8	Boston 1

During Pipp's 21-game hitting streak the Yankees won 18 and lost 3, including nine straight victories from May 8 through May 22. They also increased their first-place lead from one game to five games.

Appendix F:
Lou Gehrig's First Season

Date	Hits	Firsts	Opponent
June 15	No At Bats*	First Game	St. Louis Browns
June 17	No At Bats		Detroit Tigers
June 18	0–1	First At Bat	Detroit Tigers
July 2	0–1		Washington Senators
July 7	1–1	First Hit	St. Louis Browns
July 17	0–1		Cleveland Indians
July 19	0–1		Detroit Tigers
September 25	0–1		Detroit Tigers
September 26	1–1		Detroit Tigers
September 27	1–2	First Home Run	Boston Red Sox†
September 28	4–7		Boston Red Sox
September 29	2–4		Boston Red Sox
September 29	2–6		Boston Red Sox
	11–26 (.423)		

*Played top of the ninth for Pipp; one put out.

†On the same date 15 years later, Gehrig would hit his 493rd and last home run off Dutch Leonard of the Washington Senators.

Appendix G:
New York Yankees
World Series Record,
1921–2009

Year	Winner	Loser	Yankee Manager
1921	New York Giants (5)	New York Yankees (3)	Miller Huggins
1922	New York Giants (4)	New York Yankees (0) 1 tie	Miller Huggins
1923	New York Yankees (4)	New York Giants (2)	Miller Huggins
1926	St. Louis Cardinals (4)	New York Yankees (3)	Miller Huggins
1927	New York Yankees (4)	Pittsburgh Pirates (0)	Miller Huggins
1928	New York Yankees (4)	St. Louis Cardinals (0)	Miller Huggins
1932	New York Yankees (4)	Chicago Cubs (0)	Joe McCarthy
1936	New York Yankees (4)	New York Giants (2)	Joe McCarthy
1937	New York Yankees (4)	New York Giants (1)	Joe McCarthy
1938	New York Yankees (4)	Chicago Cubs (0)	Joe McCarthy
1939	New York Yankees (4)	Cincinnati Reds (0)	Joe McCarthy
1941	New York Yankees (4)	Brooklyn Dodgers (1)	Joe McCarthy
1942	St. Louis Cardinals (4)	New York Yankees (1)	Joe McCarthy
1943	New York Yankees (4)	St. Louis Cardinals (1)	Joe McCarthy
1947	New York Yankees (4)	Brooklyn Dodgers (3)	Bucky Harris
1949	New York Yankees (4)	Brooklyn Dodgers (1)	Casey Stengel
1950	New York Yankees (4)	Philadelphia Phillies (0)	Casey Stengel
1951	New York Yankees (4)	New York Giants (2)	Casey Stengel
1952	New York Yankees (4)	Brooklyn Dodgers (3)	Casey Stengel
1953	New York Yankees (4)	Brooklyn Dodgers (2)	Casey Stengel
1955	Brooklyn Dodgers (4)	New York Yankees (3)	Casey Stengel
1956	New York Yankees (4)	Brooklyn Dodgers (3)	Casey Stengel
1957	Milwaukee Braves (4)	New York Yankees (3)	Casey Stengel
1958	New York Yankees (4)	Milwaukee Braves (3)	Casey Stengel

1960	Pittsburgh Pirates (4)	New York Yankees (3)	Casey Stengel
1961	New York Yankees (4)	Cincinnati Reds (1)	Ralph Houk
1962	New York Yankees (4)	San Francisco Giants (3)	Ralph Houk
1963	Los Angeles Dodgers (4)	New York Yankees (0)	Ralph Houk
1964	St. Louis Cardinals (4)	New York Yankees (3)	Yogi Berra
1976	Cincinnati Reds (4)	New York Yankees (0)	Billy Martin
1977	New York Yankees (4)	Los Angeles Dodgers (2)	Billy Martin
1978	New York Yankees (4)	Los Angeles Dodgers (2)	Bob Lemon
1981	Los Angeles Dodgers (4)	New York Yankees (2)	Bob Lemon
1996	New York Yankees (4)	Atlanta Braves (2)	Joe Torre
1998	New York Yankees (4)	San Diego Padres (0)	Joe Torre
1999	New York Yankees (4)	Atlanta Braves (0)	Joe Torre
2000	New York Yankees (4)	New York Mets (1)	Joe Torre
2001	Arizona Diamondbacks (4)	New York Yankees (3)	Joe Torre
2003	Florida Marlins (4)	New York Yankees (2)	Joe Torre
2009	New York Yankees (4)	Philadelphia Phillies (2)	Joe Girardi

Chapter Notes

Preface

1. Henry D. Fetter, *Taking on the Yankees* (New York: W.W. Norton, 2003), p. 18.

Chapter 1

1. Jim Reisler, *Babe Ruth: Launching the Legend* (New York: McGraw-Hill, 2004), p. 137.
2. Donald Honig, *The New York Yankees* (New York: Crown, 1987), p. 6.
3. *Ibid.*, p. 7.
4. Tom Meany, *The Yankee Story* (New York: E. P. Dutton, 1960), p. 29.
5. *The Sporting News*, October 20, 1921, p.1.
6. Daniel R. Levitt, *Ed Barrow: The Bulldog Who Built the Yankees' First Dynasty* (Lincoln: University of Nebraska University Press, 2008), p. 196.
7. *The Stadium, Part One: The House That Ruth Built* (New York: Daily News, 2008), p. 4.
8. John J. McGraw, *My Thirty Years in Baseball* (New York: Arno Press, 1974), p. 5.
9. Noel Hynd, *The Giants of the Polo Grounds: The Glorious Times of Baseball's New York Giants* (New York: Doubleday, 1988), p. 241.

Chapter 2

1. *The New York Times*, February 16, 1923, p. 11.
2. *The New York Times*, March 4, 1923, p. 1.
3. *The New York Times*, March 9, 1923, p.11
4. *The New York Times*, April 19, 1923, p. 1.
5. *Ibid.*, p.1.
6. Waite Hoyt as told to Stanley Frank, "Why the American League Wins," *Saturday Evening Post*, April 2, 1938, p. 34.
7. Mike Sowell, *The Pitch That Killed* (New York: Macmillan, 1989), p. 5.

8. *Ibid.*, p. 20.
9. *Ibid.*, pp. 185–86.
10. Fred Lieb, *Baseball As I Have Known It* (New York: Coward, McCann & Geoghegan, 1977), p. 131.
11. Daniel R. Levitt, *Ed Barrow: The Bulldog Who Built the Yankees' First Dynasty* (Lincoln: University of Nebraska Press, 2008), p. 153.
12. Lieb, *Baseball As I Have Known It*, p. 136.
13. Ray Robinson, *Iron Horse* (New York: W.W. Norton, 1990), p. 45.
14. Lawrence S. Ritter, *The Glory of Their Times* (New York: William Morrow, 1984), pp. 242–43.
15. *Ibid.*, p. 244.
16. Bill Nowlin, ed., *When Boston Still Had The Babe* (Boston: Rounder, 2008), p. 69.
17. Ritter, *The Glory of Their Times*, p. 244.

Chapter 3

1. Paul Adomites *et al.*, *Cooperstown: Hall of Fame Players* (Lincolnwood, Ill.: Publications International, 2001), p. 119.
2. Donald Honig, *The Greatest Pitchers of All Time* (New York: Crown, 1988), p. 39.
3. *The New York Times*, May 6, 1923, p. 1.
4. Timothy M. Gay, *Tris Speaker: The Rough-and-Tumble Life of a Baseball Legend* (Lincoln: University of Nebraska Press, 2005), p. 6.
5. David Pietrusza *et al.*, *Baseball: The Biographical Encyclopedia* (Kingston, N.Y.: Total Sports Publishing, 2000), p. 312.
6. *The New York Times*, January 11, 1922, p. 24.
7. *The New York Times*, July 24, 1922, p. 11.
8. *Ibid.*

9. Donald Honig, *The Man in the Dugout* (Chicago: Follett, 1977), p. 171.

10. Lawrence S. Ritter, *The Glory of Their Times* (New York: William Morrow, 1984), p. 245.

11. Jonathan Fraser Light, *The Cultural Encyclopedia of Baseball* (Jefferson, N.C.: McFarland, 1997), p. 685.

12. *The New York Times*, May 20, 1923, p. 2.

13. *The New York Times*, May 22, 1923, p. 15.

14. *Ibid.*

15. Rich Westcott, *Diamond Greats* (Westport, Conn.: Meckler, 1988), p. 118.

16. *Ibid.*, p. 119.

17. *Ibid.*, p. 120.

18. Robert W. Creamer, *Babe: The Legend Comes To Life* (New York: Simon and Schuster, 1974), p. 265.

Chapter 4

1. David Pietrusza *et al.*, *Baseball: The Biographical Encyclopedia* (Kingston, N.Y.: Total Sports Publishing, 2000), p. 876.

2. David L. Porter, ed. *Biographical Dictionary of American Sports: Baseball* (Westport, Conn.: Greenwood Press, 1987) p. 443.

3. Gerald Astor, *The Baseball Hall of Fame 50th Anniversary Book* (New York: Prentice-Hall, 1988), p. 134.

4. *The New York Times*, June 11, 1923, p. 9.

5. Barry Sparks, *Frank "Home Run" Baker* (Jefferson, N.C.: McFarland, 2006), p. 213.

6. *The New York Times*, February 22, 1920, p. 19.

7. Article in Aaron Ward collection, Giamatti Research Library, Cooperstown, N.Y.

8. "Big League Timber from Arkansas," *Baseball Magazine* 36 (February 1926), p. 402.

9. Article in Aaron Ward collection, Giamatti Research Library, Cooperstown, N.Y.

10. Ray Robinson, *Iron Horse* (New York: W.W. Norton, 1990), p. 62.

11. Wayne Stewart, "The Man Who 'Owned' Babe Ruth and Other Tales of Success Against the Babe," *Baseball History* 2 (1989), p. 79.

12. Christy Mathewson, *Pitching in a Pinch* (New York: Grosset & Dunlap, 1912), pp. 8–9.

13. Wayne Stewart, "The Man Who 'Owned' Babe Ruth and Other Tales of Success Against the Babe," p. 79.

14. *Ibid.*, p. 81.

15. David Jones, ed., *Deadball Stars of the American League* (Dulles, Va.: Potomac Books, 2006), p. 726.

16. Tom Meany, *The Yankee Story* (New York: E.P. Dutton, 1960), pp. 85–86.

17. David Jones, ed., *Deadball Stars of the American League*, p. 728.

18. Bruce Anderson, "Just a Pipp of a League," *Sports Illustrated*, June 1987, p. 90.

19. Fred Lieb, *Baseball As I Have Known It* (New York: Coward, McCann & Geoghegan, 1977), p. 102.

20. *The New York Times*, June 26, 1923, p. 5.

21. Donald Honig, *The Man in the Dugout* (Chicago: Follett, 1977), p. 174.

22. Robert W. Creamer, *Babe: The Legend Comes To Life* (New York: Simon and Schuster, 1974), p. 18.

Chapter 5

1. Donald Honig, *The Man in the Dugout* (Chicago: Follett, 1977), p. 167.

2. "The Veteran of the Yankees Hurling Staff," *Baseball Magazine* 27 (July 1926), p. 349.

3. Daniel R. Levitt, *Ed Barrow: The Bulldog Who Built the Yankees' First Dynasty* (Lincoln: University of Nebraska Press, 2008), p. 247.

4. Donald Honig, *The Man in the Dugout,* p. 178.

5. William A. Cook, *Waite Hoyt* (Jefferson, N.C.: McFarland, 2004), p. 6.

6. Tom Knight, "Remembering Waite Hoyt," *The National Pastime* 15 (1995), p. 100.

7. Waite Hoyt as told to Stanley Frank, "Why The American League Wins," *The Saturday Evening Post*, April 2, 1938, p. 17.

8. Tom Knight, "Remembering Waite Hoyt," p. 100.

9. Ted Patterson, "Waite Hoyt, Broadcaster," *Baseball Research Journal* 1 (1974) p. 74.

10. *The New York Times*, July 12, 1923, p. 14.

11. Paul Adomites *et al.*, *Cooperstown: Hall of Fame Players* (Lincolnwood, Ill.: Publications International, 2001), p. 145.

12. *The New York Times*, July 13, 1923, p. 2.

13. *Jersey City Reporter*, July 16, 2001, Jersey City Past and Present website.

14. *The New York Times*, July 16, 1923, p. 7.

15. Leonard Koppett, *The Man in the Dugout: Baseball's Top Managers and How They Got That Way* (New York: Crown, 1993), p. 106.

16. Donald Honig, *The Man in the Dugout,* p. 172.

17. Leonard Koppett, *The Man in the Dugout*, p. 112.

18. Leigh Montville, *The Big Bam: The Life and Times of Babe Ruth* (New York: Doubleday, 2006), p. 207.

19. *The New York Times*, September 26, 1929, p. 22.

Chapter 6

1. *The New York Times*, July 24, 1923, p. 1.

2. John Kuenster, ed., *The Best of Baseball Digest* (Chicago: Ivan R. Dee, 2006), p. 15.

3. Ray Robinson, *Iron Horse* (New York: W.W. Norton, 1990), p. 73.

4. *The New York Times*, August 3, 1923, p. 1.

5. *The New York Times*, August 4, 1923, p. 8.

6. Norman L. Macht, *Connie Mack and the Early Years of Baseball* (Lincoln: University of Nebraska Press, 2007), p. 589.

7. Bill Nowlin, ed., *When Boston Still Had The Babe* (Boston: Rounder, 2008), p. 33.

8. Fred Lieb, *Baseball As I Have Known It* (New York: Coward, McCann & Geoghegan, 1977), p. 132.

9. Leigh Montville, *The Big Bam: The Life and Times of Babe Ruth* (New York: Doubleday, 2006), p. 181.

10. Al Stump, *Cobb* (Chapel Hill, N.C.: Algonquin, 1994), p. 351.

11. Joe Falls, *The Detroit Tigers* (New York: Walker, 1989), p. 39.

12. David Jones, ed., *Deadball Stars of the American League* (Dulles, Va.: Potomac Books, 2006), p. 632.

13. Skip Goforth, "My Friend Wally Schang," Wally Schang McFarland website.

Chapter 7

1. John Kuenster, ed., *The Best of Baseball Digest* (Chicago: Ivan R. Dee, 2006), p. 285.

2. Blake Sebring, "Our Own Iron Horse," News-Sentinel.com website.

3. Bill Nowlin, ed., *When Boston Still Had The Babe* (Boston: Rounder, 2008), p. 115.

4. Bill James, *The New Bill James Historical Baseball Abstract* (New York: The Free Press, 2001), p. 647.

5. *The New York Times*, May 7, 1925, p. 13.

6. Lawrence S. Ritter, *The Glory of Their Times* (New York: William Morrow, 1984), p. 249.

7. Erik Strohl, *Curator's Corner: Memories and Dreams* 25 (2000), p. 27.

8. *The New York Times*, September 15, 1923, p. 1.

9. Jack Dempsey with Barbara Piattelli Dempsey, *Dempsey* (New York: Harper & Row, 1997), p. 150.

10. *The New York Times*, September 16, 1923, p. 1.

11. *The New York Times*, October 3, 1923, p. 18.

12. John J. McGraw, *My Thirty Years in Baseball* (New York: Arno Press, 1974), p. 132.

13. David Pietrusza, et al., *Baseball: The Biographical Encyclopedia* (Kingston, N.Y.: Total Sports Publishing, 2000), p. 752.

14. John J. McGraw, *My Thirty Years in Baseball*, p. 175.

15. Frank Frisch as told to J. Roy Stockton, *Frank Frisch: The Fordham Flash* (New York: Doubleday, 1962), p. 29.

16. Ray Robinson, *Iron Horse* (New York: W.W. Norton, 1990), p. 76.

17. Frank Frisch as told to J. Roy Stockton, *Frank Frisch: The Fordham Flash*, p. 43.

18. *The New York Times*, October 10, 1923, p. 17.

19. *Ibid.*

Chapter 8

1. Joseph Durso, *The Days of Mr. McGraw* (Englewood Cliffs, N.J.: Prentice-Hall, 1969), p. 153.

2. *Ibid.*, p. 158.

3. *The New York Times*, October 11, 1923, p. 1.

4. Joseph Durso, *The Days of Mr. McGraw*, p. 166.

5. Joseph Durso, *Casey & Mr. McGraw* (St. Louis, Mo.: The Sporting News, 1989), p. 149.

6. *The New York Times*, October 12, 1923, p. 12.

7. *The New York Times*, October 13, 1923, p. 10.

8. Lawrence S. Ritter, *The Glory of Their Times* (New York: William Morrow, 1984), p. 249.

9. *The New York Times*, October 13, 1923, p. 11.

10. *The New York Times*, October 14, 1923, sec 1, part 2, p. 1.

11. *The New York Times*, October 15, 1923, p. 12.

12. Joseph Durso, *Casey & Mr. McGraw*, pp. 152–53.

13. *Ibid.*, p. 153.

14. *The New York Times*, October 16, 1923, p. 15.

15. *Ibid.*

16. *The Sporting News*, October 25, 1923, p. 1.

17. *The New York Times*, October 17, 1923, p. 16.

Bibliography

Books

Adomites, Paul, *et al. Cooperstown: Hall of Fame Players*. Lincolnwood, Ill.: Publications International, 2001.

Allen, Maury. *You Could Look It Up*. New York: Times Books, 1979.

Astor, Gerald. *The Baseball Hall of Fame 50th Anniversary Book*. New York: Prentice-Hall, 1988.

Aylesworth, Thomas G. *The World Series*. New York: Gallery Books, 1988.

Cook, William A. *Waite Hoyt*. Jefferson, N.C.: McFarland, 2004.

Creamer, Robert W. *Babe: The Legend Come To Life*. New York: Simon and Schuster, 1974.

Daniel, Harrison W., and Scott P. Mayer. *Baseball and Richmond: A History of the Professional Game, 1884–2000*. Jefferson, N.C.: McFarland, 2003.

Dempsey, Jack, with Barbara Piattelli Dempsey. *Dempsey*. New York: Harper & Row, 1977.

Eig, Jonathan. *Luckiest Man: The Life & Death of Lou Gehrig*. New York: Simon and Schuster, 2005.

Falls, Joe. *The Detroit Tigers: An Illustrated History*. New York: Walker, 1989.

Fetter, Henry D. *Taking on the Yankees*. New York: W.W. Norton, 2003.

Fimrite, Ron. *The World Series*. Birmingham, Alabama: Oxmoor House, 1993.

Frisch, Frank, as told to J. Roy Stockton. *Frank Frisch: The Fordham Flash*. New York: Doubleday, 1962.

Frommer, Harvey. *Five O'Clock Lightning*. Hoboken, N.J.: Wiley, 2008.

Gay, Timothy M. *Tris Speaker: The Rough-and-Tumble Life of a Baseball Legend*. Lincoln: University of Nebraska Press, 2005.

Ginsburg, Daniel E. *The Fix Is In*. Jefferson, N.C.: McFarland, 1995.

Hanks, Stephen, *et al. 150 Years of Baseball*. Lincolnwood, Ill.: Publications International, 1989.

Honig, Donald. *The Greatest Pitchers of All Time*. New York: Crown, 1988.

_____. *The New York Yankees*. New York: Crown, 1987.

Hynd, Noel. *The Giants of the Polo Grounds: The Glorious Times of Baseball's New York Giants*. New York: Doubleday, 1988.

James, Bill. *The New Bill James Historical Baseball Abstract*. New York: The Free Press, 2001.

Jones, David, ed. *Deadball Stars of the American League*. Dulles, Va.: Potomac Books, 2006.

Koppett, Leonard. *The Man in the Dugout: Baseball's Top Managers and How They Got That Way*. New York: Crown, 1993.
Kuenster, John, ed. *The Best of Baseball Digest*. Chicago: Ivan R. Dee, 2006.
Leventhal, Josh. *Take Me Out To The Ballpark*. New York: Black Dog & Leventhal, 2000.
Levine, Peter, ed. *Baseball History* 2. Westport, Connecticut: Meckler Books, 1989.
Levitt, Daniel R. *Ed Barrow: The Bulldog Who Built the Yankees' First Dynasty*. Lincoln: University of Nebraska Press, 2008.
Lieb, Frederick A. *The Story of the World Series*. New York: G.P. Putnam's Sons, 1950.
Light, Jonathan Fraser. *The Cultural Encyclopedia of Baseball*. Jefferson, N.C.: McFarland, 1997.
Markol, Arnold, ed. *The Scribner Encyclopedia of American Lives: Sports Figures*, Volume Two. New York: Charles Scribner's Sons, 2002.
Mathewson, Christy. *Pitching in a Pinch*. New York: Grosset & Dunlap, 1912.
Mayer, Ronald A. *Christy Mathewson*. Jefferson, N.C.: McFarland, 1993.
_____. *The 1937 Newark Bears*. Newark, N.J.: Rutgers University Press. 1985.
McGraw, John J. *My Thirty Years in Baseball*. New York: Arno Press, 1974.
Meany, Tom. *The Yankee Story*. New York: E.P. Dutton, 1960.
Montville, Leigh. *The Big Bam: The Life and Times of Babe Ruth*. New York: Doubleday, 2006.
Nowlin, Bill, ed. *When Boston Still Had the Babe*. Boston: Rounder, 2008.
Pietrusza, David, *et al. Baseball: The Biographical Encyclopedia*. Kingston, N.Y.: Total Sports Publishing, 2000.
Porter, David L., ed. *Biographical Dictionary of American Sports: Baseball*. Westport, Conn.: Greenwood Press, 1987.
Reichler, Joseph L., ed. *The Baseball Encyclopedia*. New York: Macmillan, 1988.
Reisler, Jim. *Babe Ruth: Launching the Legend*. New York: McGraw-Hill, 2004.
Ritter, Lawrence. *The Glory of Their Times*. New York: William Morrow, 1984.
Robinson, Ray. *Iron Horse*. New York: W.W. Norton, 1990.
Russell, Francis. *The Shadow of Blooming Grove: Warren G. Harding in His Times*. New York: McGraw-Hill, 1968.
Smelser, Marshall. *The Life That Ruth Built*. New York: Quadrangle/The New York Times, 1975.
Smith, Robert. *Babe Ruth's America*. New York: Thomas Y. Crowell, 1974.
Sowell, Mike. *The Pitch That Killed*. New York: Macmillan, 1989.
Sparks, Barry. *Frank "Home Run" Baker*. Jefferson, N.C.: McFarland, 2006.
Stein, Fred. *And The Skipper Bats Cleanup*. Jefferson, N.C.: McFarland, 2002.
Stout, Glenn. *Yankees Century*. Boston: Houghton Mifflin, 2002.
Thorn, John *et al.*, eds. *Total Baseball*. Sixth Edition. Kingston, N.Y.: Total Sports Publishing, 2001.
Wallerstein, Jane. *Voices From the Paterson Silk Mill*. Charleston, S.C.: Arcadia, 2000.
Wescott, Rich. *Diamond Greats*. Westport, Conn.: Meckler, 1988.

Newspapers

The Jersey Reporter, July 16, 2001.
The New York Times, February–October, 1923.
The Sporting News, April–October, 1923.
The Star Ledger, July 4, 2008.

Articles and Periodicals

Anderson, Bruce. "Just a Pipp of a Legend," *Sports Illustrated* (June 1987), p. 90.
Coffey, Wayne. "The Stadium, Part One: The House That Ruth Built," (2008), pp. 1–43.

Farmer, Ted. "Carl Mays Dominates the A's," *Baseball Research Journal* 28 (1999), pp. 67–68.
Hoyt, Waite as told to Stanley Frank. "Why the American League Wins," *Saturday Evening Post*, April 2, 1938, pp. 16–36.
Knight, Tom. "Remembering Waite Hoyt," *The National Pastime* (1995), pp. 100–101.
Patterson, Ted. "Waite Hoyt, Broadcaster," *Baseball Research Journal* 1 (1974), p.3.
Payne, Marty. "Frank 'Home Run' Baker," *Baseball Research Journal* 29 (2000), pp. 65–72.
Richard, Kenneth, D. "Remembering Carl Mays," *Baseball Research Journal* 30 (2001), pp. 122–126.
Strohl, Erik. "Curator's Corner," *Memories and Dreams* (2003), p. 27.

Internet Resources

Baseball Almanac.com
Baseball Digest Daily.com
Baseball-reference.com
Jersey City Past & Present Website
News-Sentinel.com
Paterson: History—Early Industrial Development, Early Labor Problems.
The Baseball Page.com
wallie schang mcfarland
w.w.w.SABR.org

Other

Aaron Ward Collection, Giamatti Research Library, Cooperstown, New York.
E-Mail Correspondence with Marcie Beck, Grand Rapids Public Library.

Index

Numbers in **bold italics** indicate pages with photographs.